Ressourcement Theology

Ressourcement Theology

A Sourcebook

Patricia Kelly

LONDON • NEW YORK • OXFORD • NEW DELHI • SYDNEY

T&T CLARK
Bloomsbury Publishing Plc
50 Bedford Square, London, WC1B 3DP, UK
1385 Broadway, New York, NY 10018, USA
29 Earlsfort Terrace, Dublin 2, Ireland

BLOOMSBURY, T&T CLARK and the T&T Clark logo are trademarks
of Bloomsbury Publishing Plc

First published in Great Britain 2021
This paperback edition published in 2022

Copyright © Patricia Kelly, 2021

Patricia Kelly has asserted her right under the Copyright, Designs and Patents Act,
1988, to be identified as Author of this work.

For legal purposes the Acknowledgements on p. vii constitute an extension
of this copyright page.

Cover design: Terry Woodley
Cover image: © oneclearvision / iStock

All rights reserved. No part of this publication may be reproduced or
transmitted in any form or by any means, electronic or mechanical,
including photocopying, recording, or any information storage or retrieval
system, without prior permission in writing from the publishers.

Bloomsbury Publishing Plc does not have any control over, or responsibility for, any
third-party websites referred to or in this book. All internet addresses given in this
book were correct at the time of going to press. The author and publisher regret any
inconvenience caused if addresses have changed or sites have ceased to exist, but can
accept no responsibility for any such changes.

A catalogue record for this book is available from the British Library.

A catalog record for this book is available from the Library of Congress.

ISBN: HB: 978-0-5676-7249-0
PB: 978-0-5676-9990-9
ePDF: 978-0-5676-7250-6
eBook: 978-0-5676-7251-3

Typeset by Newgen KnowledgeWorks Pvt. Ltd., Chennai, India

To find out more about our authors and books visit www.bloomsbury.com
and sign up for our newsletters.

Contents

Acknowledgements	vii
A note on translation	viii
Introduction	1
Part One The sources of theology	11
Introduction	
1 Marie-Dominique Chenu, 'Theology'	15
2 Henri Bouillard, 'Conversion and grace in Aquinas'	33
3 Jean-Marie Le Blond, 'The analogy of truth'	41
4 Henri de Lubac, 'Supernatural and superadded'	49
5 Jean Daniélou, 'Current trends in religious thought'	61
6 Anon. 'Response to "The sources of Theology"'	73
Part Two Attacks on 'the new theology'	83
Introduction	
7 Pietro Parente, 'New tendencies in theology'	85
8 Réginald Garrigou-Lagrange, 'Where is "new theology" going?'	89
9 Marie-Michel Labourdette, 'Theology and its sources'	101
10 Marie-Michel Labourdette and Marie-Joseph Nicolas, 'The analogy of truth and the unity of the theological method'	115
Part Three Further thoughts on *ressourcement*	149
Introduction	
11 Jules Lebreton 'The "sources chrétiennes"'	151

| 12 | Henri de Lubac, 'Memories of 1940–1945' | 155 |
| 13 | Yves Congar, 'Collective responsibility' | 159 |

Bibliography and further reading 171
Index of names 175

Acknowledgements

My thanks are due to the following for permission to publish these translations:

Les éditions du Cerf (Marie-Dominique Chenu, 'La Théologie', *Une École de théologie: Le Saulchoir*; Yves Congar, 'Responsabilité collective', *Vraie et fausse réforme dans l'Église*; Henri de Lubac, 'Souvenirs (1940–1945)', ΑΛΕΞΑΝΔΡΙΝΑ: *mélanges offerts à Claude Mondésert SJ*);

Jésuites de l'Europe Occidentale Francophone (Henri Bouillard, 'Conclusion', *Conversion et grâce dans S. Thomas d'Aquin. Étude historique*);

Recherches de Science Religieuse (Henri Le Blond, 'L'analogie de la vérité'; Anon, 'La théologie et ses sources: réponse'; Jules Lebreton 'Les «sources chrétiennes»');

Études (Jean Daniélou, 'Les orientations présentes de la pensée religieuse');

L'Osservatore Romano (Pietro Parente, 'Nuove tendenze teologiche');

Revue Thomiste (Marie-Michel Labourdette, 'La théologie et ses sources'; Marie-Michel Labourdette and Marie-Joseph Nicolas, 'L'analogie de la vérité et l'unité de la Science Théologique');

Angelicum (Réginald Garrigou-Lagrange, 'La nouvelle théologie, où va-t-elle?').

Henri de Lubac, 'Surnaturel et surajouté', *Surnaturel. Études historiques*. Every effort has been made to trace the copyright holders of this work and to obtain their permission for the use of this copyright material.

I would also like to thank Anna Turton, Sarah Blake and Veerle Van Steenhuyse at T&T Clark, who have been unfailingly kind and patient, despite delays. Marcus Pound, my *Doktorvater*, encouraged and sustained my interest in the *ressourcement* theologians through my doctoral studies at Durham University. Professor Lewis Ayres and Rev. Dr Gabriel Flynn, my unofficial *Doktorväter*, have read and commented on drafts, made helpful suggestions and amendments, and generally encouraged me to keep going. Rev. Dr James P Green and Rev. Dr Ashley Beck kindly translated the Latin texts for me. Rev. Conor McDonough OP, my mother Moira Pavelin, and David Bone all patiently read through drafts, offering comments and corrections.

Liam Kelly, as always, has been a tower of strength and a rock of support. Thank you, my love.

A note on translation

Some readers will be aware of the difficulties inherent in translation: the Italian phrase 'to translate is to betray' (*traduttore traditore*) indicates the difficulties involved in the enterprise! Translating academic French from the mid-twentieth century into English adds an extra layer of complexity. First, as in other Romance languages, what is considered good style in French is significantly more prolix than the English equivalent – even adjusting for the differences in style between the 1940s and today. Occasionally, where there is excessive redundancy or repetition, I have opted for simplicity to save the reader's nerves.

Second, I have made some choices which may strike the reader as odd but which make sense in French. I have translated the French *science* and *scientifique* throughout as 'science' and 'scientific', following French usage where *science*, as with the Latin *scientia*, is understood as 'a field of academic knowledge' (akin to German *Wissenschaft*). In English, by contrast, for the last two centuries 'science' has been used overwhelmingly to refer to a few subject areas, rather than to intellectual endeavour as a whole. Similarly, French *intellectuel* and cognates, deriving from Latin *intellectum*, understanding, have been translated as 'understanding' rather than 'intellectual'. An odd phrase, the 'data of divine revelation' or 'the revealed data', makes an appearance in a number of texts. This phrase, *le donné révélé de théologie*, was first used by Ambroise Gardeil OP (1859–1931), co-founder of the *Revue Thomiste* and Regent of Le Saulchoir to describe the concept of Christian revelation.

Finally, readers will note that some footnotes do not follow what one might think of as contemporary scholarly style: I have followed the information given by the authors, which is in some cases less full than current style would require.

Introduction

In the last decade, *ressourcement* theology (also known as *la nouvelle théologie*) has undergone its own revival in English-language theology. Works such as Fergus Kerr's *Twentieth-Century Catholic Theologians*,[1] Hans Boersma's *Nouvelle Théologie and Sacramental Ontology*,[2] Jürgen Mettepennigen's *Nouvelle Théologie New Theology*,[3] Gabriel Flynn and Paul Murray's *Ressourcement: A Movement for Renewal*[4] and a special issue of the *International Journal for Systematic Theology*,[5] alongside translations of key works and studies of individual scholars,[6] have brought this development in twentieth-century theology to a wider audience.

Ressourcement theology is the name given to the work of a number of French theologians, who were active from the interwar period until and including the Second Vatican Council (1962–65). These scholars – Dominicans including Marie-Dominique Chenu (1895–1990) and Yves Congar (1904–1995), based at the Dominican house of studies Le Saulchoir, just outside Tournai in Belgium, and Jesuits including Henri de Lubac (1896–1991), Jean Daniélou (1905–1974) and Henri Bouillard (1908–1981), based at the Jesuit house of La Fourvière in Lyon – sought to 'refresh' Catholic theology by 'retrieving' or 'returning to' the sources of theology – all captured in the French term *ressourcement*. They were attacked by their theological opponents and censured by their Religious superiors for what was seen as their 'new' approach to Catholic theology, particularly as they were also suspected and accused of wanting to abandon the work of St Thomas Aquinas. Leo XIII's 1879 encyclical *Aeterni Patris*[7] had insisted that the curriculum of Catholic seminaries be founded on the philosophy and theology of Thomas and, by implication, the interpretations of his sixteenth- and seventeenth-century commentators, such as the Italian Dominican Thomas Cajetan (1469–1534),

---

[1] Fergus Kerr, *Twentieth-Century Catholic Theologians* (Oxford: Blackwell, 2005).
[2] Hans Boersma, *Nouvelle Théologie and Sacramental Ontology* (Oxford: Oxford University Press, 2009).
[3] Jürgen Mettepenningen, *Nouvelle Théologie New Theology* (London: T&T Clark, 2010).
[4] Gabriel Flynn and Paul D. Murray, *Ressourcement: A Movement for Renewal* (Oxford: Oxford University Press, 2012).
[5] *International Journal for Systematic Theology* 7/4 (2005).
[6] For further details, see the 'further reading' section.
[7] Leo XIII, Encyclical Letter on the Restoration of Christian Philosophy, *Aeterni Patris* (4 August 1879); http://w2.vatican.va/content/leo-xiii/en/encyclicals/documents/hf_l-xiii_enc_04081879_aeterni-patris.html (accessed 16 August 2019).

the Spanish Dominican Melchior Cano (1509–1560) and his Jesuit compatriot Francisco Suárez (1548–1617).

Ressourcement theology remains the most significant development in twentieth-century Catholic theology. It has been compared to Modernism,[8] that nebulous 'movement' of the first decade of the twentieth century condemned by the 1907 Encyclical *Pascendi*.[9] It remains unclear whether those described as Modernists considered themselves a movement or whether that concept was externally imposed. Likewise it is unclear whether the *ressourcement* theologians formed a definite 'movement'. Jodock has argued that '[i]n the face of the rigidities of neo-scholastic versions of Catholicism and its resistance to notions of historical development and change, these Catholics [Modernists] were seeking an alternative way of interpreting the faith.'[10] Not dissimilar criticisms would be made of the *ressourcement* theologians, and accusations of 'Modernism' were frequently hurled at them by their opponents. Some, such as Chenu, took a deliberately provocative delight in referring to the positives of Modernist scholarship. Like their 'Modernist' predecessors, many of the *ressourcement* theologians were implicitly condemned in Pius XII's 1950 encyclical *Humani Generis*, which warned of 'novelties [bearing] their deadly fruit in almost all branches of theology.'[11] As a result of this encyclical, Congar, de Lubac and Bouillard were barred from teaching and some of their works, along with Le Blond's article in this volume, removed from seminaries.

There is debate about the most pertinent term to describe *ressourcement* theology. The provenance and use by its opponents of the term *nouvelle théologie* implied a break with Catholic tradition. De Lubac wrote to his superiors in 1947 that 'far from having had the idea of promoting a "new theology"', he had not even known such a term existed.[12] The great historian of the French interwar Church, Étienne Fouilloux, cautiously avoids the contentious *nouvelle théologie*, preferring '*la théologie nouvelle*'.[13] Boersma nuances the terms, noting the 'character [of *nouvelle théologie*] as a movement of *ressourcement*' and suggesting that *ressourcement* – the recovery or retrieval of the ancient sources of theology – developed from the return to the mystery of theology, as expressed in the nature–supernature debate which was part of the project of *nouvelle*

---

[8] For a comprehensive account of 'Modernism' and its condemnation, see Darrell Jodock (ed.), *Catholicism Contending with Modernity* (Cambridge: Cambridge University Press, 2000); see also Stephen Bullivant, 'Newman and Modernism: The *Pascendi* Crisis and Its Wider Significance', *New Blackfriars* 92, no. 1038 (2011), 189–208; and Gerard Loughlin, '*Nouvelle Théologie*: A Return to Modernism', in G. Flynn and P. D. Murray (eds), *Ressourcement*.

[9] Pius X, Encyclical Letter on the Doctrines of the Modernists, *Pascendi Dominici Gregis* (8 September 1907); http://w2.vatican.va/content/pius-x/en/encyclicals/documents/hf_p-x_enc_19070908_pascendi-dominici-gregis.html (accessed 16 August 2019).

[10] Jodock, *Catholicism Contending with Modernity*, 3.

[11] Pius XII, Encyclical Letter Concerning Some Opinions Threatening to Undermine the Foundations of Catholic Doctrine, *Humani Generis* (12 August 1950); http://w2.vatican.va/content/pius-xii/en/encyclicals/documents/hf_p-xii_enc_12081950_humani-generis.html (accessed 16 August 2019), #25.

[12] Henri de Lubac, *At the Service of the Church: Henri de Lubac Reflects on the Circumstances That Occasioned His Writings*, trans. Anne Elizabeth Englund (San Francisco: Ignatius, 1993), 269.

[13] Étienne Fouilloux, ' « *Nouvelle théologie*» *et la théologie nouvelle*', in *L'histoire religieuse en France et en Espagne*, ed. Benoît Pallistrandi (Madrid: Casa Velasquez, 2004).

théologie.¹⁴ I have chosen to use the term *ressourcement* which to my mind better reflects the retrieval of the biblical, patristic, liturgical and medieval texts which form the sources of Christian theology in order to 'refresh' theology.

In the articles translated here, it is clear that 'new theology' is a term used by its self-described opponents. Pietro Parente's (1891–1986) 1942 article denouncing the work of Chenu and his confrere Louis Charlier (1898–1981) introduced the phrase to the wider public, and it was soon re-employed by Réginald Garrigou-Lagrange OP (1877–1964) and Marie-Michel Labourdette (1908–1990). In all three cases, the term was used polemically to imply that 'new' theology was rejecting, rather than retrieving, the Catholic tradition. Labourdette's article took aim at the '*Sources chrétiennes*' and '*Théologie*' series, reserving his fiercest condemnation for the historical methodology at the centre of *ressourcement*, which he attributed to relativism. As Holsinger has pointed out, '[e]ven seemingly innocent editorial projects, such as the series *Sources chrétiennes*, threatened to undermine the centrality of Thomas Aquinas and scholastic theology to the spiritual and intellectual mission of the Church.'¹⁵ Labourdette's article was anonymously rebutted by de Lubac and others in the *Recherches de science religieuse*, where his misinterpretation was ridiculed and the Jesuit authors insisted on their fidelity to the Church and to Tradition, emphasizing the methodological differences between 'history' and 'dogma'. There was a further response to this anonymous article, penned by Labourdette and Nicolas, which took aim at the new series, de Lubac, Bouillard, and Le Blond.

Discussing Pius XII's use of the term 'new theology' in an address to the Jesuit Congregation in 1946, de Lubac later insisted that 'none of the members of what was called the "Fourvière School", as far as I know, ever used that expression'.¹⁶ Here we may note the similarities with the interpretation of Vatican II offered by Benedict XVI in his address to the Curia in December 2005. He suggested that, while many saw the Council as a break with the past (what he described as a 'hermeneutic of rupture'), he viewed it as a renewing and continuing of the tradition, or a 'hermeneutic of continuity'.¹⁷ In a similar way, the *ressourcement* scholars saw themselves as retrieving the ancient texts in order to renew tradition (hermeneutic of continuity) while their opponents' use of the term '*nouvelle théologie*' sought rather to imply that they were breaking with tradition (hermeneutic of rupture).

The resistance to both *ressourcement* and Modernism must be placed within the wider context of the troubles assailing the Church during the 'long nineteenth century' (1789–1914). Under the Terror which followed the French Revolution, significant numbers of clergy and Religious had been executed, and during the Napoleonic wars which ravaged continental Europe until 1815, churches and religious houses

---

¹⁴ Boersma, *Nouvelle Théologie and Sacramental Ontology*, p. viii, and ch. 1, and Boersma, *Heavenly Participation: The Weaving of a Sacramental Tapestry* (Grand Rapids, MI: Eerdmans, 2011), 9.
¹⁵ Bruce Holsinger, *The Premodern Condition: Medievalism and the Making of Theory* (Chicago: University of Chicago Press, 2005), 40.
¹⁶ De Lubac, *At the Service of the Church*, 60.
¹⁷ Benedict XVI, 'Christmas Greetings to Members of the Roman Curia and Prelature' (22 December 2005); http://w2.vatican.va/content/benedict-xvi/en/speeches/2005/december/documents/hf_ben_xvi_spe_20051222_roman-curia.html (accessed 16 August 2019).

were deliberately targeted by French troops. The 1801 Concordat between Rome and Napoleon placed the French Church firmly under state control, and its fortunes waxed and waned with changes of government through the century. The Europe-wide 'year of revolutions' of 1848 and the chaos of 1870 merely added to the Church's perception of being 'under siege' from modernity: a perception which gave rise to Pius IX's 1851 *Syllabus of Errors* and his dogmatic constitution *Pastor Aeternus* on papal infallibility (1870),[18] as well as the violent over-reaction to Modernism under Pius X.

What was referred to and condemned as 'Modernism' was a very nineteenth-century approach to theology. Some of the Modernists were over-enthusiastic about the new approaches to biblical study opened up by archaeology, philology and the work of a number of German scholars, such as Julius Wellhausen (1844–1918), author of the documentary hypothesis of Pentateuch authorship, and Johan Griesbach (1745–1812), who proposed the four- or two-source theory of the Gospels. Marie-Joseph Lagrange OP (1855–1938), a Dominican of the Toulouse Province, who had founded the *École biblique et archéologique de Jérusalem*, was one unfortunate victim of the over-reaction to biblical studies, temporarily recalled and under some suspicion for the remainder of his life, although he remained faithful to the strictures of Leo XIII's encyclical on the Bible, *Providentissimus Deus* (1893).[19]

The work of the English scholar John Henry Newman (1801–1891) was also deeply suspect, particularly his essay on the development of doctrine.[20] Here Newman argued that while the truth of divine revelation is unchanging – indeed, revelation ends and is complete with the death of the last Apostle – revelation itself slowly unveils its truths over time, as and when Providence dictates appropriate. It was this sense that the *ressourcement* scholars latched onto and indeed developed, as they argued about the language and philosophical underpinnings on which neo-scholastic theology depended. Like his near contemporaries at Tübingen, Johann Adam Möhler (1796–1838) and Sebastian Drey (1777–1853), Newman – a convert – had studied theology in a Protestant university, with a focus on Scripture and the Church Fathers rather than the neo-scholastics. The so-called 'Tübingen School' of Catholic theology grew out of the integration of the regional seminary into the Protestant university at Tübingen. Both Newman and Möhler wrote early works on Athanasius of Alexandria and the Arian crisis; both remained suspect in a Church which was increasingly influenced by the Roman School and its devotion to neo-scholasticism. A French translation of Möhler's *Unity in the Church* was the second volume in the '*Unam Sanctam*' series on ecclesiology edited by Congar. Building on the Vatican I statement that 'God ... can be known with certainty ... by the natural power of human reason',[21] the 'unitary method'

---

[18] Pius IX, Dogmatic Constitution *Pastor Aeternus* (18 July 1870); http://w2.vatican.va/content/pius-ix/la/documents/constitutio-dogmatica-pastor-aeternus-18-iulii-1870.html (accessed 16 July 2019).

[19] Leo XIII, Encyclical Letter on Holy Scripture *Providentissimus Deus* (18 November 1893); http://w2.vatican.va/content/leo-xiii/en/encyclicals/documents/hf_l-xiii_enc_18111893_providentissimus-deus.html (accessed 16 August 2019).

[20] See Ian Ker and Terence Merrigan (eds), *The Cambridge Companion to John Henry Newman* (Cambridge: Cambridge University Press, 2009).

[21] 'Dogmatic Constitution on the Catholic Faith *Dei Filius*', 2, in Norman P. Tanner SJ (ed.), *Decrees of the Ecumenical Councils* (London: Sheed & Ward, 1990), II.806.

was an attempt to strengthen the Church's stance in relation to modernity by proposing a single methodological foundation to underpin philosophy and thus theology.[22]

The long nineteenth century came to a dramatic and tragic end with the First World War. The influential scholar Pierre Rousselot (1878–1915) lost his life on the battlefield; de Lubac suffered a serious head injury which plagued him for the rest of his life; Chenu avoided military service only because his poor health caused him to fail three medicals. The fact that clergy and Religious were compulsorily called up for military service was due to the collapse of Church–State relations in France under the Combes government in 1904 and 1905, as a result of which privileges were withdrawn and thousands of Religious forced into exile.[23] The Jesuits combined forces and sent their students to study in Hastings and Jersey, while the Paris Dominican Province found refuge near Tournai. Sorrel has pointed out that this exile had an important effect on the *ressourcement* generation, due both to the stronger community life and to the increased flexibility in what reading material was available to students. Access to the ancient sources of theology such as Migne's *Patrologia Latina* and *Patrologia Graeca* instilled the familiarity with and love for these texts which would lead to their retrieval by the young theologians during the 1920s, 1930s and 1940s.

The upheavals of the First World War and the seismic social changes in its wake had an additional social impact on Religious and clergy. They suddenly had significantly more contact with their contemporaries then they would normally have had in a seminary or novitiate both on and off the battlefield. This in turn made them profoundly aware of the atheism, anti-clericalism and contempt for religion which stalked France, and above all they became aware of the impossibility of convincing their peers that knowledge of God was reasonable while locked into the neo-scholastic categories of Aristotelian philosophy. This explains the enthusiasm with which they would later greet Newman's concept of the development of doctrine and their desire for a new theological language which would speak to their contemporaries. Numerous scholars have pointed to the profound shock which 'total war' brought about among theologians from all churches, whether in France, Britain or Germany, leading them to question the assumptions on which nineteenth-century theology had been constructed.

The return to the sources of Christian theology practised by the students who would become the *ressourcement* theologians must be the primary characteristic of *ressourcement* theology. What Chenu and others derided as 'Baroque scholasticism' had in many cases shrivelled still further, with Scripture, scholastic texts and the commentaries plundered for a theology which remained largely apologetic, often anti-Protestant and concerned at all time to demonstrate its adherence to Magisterial statements of faith. Hence the derisory description, 'Denzinger-theology'. 'Denzinger', or the *Enchiridion Symbolorum et Definitionem*, is a collection of conciliar statements, creeds and definitions from the Magisterium, now in its 43rd (2010) edition, originally compiled by the German theologian in 1854. 'Denzinger-theology' refers to a style of

---

[22] See Gerald A. McCool SJ, *Nineteenth-Century Scholasticism: The Search for a Unitary Method* (New York: Fordham University Press, 1989).

[23] See Christian Sorrel, *La république contre les congrégations: Histoire d'une passion francçaise 1899–1904* (Paris: Cerf, 2003), 199.

pedagogy which emphasizes the study of extracts from this compendium – often taken out of context – which were then made to dovetail with other Denzinger quotations – see for instance Garrigou-Lagrange's text here. One of the hallmarks of *ressourcement* scholars would be their reading and close study of entire texts, from the liturgical texts of the early Church, to patristic texts, to the writings of Aquinas, along with an awareness of and sensitivity to the cultural contexts in which these texts had been created.

This was precisely the path taken, not only by de Lubac, Bouillard and Daniélou (see the translations in this volume from de Lubac's *Surnaturel*, Bouillard's *Conversion et grâce chez S. Thomas d'Aqin* and Daniélou's article) but also by Chenu. In addition to teaching a course on the 'history of doctrine', as did de Lubac, Chenu was one of the first subscribers to the historical journal *Annales*, which sought to do for history what the *ressourcement* theologians were doing for theology. Where the *Annales* historians focused, not on battles and monarchs but on private journals, tax records and archives which spoke about the context and the warp and weft of daily life, the *ressourcement* theologians focused less on creedal statements and Magisterial definitions and more on the intellectual, social and economic conditions which had produced particular theological writings, whether they be the Cappadocian Fathers of the fourth century, the early scholastics of the twelfth-century renaissance or Aquinas himself. This passion for the sources bore fruit in the various series of books sponsored and edited by the *ressourcement* theologians and their Orders: '*Unam Sanctam*', '*Théologie*' and '*Sources chrétiennes*'.

One of the aims of all these series was to bring the sources of theology to a wider audience. '*Sources chrétiennes*', far from being an attack on and undermining of the writings of Thomas, sought to provide contemporary French translations of some of the major works of the Christian Tradition of the East and West which lay in the hinterland of scholastic thought. The idea that such texts should be available to the 'interested reader' and the wider public, rather than reserved to the study of the specialist, was an offence and outrage to critics such as Labourdette, Garrigou-Lagrange and Nicolas, as may be seen in the translations of their articles below. '*Unam Sanctam*', which included Möhler's *L'unité dans l'Église*, de Lubac's *Catholicisme* and Congar's *Vraie et fausse réforme dans l'Église*, has recently been restarted by *Éditions du Cerf*, with two 'new series', one on recent theology and one on Vatican II, which is indicative of the importance of *ressourcement* theology both to the Second Vatican Council and to its ongoing influence in contemporary Catholic theology.

The publishing series are among the many examples of the second characteristic of *ressourcement* theology: what I call *théologie engagée*. The term *engagement* will be familiar to those who have read or studied Jean-Paul Sartre and the other existentialist philosophers who were the contemporaries of the *ressourcement* theologians, as an insistence that life should be lived rooted in reality, with a 'commitment' to change, improvement and 'making a difference'. One aspect of *théologie engagée* undertaken by *ressourcement* theologians was indeed the publication of heretofore unpublished and inaccessible material which might shed light on both the early Church and how the Church could and should respond to contemporary crises, such as the rise of totalitarianism and economic collapse.

Another aspect of *théologie engagée* was a desire to be involved in the realities of daily life as experienced by their contemporaries. This might be, as for Chenu and Congar, involvement with groups such as the *Jeunesse Ouvrière Chrétienne* (Young Christian Workers), which sought to bring young working-class people back to the Church,[24] or, as for de Lubac and his confrere Yves de Montcheuil, involvement with clandestine publishing and other resistance groups during the Second World War. De Lubac spent time on the run, while de Montcheuil lost his life as a result of his activities. Chenu and Congar were censured in 1953 as much for their work with the Worker Priest movement as for any reaction to *Humani Generis*. Either way there was no question that these theologians would not refrain from 'getting their hands dirty'. They were convinced that theology should be a part of, and relatable to, the world of the everyday reality lived by those around them, whether or not they were faithful Catholics.

The *engagement* of *ressourcement* theologians during the Second World War drove a further wedge between them and their theological opponents in the post-war period. In the anonymous 'Response' to Labourdette's 'The sources of theology', the authors lament that 'while the dark days of Modernism are, thank God, now long gone, the dark days of *intégrisme* are only too close to returning', referring to a world view of unchanging and unchangeable religious doctrine associated with political support for right-wing or totalitarian regimes. The official support of the Catholic hierarchy for the Vichy regime is not the French Church's finest hour. However, it must also be understood in the context of seventy years of the avowedly secularist Third Republic, which viewed the Church in general, and Religious in particular, as a threat to the modern, secular Republic. Anti-Church measures relating to clerical and Religious involvement in education and charitable works had culminated in 1905 with the separation of Church and State, the breakdown of diplomatic relations with the Vatican and the expulsion of Religious from France. Vichy's promotion of the Church and support of Church involvement in education were seen by many Catholics as a breath of fresh air. The *ressourcement* theologians by contrast were appalled by what they saw as Vichy's collaboration with the evils of National Socialism. De Lubac's *At the Service of the Church* and *Theology in History* offer an excellent commentary on this time.[25]

A third characteristic of *ressourcement* theology, and the one which will undoubtedly strike readers of this book as the most significant, is the nature–supernature, or nature–grace question. Of course, the question of how God's grace intervenes to save humanity and the interconnected question of how humanity participates in the divine nature have been a part of Christian theology since its earliest days. There are two related questions which the *ressourcement* scholars tackled. The first is the question of the *analogia entis* – the analogy of being – which seeks to describe how creation and humanity relate to God through their being. The second is the question of nature and

---

[24] For an account of the *Jeunesse Ouvrière Chrétienne* as *théologie engagée* and of Chenu's involvement in this movement and the worker priests, see my PhD thesis, 'Taking Theology to Work: *Ressourcement* Theology and Industrial Work in Interwar France and Belgium' (Durham University, 2016). http://etheses.dur.ac.uk/11819/.

[25] De Lubac, *Service*; Henri De Lubac, *Theology in History*, trans. Anne Englund Nash (San Francisco: Ignatius, 1996).

supernature – in other words, how God acts on and in humanity to bring people to salvation.

Let us turn first to the *analogia entis*. This question is at the heart of much patristic theology: how to balance the idea, central to Judaeo-Christian theology, that the human person is created in the image of God, with the concept of divine transcendence? God is infinite; humanity finite. Not only is the human person incapable of describing the divine nature – hence the rise of apophatic theology and the 'Names of God' in the Tradition – the human person, while created in the image of God and dependent on the act of God to keep her in existence, is not in any way divine. Humanity thus participates in the divine by analogy: as God is the fullness of Being, so humanity participates analogically, partially and imperfectly, in Being.

At this point it is important to note the external philosophical influences which came to bear on the expression of both patristic and scholastic theology. The theology of the early Church developed around the Mediterranean in conjunction with neo-Platonic thought. 'What has Athens [philosophy] to do with Jerusalem [theology]?' Tertullian famously taunted. The answer was: quite a lot! First neo-Platonic and then Aristotelian metaphysics, or the ways in which we categorize the world, has offered the categories for Christian theology since the first century. The neo-Platonic Transcendentals offered Christians a way of describing an otherwise ineffable, or indescribable, God: he was all goodness and truth, all beauty, all Being. The divine Being represented the fullest, most perfect way of Being there could be, just as divine Truth represented the fullest, most perfect Truth there could be. Human truth, like human beauty, goodness and being, could only participate in a limited and imperfect way in the divine fullness, just as human speech could only describe the divine fullness of beauty, truth, goodness and being, in a limited and imperfect way. This became known as the *analogia entis*: the way in which humans participated, in an imperfect and analogous way, in the divine mode of being.

The neo-Platonic world view which had held sway during the early period of Christianity continued to dominate until the eleventh century. This period, which saw the development of loose confederations of scholars which would later be described as universities, may be considered to be the start of the scholastic period. First, the 'dialectical method' of disputation, as seen for instance in the *Summa theologiae*, became widespread as a pedagogical method. Second, of key importance for Catholic theology, the work of Aristotle made its way via Jewish and Islamic scholarship to the university curriculum. As Bouillard pointed out, Aquinas's use of Aristotelian metaphysics was daring in its novelty (so daring, in fact, that the great Doctor narrowly avoided being accused of heresy). Where patristic thought had relied on neo-Platonic philosophy, scholastic thought was constructed on Aristotelian categories. As Bouillard demonstrated, this raised questions about the appropriateness of Thomist and neo-Thomist concepts of grace; yet as Le Blond showed, the neo-Platonic categories on which patristic thought had developed were not necessarily helpful to the twentieth century either.

De Lubac's critique of neo-Scholastic understandings of grace, *Surnaturel*, now added further fuel to the fire. Just as Bouillard's chronological reading of Aquinas had demonstrated that he had changed his theology of grace over his career, so de Lubac's painstaking investigations of the sources revealed that the concept of 'pure nature', far from being intrinsic to Christian theology on grace, was in fact an invention – not to say a deformation – of the Thomist commentators of the Counter-Reformation. For much of the Christian period, it has been assumed that nature was 'graced' with the divine presence – absolutely not as a pantheism, and still less panentheism, but an acknowledgement that the Judaeo-Christian Creator God, 'in whom we live and breathe and have our being', holds all of creation in continuous being. De Lubac spent much of *Surnaturel* arguing that the development of the concept of pure nature by neo-scholastics of the sixteenth and seventeenth centuries was both theologically incoherent and ahistorical. The doctrine of 'pure nature' had arisen as a debating device to contemplate what a world devoid of divine grace would look like; some theologians suggested that grace – an entirely gratuitous gift of God – was only necessary in a postlapsarian world and that humanity was created only in a state of 'pure nature'. De Lubac pointed out that, first, this in fact went against the whole of Christian tradition, from Ireneaus to Aquinas; and, second, this abandoned the idea of the *desiderium naturale*, the natural desire for God and the beatific vision which the whole of Christian tradition had taken for granted as an innate characteristic of human nature. As de Lubac not very subtly demonstrated, it was the sixteenth-century scholastics, and their nineteenth- and twentieth-century followers, whose approach to theology was 'new'.

The articles and chapters translated in this book are some of the key articles of *ressourcement* theology, but as yet they are unavailable in English. In the first part, 'the sources of theology' are articles which challenge the neo-scholastic understanding and method of theology. Part Two contains a number of attacks on 'new theology', while the third part has articles which offer a wider perspective. Introductions to each article may be found at the start of each section. Suggestions for further reading may be found towards the end of the book.

Part One

The sources of theology

Introduction

1 Marie-Dominique Chenu, 'Theology'

Marie-Dominique Chenu (1895–1990) was at one time possibly the most notorious of the *ressourcement* scholars, variously seen as a rigorously academic Church historian and as a trouble-making 'young Turk'. Having joined the French Dominicans at Le Saulchoir in 1913, he studied in Rome at the Dominican 'Angelicum' university, ending with a doctorate on 'Contemplation in Aquinas' supervised by none other than Réginald Garrigou-Lagrange. Garrigou-Lagrange, indeed, had wanted Chenu to stay on in Rome to teach; but Chenu was drawn back to Le Saulchoir, where he joined the teaching team, becoming Regent of Studies in 1932 – successor, as he noted, to Thomas Aquinas, who had been the Regent of Studies at the Dominican house of study in Paris.

It was as Regent that Chenu gave the annual celebratory address for the Feast of St Thomas in 1937, which became *Une école de théologie: Le Saulchoir*. Privately published by the Dominican press, only some 800 copies were printed,[1] although it found its way quickly enough to Rome, where it was added to the Index of Prohibited Books in 1942 – famously, Chenu heard the news on the radio. The work should be considered to be his charter for theological education: starting with the general context, it moves first to theology and then to philosophy, in marked contrast to the neo-scholastic curriculum of the time. Chenu also fired a number of salvos at what he described as 'baroque' scholasticism – the scholasticism of the sixteenth- and seventeenth-century commentators, whose accretions had covered and destroyed the original work of Thomas – and he took not a little provocative pleasure in naming and praising those who had been condemned a few decades earlier as 'Modernists'.

As observed in the 'Note on Translations' above, a key phrase in this text, and elsewhere in Chenu's writing on theology, is *le donné révélé*, which I have translated variously as 'the data of revelation', 'the data of divine revelation', 'divinely revealed data', or 'revealed data'. He took this phrase from his predecessor as Regent at Le Saulchoir, Antoine Gardeil.

---

[1] See Fergus Kerr, 'Chenu's Little Book', *New Blackfriars* 66 (1985), 108–12; and Francesca Murphy, 'Gilson and Chenu: The Structure of the *Summa* and the Shape of Dominican Life', *New Blackfriars* 85/997 (2004), 290–303 (298–9).

2 Henri Bouillard, 'Conversion and grace in Aquinas'

Henri Bouillard (1908–1981) joined the Jesuits in his twenties and was sent to Rome to complete his theological studies at the Gregorian university. His doctoral thesis, '*Conversion et grâce chez S. Thomas d'Aquin. Étude historique*', completed in 1940, was defended in Lyon after he had returned to France following the outbreak of war. In 1944 it was published as the first in the new '*Théologie*' series sponsored and edited by the Lyon Jesuits, and the resulting backlash may be followed in the articles by Labourdette, Garrigou-Lagrange, and Labourdette and Nicolas in Part Two of this book.

It is fair to say that *Conversion et grâce* dealt a veritable body blow to the certainties of neo-scholastic thought. The latter took what Bouillard described as the 'manualist' position – the study of theological statements, discussed in a scholastic manner – and entirely rejected a historical or developmental approach. Theology, particularly the writings of St Thomas, was seen as a monolithic, unchanging structure. Bouillard's painstaking historical analysis of Aquinas's position on grace and how it leads first to the conversion of the human person to God, and ultimately to their justification, blew this unchanging monolith out of the water. If his analysis were correct, Thomas's position had changed significantly between his *Commentary on the Sentences* and the *Summa theologiae*, particularly following his discovery of the semi-Pelagian controversy while he was writing the *Summa Contra Gentiles*. Bouillard insisted that Thomas's works needed to be read in chronological order, located in the context of Aquinas's life, and with an awareness of the intellectual context in which he was working.

By 1946 Bouillard's position would be battered by two of the French Dominican neo-Thomist heavyweights, Garrigou-Lagrange and Labourdette. First, the emphasis on 'context' appeared to them to be, in Garrigou's words, a 'return to Modernism', not to mention to whiff of relativism. Second, Bouillard was relatively critical of Aquinas's use of Aristotle, suggesting this was something of a novelty. Finally, they were deeply concerned that Bouillard's description of grace removed its gratuitous nature and forced God into making this gift.

3 Jean-Marie Le Blond, 'The analogy of truth'

Unlike his Jesuit confreres whose work also appears in this book, Jean-Marie Le Blond SJ (1899–1973) was neither a theologian nor an academic. The philosopher, whose 1936 Paris thesis, *Logique et méthode chez Aristote* ('Logic and method in Aristotle'), was published in 1939, at the same time as a shorter work, *La definition chez Aristote* ('Definition in Aristotle'), had taught at the Gregorian university and by 1947 was teaching philosophy at the Jesuit collège of Mongré. Much of his life's work was dedicated to producing translations and commentaries of Aristotle's works (*Physics* and *Treaty on the parts of animals*), although he also published on St Augustine and the knowledge of God.

With its critique of Aquinas's 'novel' introduction of Aristotelian categories into Christian theology, Bouillard's *Conversion et grâce chez St Thomas d'Aquin* was clearly attractive and interesting to Le Blond, who penned a discreet rebuttal of Labourdette's attack on Bouillard. Bouillard is not named in the article; rather, Le Blond takes *Conversion et grâce* as his starting point for a discussion on the appropriateness of Aristotelian philosophy as the basis for twentieth-century theology. In particular, he moved the discussion away from the *anaologia entis*, or 'analogy of being', insisting that the concept of analogy should be extended to all the 'Transcendentals', including Truth. The suggestion that human truths – including those taught by the Church about God – might only be analogous and imperfect, acted, entirely predictably, like a red rag to a bull, and Le Blond's article was in turn lambasted by Labourdette and Nicolas the following year. Le Blond's article was also one of those removed from library shelves in 1950 at the orders of the Jesuit General, Jean-Baptiste Janssens, following the publication of *Humani Generis*.

4 Henri de Lubac, 'Supernatural and superadded'

Henri de Lubac (1895–1990) is perhaps the best known *ressourcement* theologian in the English-speaking world. A significant proportion of his prodigious output has been translated and is readily available. *Surnaturel. Études historiques*, his third book, remains one of the few exceptions never translated into English – perhaps because it was felt to be so obviously in the sights of *Humani Generis* and also because the later *Mystère du Surnaturel* was itself translated.

Like both *Catholicisme* (1937) and *Corpus Mysticum* (1944), the ideas in *Surnaturel* had been on de Lubac's mind since his student days. The book had its roots in articles published in *Recherches de Science Religieuse* in the early 1930s. Like *Corpus Mysticum*, much of the manuscript was completed in the extraordinary circumstances of the German invasion and occupation of France during the Second World War, *Corpus Mysticum* during the initial phase of German invasion, *Surnaturel* in 1943–4 when de Lubac was in hiding and in fear of his life due to his activities in the Resistance. And like the earlier titles with which it shares the *étude historique* epithet, *Surnaturel* drew on de Lubac's extensive and profound reading of the Greek and Latin Fathers of the Church.

At the heart of the book, de Lubac was dealing with a knotty problem at the centre of the debate between neo-Thomism and *ressourcement* theology: Can there be such a thing as 'pure nature'? As de Lubac demonstrated, the concept of 'pure nature' – a nature entirely separated from and denuded of divine grace or 'supernature' – was one which would have been completely alien to Thomas himself and to his scholastic contemporaries and successors. On the contrary, it was a device invented by commentators in the late fifteenth and early sixteenth centuries to enable hypothetical debate about grace/supernature. Could God, they wondered, have created a purely 'natural' humanity without access to the 'supernatural' divine gift of sanctifying grace?

De Lubac took the question a step further. Underpinning both the patristic and scholastic teaching on grace is the concept of the *desiderium naturale*, the desire, natural to all human beings, for the beatific vision which ultimately leads us to God. However, neo-Thomism insisted on a separation of nature and supernature, with the result that in this anthropology the *desiderium naturale* was no longer innate but must come about as the gratuitous divine gift of grace: 'supernature' or, as he refers to it, 'super-added'.

5 Jean Daniélou, 'Current trends in religious thought'

Études, founded in 1856, was the 'house journal' of the French Jesuits. Originally focused on theology and philosophy, the journal expanded its reach to include art, literature and other aspects of culture, particularly with regard to their interaction with theology and philosophy. Daniélou's article, with its sharp critique of the 'rupture' between theology and real life, was itself the cause of a huge rupture in French academic theology in the 1940s, between those who, like Daniélou, argued that theologians and the Church had an obligation to try to meld theology to the reality of daily life in the twentieth century and those who, like Labourdette, Garrigou-Lagrange and other neo-Thomists, insisted that the natural and supernatural – heaven and earth – should be strictly separated in theology and in the life of faith. In reality, of course, the argument had been brewing for a number of years, with Chenu's blistering attacks on the neo-scholastic methodology in 'Theology' only the tip of the iceberg. The 'historical studies' published by de Lubac and Bouillard were further grist to the mill, and Daniélou's approving comments about Modernism, Marxism, existentialism, the *Formgeschichte* school of biblical studies, Kierkegaard and other proscribed ideas seem deliberately provocative.

6 Anon. 'Response to "The sources of theology"'

Daniélou's article and Bouillard's book were apparently the triggers for the virulent attacks by Garrigou-Lagrange, Labourdette and Nicolas which may be found in Part Two of this book. Labourdette's article, 'Les sources de la théologie', was taken personally by the Fourvière Jesuits he had in his sights. The 'response' penned by de Lubac, Bouillard and Daniélou, in which de Lubac let rip the sarcasm for which he was well known, lacerated Labourdette. They pointed out that he was calling into question not only their own orthodoxy but also that of their Religious superiors and censors, without whose permission and approval they were unable to publish. In the climate of the late 1940s, the political differences between Toulouse and Fourvière were still raw, which only added to the violent language on both sides. Crucially, however, de Lubac records that Fr Nicolas, Provincial of the Toulouse Dominicans, visited Fourvière in late 1947 when the troubled waters were smoothed over.[2]

---

[2] See de Lubac, *Service*, 195.

1

'Theology'

'Theology'. Chapter 3 of *Une école de théologie: Le Saulchoir* (Kain-Lez-Tournai: Le Saulchoir, 1937; republished Paris: Cerf, 1985), 129–50.

Marie-Dominique Chenu OP

'*Le Donné révélé et la Théologie*' ['*The data of divine revelation and theology*'] was not just any title for one of the works of Fr Gardeil, whose role at Le Saulchoir we discussed in chapter 2 [of *Une École* …] above. This antithetical statement defines the axis along which the work was organized, the principle on which he divided up and described the subjects and methods of a teaching in its educational and religious pathway, from the data of revelation to dogma, from dogma to theological data, from academic theology to theological systems. It is, furthermore, a decisive choice in favour of this teaching being organized in a concrete manner. The design explicitly treats all subjects and methods with respect and curiosity, and each has a place in the plans of work. Its irreducible diversity, encompassing history and speculation, establishes the original structure of theological science.

While at every stage the Modernist controversy gave a sense of urgency to the 'reform of theology', as it was known, in reality the problems raised had much deeper roots, encompassing the whole of the history of modern theology. *The state of the theological disciplines which we study is that of the sixteenth and seventeenth centuries, not that of the medieval Summae.* There is nothing abnormal about this, and no one would dream of regretting that the requirements of defending the faith and the influence of new cultural and spiritual movements have led the theological body to develop not just new emphases, shifts and balances but also a gradual diversity of functions and methodologies. Yet precisely for anyone rooted in a familiarity with the medieval *Summae*, this very reference constructs an independence with regard to polemic and transient interests, which often closely controlled the division of subject matter, mental categories and ways of moving forward in the most legitimate manner. Firmly and solidly fixed as we are in our educational routines, we risk less by taking what are but occasional needs for our structural values. Theology is not constructed by *anti*-statements, but according to its own principles and the internal hierarchy of its objectives: this is the essential law to hold on to when methodologies are questioned.

This is probably the reason for the freedom with which Fr Gardeil undertook what he himself somewhat crudely referred to as 'a work of purification of the field of theology'.

The primacy of the revealed data

Any inventory of the revealed data is a speculative construction. By their very depth, these two functions of theology have often developed within themselves, and, far from being a shared resource through an appropriate distribution of work, the encounter between 'positive' and 'speculative' became an occasion for discord. Furthermore, and most seriously, at the heart of this rivalry is a dispute about the very value of the intellectualism set in train by speculative theology, while it was not in vain that positive theology raised the question of the precise insertion of reason into data which must be not only the rule but the soul of such speculation.

Theological 'reason' only has the desire or the right to be exercised where and to the extent that, in the light of faith, it enters, unceasingly, into a religious possession of the revealed data, the 'Word of God'. It is only according to this strict and total coherence that a theology may be constructed, for only in this way is its indispensable spiritual homogeneity ensured. Such homogeneity, moving from communion with the divine thought to the ultimate theological conclusion, is relative but sufficient. This is an essential principle, not only a favourable condition: once this coherence between religious perception and scientific conceptualization is relaxed, once their shared theatre of operations is broken, theology fails in its very nature of being the object of faith, which is at one and the same time human discourse and divine blessing. For theology is truly faith with the status of knowledge (*in statu scientiae*).

From the start, therefore, this means breaking with *anti*-Lutheran theologies which, on the pretext of blocking the progress of Protestant 'mysticism' and proclaiming the faith of authority with all its ecclesiastical formulas, feared theology should have to reduce the interior mystery of the knowledge of the divine and water down the role of supernatural enlightenment, supported by propositions of assent. Faith was no longer intrinsically supernatural and, at its most extreme, we are taught we can believe solely by force of reason, giving in to the incontestable authority of God. It was only de facto, to be meritorious, that this acquired faith was surrounded by pious confidence. Thus the assimilation of an intimate knowledge of God was weakened by faith. The subject of this faith now held only the slightest importance, as the decisive value of faith was no longer in its content and objects, but in dogmatic submission.

A theology or theological science which begins from such an understanding of faith would obviously lose its interest and its influence, having lost its living source. And it well and truly lost its source, since many theologians came to hold that theology does not need supernatural faith. Once theology was *powerful* in faith, because the assent of faith included a real supernatural perception within the agreed proposition, and this divine realism infused in a real sense the argument developed from the proposition, beyond the rational effectiveness being used. Now, a purely formal assent to the dogmatic formula is sufficient, and the non-believer may construct a good argument on this, as long as her syllogism respects the rule of the three terms. Theology would no longer be pious but would remain true. What derisory theology – *theo-logia*, the 'word of God' no longer talks in theology.

The data of divine revelation thus has primacy always and everywhere: the primacy of the object in the all-powerful primacy of the interior light of faith. Speculative construction is not a conceptual edifice superimposed on a prior perception acquired once for all. It is a living incorporation into rational structures in the light of faith, as in admirable spiritual writings. It is a permanent presence, like that of sap in a tree. It is an enveloping presence, for it is not the 'construction' which surrounds the 'data' with its subtle armour, but the 'data' which, as a spiritual environment overflowing in every direction, collapses internally and under its own pressure. It is contemplation which ignites theology; theology does not bring about contemplation. Thus the data – light and principles, light of faith and revealed truths – has primacy in all things, and even when theological science has pushed its rational effort to its furthest conclusion, its richness remains fresh and unstained to itself. There can be no worse blunder than to believe that one has enriched the 'data' and its native perception by 'reasons' and deductions. Even the most perfect theological systematizing would not add a jot of light or a tittle of truth to the Gospel.

This is how to stick to one's guns in the main discipline, studying the sources of faith, when organizing theological work. Where those who 'speculate' have shown indifference or even rage towards such study, it is because, subconsciously at least, they regard their systematic construction as having a meaning which is consistent in itself, definitively acquired and the fruit of an argument whose logical content is autonomous. Thus the 'speculative' scholars ignore and sometimes condemn everything surveyed by those exegetes, historians and theologians whom we are calling 'positive', with their greater attention to the data, unless the speculatives can find a way of introducing it into their closed system. This is not simply technical clumsiness, but an error against the rules of their knowledge, cutting it off from its ever-fresh, ever-bubbling source. Philosophy, or at least the history of philosophy, can ignore this without a problem, for its subject matter is not provided by historians, but is rather things themselves. The theologian, however, has no subject matter beyond the *auditus fidei*, for which the historian, without the light of faith, provides the survey – not simply a catalogue of propositions listed in some Denzinger, but a living subject, overflowing, always alive in a Church which is a repository, pregnant with divine intelligibility.

If Christianity draws its reality from history rather than metaphysics, the theologian's first concern, in dignity as well as in order, is to know that history and to equip himself to this effect. This is no transitory requirement, which one can hurriedly abandon to specialists at the door of the laboratory of speculation, but a permanent application in which the mind complies. Nor is it utilitarian apologetics, the subject matter of flunkeys tasked with defending the holy barque against heretics and dogma-deniers, but the substantial food of the very word of God. Texts are to theology what experiments are to science, as Thomas said; they are the soil in which theology incessantly comes back to life and grows in understanding. And this coming back, this 'resolution' of the revealed data as of the *principles* in themselves, light and object, is required even more than in science, so that every construction finds foundation and meaning.

In this conception of theology, Holy Scripture and Tradition are not primarily a collection of arguments to be used in the Schools for disputations and conclusions. They are primarily the *data of divine revelation*, to be scrutinized, known and loved for themselves. Any further speculation would be in vain if they do not aim at a better understanding of this revelation, using all the reserves of religious understanding. Exploiting St Paul's writings *in order* to demonstrate the physical causality of the sacraments is going in the wrong direction, for the physical causality is simply a means to fully understand Paul's sacramental realism. If I hold to Christ's unity of being, it is not to apply the real distinction between essence and existence to a particular case, but to assure myself of the benefits of the magnificent Christological mysticism of the Alexandrians, one of the most robust riches of the Tradition of the Eastern Churches. They are simple truisms, but they express the inviolable order of values, as opposed to the outline of so many theological manuals, in which it really seems that the Bible was only given to us to provide arguments for the Schoolmen. The infamous triple outline, according to which a theological 'thesis' was established by *proof through Scripture, proof through Tradition, proof through Reason*, is nothing more than the remains of a compromise between speculative theology and positive theology. In reality it compromises both in a false symmetry to which the primacy of revelation and the value of speculation adjust poorly. Above all, by reducing it to the establishment of outlines for 'proofs', it compromises the full and flavoursome assimilation of the inexhaustible riches of Christian thought and experience, past and present, with which texts and establishments are filled.

Anyone who undertakes to fill his essay on an article of Thomas's *Summa* with this positive revelation, in order to make the most of his new acquisitions in biblical or patristic theology, would be proceeding in a similarly clumsy manner. The intention is right, but its application is wrong. Revelation was not given in order to flow through Thomas's theological system; Thomas's theological system was given us to offer an intelligible account of a faith which is much greater than its perception.[1] Anyone who failed in the plan, mentioned elsewhere, of editing the *Summa* with a so-called positive annotation would be pleased; this would have been the wrong methodology.

If this is the place of revelation, the word of God perceived in faith and expressed in a multitude of ways, beginning with the very Incarnation of the Word, we can understand how the criticism brought against certain positive theology and the importance attributed to it falls down. It is seen as a huge survey of history, which, after lengthy and inextricable research, can only end in a collection of often disparate testimonies and opinions, incapable in themselves of constituting organic theological knowledge: 'authorities', perhaps, but not interior knowledge and living nourishment for the mind. Such an objection could only have taken root in opposition to a particular way of understanding positive theology. If we followed such a significant objection to its logical conclusion we would end up denouncing the roots of the working status

---

[1] From 1905, according to a note to Fr Gardeil, who was then a member of the commission for theological study of the Dominican Order, Fr Lemonnyer asked that this apparently progressive but poorly designed way of proceeding should be avoided, both in itself and as a way of understanding Thomas.

based on the division between the two organic functions of theology. Faith alone is the place where, psychologically and scientifically, documentation and speculation, 'authority' and 'reason' can be joined together in the unity of one subject area. This alone is both realistic perception at the beginning of contemplation of the divine and assent to the permitted propositions. We return to what was said at the start: outside of faith, in its most supernatural sense, theology has no coherence; it literally falls to pieces. But *in* faith, a demanding appetite for the *intellectus fidei* (understanding of the faith; Anselm) is born and grows in the believer which, with an ongoing interest in the divine revelation, leads to a religious and academic respect for those disciplines which investigate it. This is in fact a huge and wholesome subject, which it would be disastrous to reduce to a list of propositions and ancient texts, for the 'sources' of the theologian and the believer are the whole of the positive life of the Church – its customs and ways of thought; its devotional and sacramental life; its spiritualities, institutions, philosophies, according to the broad catholicity of the faith, through all of history and across the range of cultures.

As Melchoir Cano wrote, 'indeed, in relation to my judgements, no one could be praised as a total theologian unless he were also to pursue knowledge of all situations, and to prepare something timely to use in argument.'[2] And Noël Alexandre, one of the glories of the old convent of Saint-Jacques, concluded that

> I would concede that only a man versed in scholarly enquiry, in Sacred Scripture, in Church History, in the Councils, a man who is a pilgrim in the teachings of the holy Fathers and one who makes a home for them in his heart, is hardly half a theologian; I will firmly pronounce that he, indeed, who would be engaged in uncultured studies and untrained, would be of almost no use to the Church.[3]

Le Saulchoir remains faithful to the tradition of Saint-Jacques, and the Regent, Fr Gardeil, held the role of Cano.

Faith and history

If Revelation integrates itself in this way into time, the length of history, sacred history, centred on the historical fact of the Resurrection, and if from then on the revealed data is inscribed and presented in historical texts and facts, we are directly and brutally faced with this question: Are not theology, and the faith which inspires it, answerable to historical criticism? In principle, this would appear to throw faith open to relativism and thus to commit theology and its works to an inner circle from which the word of God cannot be reached.

This is precisely the problem of the historical method and of the effective arrangement of exegesis and the history of dogmas in theological knowledge. We

---

[2] *De locis theologicis* Bk XII Ch 2.
[3] *Historia ecclesiastica* Preface to vol. 1. Paris, 1976, p. xliiii. Noël Alexandre was Regent of Saint-Jacques (1675–1685) and held a doctorate from the Sorbonne.

know the anxieties which have weighed on theology for thirty years, not only on its orthodoxy, battered and breached by Modernism, but on its interior behaviour and the balance of its teaching programme. It is the whole notion of faith and the economy of faith which enables us to deal with this problem and to establish this programme with certain serenity.

Theology emanates from faith – it is born in and of faith. It is born from its weakness, from the radical weakness which is the assent of the mind to propositions which it can neither see nor measure. But it is also born out of power, that power which is stored in a soul in search of possession of the realistic perception of the mysterious divine reality, *substantia rerum sperandarum* (the substance of things which should be hoped for). The believer's journey does not end in dogmatic proposition, but in the divine reality as it is humanly expressed. It is, therefore, not a concept, nor formulas, nor a thought system, but the One in whom I recognize the whole of my life, the desired object of my happiness. Of course faith is an assent to propositions, which are the authentic bearers of its religious perception; but therein lies its poverty or, rather, the provisional poverty of my mind, which does not know even divine truth except through propositions. Through this and thanks to this faith is belonging to what completes all its desires, the only desire of my soul: the beatific vision in the gift of God himself.

This realism of faith, so vigorously expressed by St Paul witnessing to salvation in knowing Christ, finds its psychological reason in the strictly supernatural quality of the interior light of the 'word of God' in me. Knowledge of God in me, the word of God is all grace, personal grace, putting me in dialogue and direct contact with Him, the mysterious presence to whom the 'new man' has access, not because his reason has brought him here, but because God reveals himself, *sibi ipsis testis* (witness to his own self). 'He who believes in the Son of God has witnessed to God in him' (1 Jn 5.10). Transcendent and interior, it lies behind neither preaching nor epiphany. It is not a historical statement, it is not engaged in time, even in relation to Christ, for faith is precisely that mission which makes us 'contemporaries' of Christ. And while the Gospel comes to us through the continuity of time, it is not, in the eyes of faith, a historical text, but truly the word of God.

The theologian is a believer. He is a believer *par excellence*, and his task is formally completed in the mystery to which his faith has introduced him, not in the projection in human words of the word of God. 'Sacred doctrine': the traditional name, in its proper sense, without which it would simply become a profane science: the profanation of the word of God. It is precisely the theologian's dramatic effort to hold in radical fragility those propositions in which he gives life to the realist perception of the mysterious reality of God. This is a dialectic in which his power triumphs over his weakness: in faith. 'No theology without new birth.' Theology, in this sense, is nothing more than faith in solidarity with time; it is not rooted in history. It will hardly be the happy conclusion of a favourable historical criticism on the results of which we can build a beautiful scaffolding of 'reasons'. Revealed data, theological data, is not 'scientific': it is revealed. And if I make a scientific endeavour of this – what a nerve! – it is not through reinforcing its historical bases or its apologetic justifications. This will be a 'science of believers'. If not, we will once more only have a game of reasoning on the surface of data, theology without the word of God. This is a cardinal point on which both the organization and spirit of theology depend: Fr Gardeil and Fr Lemonnier of Le Saulchoir were fully aware of the cause, the Masters of this categorical position.

So shall we never return to history? Have we said that Christianity does not draw its reality from history? It is a paradox of faith that the 'substance of things which should be hoped for' (*substantia rerum speranduarum*) only finds its object in received teaching: 'faith through hearing' (*fides ex auditu*). The word of God is given to us in human words, and supernatural faith will be an assent to determined propositions. A dogmatic formula is not a juridical statement external to the revelation which it presents: it is the incarnation in concepts of the Word of God. This is the economy of that Word: it speaks humanly; it robes the forms of the human mind and produces in itself, according to the conditions required by the mechanism of psychology linked to the slow and heavy complexity of notions and judgements, linked to categories of time and space, as the philosophers said, engaged in a history. Things will be known in the thinking of the person who understands them as they should be by someone with understanding. (*Cognita sunt in cognoscente ad modum cognoscentis.*) To exclude God from this natural law of all knowledge, on the pretext that he is transcendent, or that he reveals himself, would really be to give in, in advance, to the spiritual disorder of a false mysticism. Faith is no more a light placed at the surface of reason than grace is in nature: faith lives in reason, grace in nature. And faith is not contaminated by this incarnation, any more than the Word was lessened by taking flesh. The dual or, rather, unique theandric mystery, the very mystery of Christ, in whom the divine and the human are one: a unique Person, in whom I pitch my tent through faith, the eternal Son of God who enters into history. The Christ of faith is in the Christ of history.

All of history comes through this. The theologian has no chance of finding her data outside of history, outside of that 'hearing of faith' (*auditus fidei*) which resounds through time, from Abraham, 'whose faith was counted to him as righteousness', until Christ, and in the Church, Christ permanently down the centuries. Of course this is sacred history, but its sacred nature neither removes it nor abstracts it from the contexts which are its subject, and the law of human history, otherwise this would not be an incarnation. If human words were structurally damaged by the coming of the Word of God, they would be unintelligible to humanity and would no longer reveal God's word. The Word truly became human when he became human, one of us. The Son of God is a historical person.

The theologian, then, works with history. Her data is not the nature of things, or their timeless forms, but events which respond to an *economy*, whose fulfilment is linked to time, just as size is linked to the body, above the order of essences. This is the *real* world, not the philosophers' abstraction. The believer, the believing theologian, enters into this plan of God through faith; the understanding he seeks is a divine initiative, in fact a series of divine, absolute initiatives, whose essential trait is that they are without 'reason'. They are general initiatives like creation, the incarnation, redemption and particular initiatives such as predestinations of grace, the sweet and terrible contingencies of a love which does not need to give any account of its benefits or its desertions. The true world of contemplation and of theological understanding is this, given over to the initiatives of a free God, who directs this huge, undefinable story, in which he is the primary character, as he alone wishes. This is so true that, if there is a problem, it is finding reasons for this freedom without reasons, 'rationalizing' this story, not knowing it in oneself in one's immediate surroundings. For it is clear that it is to be known according to the laws of history, and the word of God will be known in it. It is in the name of this very theandrism of the Word that historical criticism, with all its apparatus, became a tool appropriated by theology. To provoke such trouble in the study of the sources of revelation and the development of theological method around 1900 required the conjunction of modernist historicism and a false theology of faith. Modernist historicism, which took history to be an absolute, where only faith can be absolute; a false theology of faith, which rejected its substantial supernatural-ness due to a fear of no longer being able to make rational apologetics out of mystical assent. For Gardeil, on the other hand, completely at ease in a Thomist theology of faith, history was no longer the critical suspect which had to be held at arm's length and poorly treated, but the precious handmaid which, in the independent handling of its rules and tools, granted faith the means of sticking more fully to its own data, freed from the track of time according to the gradual economy of revelation, and not according to the logical deductions of a neo-Platonic Logos.

Hence Gardeil's disciples at Le Saulchoir warmly and fully welcomed the *historical methodology* and its resources for which Fr Lagrange, in one of his infamous seminars in Toulouse, had just claimed rights and magnificent results.[4] The best testimony of this encounter between theology and historical exegesis was the doctrine of inspiration which supported Fr Lagrange's method. The incarnation of the Word of God took place even in the letters of words – 'literal inspiration' – and the very letter with all its grammatical, literary and historical workmanship is the proper way of reaching an understanding of the faith. The word of God is *in* the human word: God's strength is revealed in this weakness. Accidents may happen during the philologist's clumsy investigations, in literary criticism or historical criticism; but a methodology is not built upon accidents, rather on the objective order of realities. Here, these are the realities of supernatural faith *in* the human mind and language. Biblical docetism is simply the false modesty of a fearful faith in an out-of-place theology.

We can see how theological work is organized on these bases, according to the complexity of its methods which guarantee – rather than reduce – unity of faith. Historical exegesis (the Bible) and the history of dogmas (Tradition) will, as their names suggest, be works of history, a history carried out according to its ways and processes, in the light of resources, in all sincerity and loyalty. Biblical theology, patristic theology, symbolic theology: in short, positive theology will develop, rather, in the light of faith, and following faith's criteria, as it is properly theology. The road from Athens to Piraeus is not the same as the road from Piraeus to Athens. If the distinction between these two routes seems entirely abstract and the cross-checking tricky, that is because it is tricky to conceive of and express the cross-checking of the divine and human in revelation: the revelation of the word of God, at the summit of which the revelation of the Word made flesh took place. As for the apparent subtlety of discernment, these are methodological abstractions which, according to the law of all scholarship, guarantee the probity of the research and the internal order of the construction. The discipline

---

[4] M.-Joseph Lagrange OP, *La Méthode historique*, Paris, 1903.

of formal objects is one of the most precious riches of Thomist pedagogy; the painful confusion of ideas, methods and vocabularies among the best theologians during the Modernist crisis has once again underlined Thomas's quality and urgency.

The freedom with which St Thomas opened his mind to Greek scholarship – against the religious and philosophical agreement which sought to prevent Christianity's access to it – comes from this same discipline and mindset. Likewise, the discreet ease with which today's Thomist kills off biblical concordance in all its forms, not only the academic concordance which has weighed down the teaching of Scripture for half-a-century but also the ethnological and historical concordances which are as annoying a compromise for faith as for scholarship. The same adversaries saw rationalism at play in the Greek scholarship of the thirteenth century and the biblical studies of the twentieth.

If the economy of revelation develops in time and if as a consequence faith finds its authentic expression in statements which are integral with history, the particular case – this is all it is – of the development of dogma within the new economy, the life of the Church, will not unsettle the theologian: it is normal, and the law of the incarnation is visible in it. To seek to camouflage it or to reduce it simply to a game of verbal equivalence, as happened with a certain fixed mindedness, in which all theology was reduced to being anti-Modernist, is not only to treat history badly (a poor way of preparing good theology) but also a poor understanding of faith. It is a strange inversion, which is a sign of error: these are the same theologians who, because they have lost the sense of transcendence of the Word of God in faith, transfer faith to the absolute in the formulas which express it in an authoritarian manner and thus subject these formulas to history. As Fr Gardeil said, *contra* those who, having rejected the analogy of the divine names, lost the anguish of the theologian before the mystery to be held in human speech, however categorical it is, this is 'an unintelligent and low conception of the divine reality'. It is faith which is an absolute and which escapes from history. Pure faith in its infused light, not dogma, is the hearing of faith (*auditus fidei*) which submits to the magisterium.

This is a real development, in full dogmatic reality, not in the continuation of the second zone. Does the believer's seeking understanding (*quaerens intellectum*) take place at the fringes of truth? This perhaps opens the door to relativism of dogmatic formulas; but this historical relativism is but the effect, following the lapse of time, of their metaphysical relativism. With the same vigour and serenity as Cajetan, Fr Gardeil proclaimed this metaphysical relativism, the very expression of the doctrine of analogical knowledge. The historical contingencies and the psychological complexities of dogmatic formulas may be coolly considered next to such a radical source of relativism.

Appealing to evolutionary theory to explain the development of dogma, as was done around 1900, is not without difficulty. In any case, transferring the mindset of vocabulary and theories from the physical sciences into another discipline is a delicate operation. In this case, it was necessary to expurgate 'evolution' from its biological meaning or Hegelian metaphysics. But the image of biological growth has long had a legitimate place in theology (Vincent of Lérins, in the fifth century); and the sense of history, on which Hegelian speculation rests, had already, in Möhler and Newman, found a rare spiritual quality in Christianity. This, then, was a wonderful case of theological 'science': it is dealt with in one of the most polished chapters of *Le donné révélé*, from which one of Fr Gardeil's friends and disciples, Fr Marin-Sola, would later draw inspiration for his own masterpiece, *L'évolution homogène du dogme catholique*.[5] Of course, one can discuss the conclusions of these two Masters, but the historian of Christian doctrine will find, in the thesis of the gradual unfolding of divine revelation, with the legitimacy of its work and method, the theological reason of her own historical observations. Mgr Battifol, who benefitted from Fr Gardeil's friendly censoring at a difficult moment in his work on the development of Eucharistic dogma, was therefore sure of having every reassurance outside of the narrow solution into which he had been blocked by certain theologians. This was a significant and comforting encounter between two Masters who, for too long, like the disciplines of which they were the leaders, had each been working for his own side.

Yet we should note this: because this historical 'growth' of dogma remains the temporal effect of a faith which remains identical through time, in souls where the word of God speaks, the crises of Christian thought – as it were – are definitively judged beyond the passage of time, according to the spiritual plan of the nearness of Christ (*propinquitas ad Christum*) (*ST* 2ae2ae a.7 ad.2, 4). This is the history of souls, not only a social memory. Such is the history of dogmas or, rather, the history of Christian doctrine which, for the theologian, is the subject of Tradition.

If we take the life of the Church in its historical and spiritual tradition as the locus of Tradition in this way, we once again encounter the primacy of the *data of revelation* in the structure of theology, as we have discussed. Just as Scripture is not a kind of external 'proof' for the truth of such-and-such a dogma, neither is Tradition; it is itself its own truth. It is a proof in the sense that it is the permanent Christian conscience in the Church, acting as a criterion to judge any innovation. It is not simply a collection of beliefs, following an empirical and static concept of places, but the presence of the Spirit in the social body of the Church, divine and human in Christ. Not only is it the conservation of dogmas described, results reached or decisions taken in the past, but it is the creating principle of understanding and the inexhaustible source of new life. Tradition is not an aggregate of traditions, but a principle of organic continuity, of which the magisterium is the infallible tool, in the theandric reality of the Church, the mystical body of Christ.

Here, in its very vocabulary,[6] is the main theme of the Catholic Tübingen theologians (Drey and Möhler). At Le Saulchoir we have been pleased to borrow from these masters of the Catholic German renaissance of the nineteenth century at the same time as, in theology and revelation of the faith, we are similarly inspired by M. J. Scheeben. With them, we reject the abstract intellectualism of the *Aufklärung* and its indifference to history: these wrongs are connected and did not avoid contaminating modern Scholasticism, where the *Aufklärung* disingenuously reinforced the host of manuals, even the Thomist ones.

---

[5] Valencia 1923/Fribourg-Paris, 1924.
[6] Cf. E. Vermeil, *J.A.Möhler et l'école catholique de Tubingue (1815–1840)*, Paris, 1913. See too some excellent words by Drey, cited in the *RSPT* 1937 (719–721).

We talked about being present to one's time. Well, here we are. Theologically speaking, that means to be present to divine revelation in the present life of the Church and the contemporary experience of Christianity. Tradition, then, is *in faith*, the very presence of revelation. The theologian lives from this: he gazes with wide eyes at Christianity at work.

So, with holy curiosity, let us see what we do:

- Missionary expansion, which in its deepest sense shows itself to be against all that narrow-mindedness in our minds and institutions, enlivened by the feeling of the new dimensions of the world, its solidarities, its independence, its adult peoples, outliers of a colonialism past its use-by date;
- the plurality of human civilization, whose disparate wealth can weigh down local Christianities, but which can also make them feel, with the transcendence of Christianity, the divine suppleness of its grace;
- the original grandeur of the East, which Islam snatched from the Gospel, dilapidated by schism, but whose loss remains an open wound for the Church, tempted for too long to hide itself in Western Latinism;
- the moving and irrepressible demand for union which is working, even more feverishly than Christianity itself, on dissident Christendoms, whose 'ecumenical' movements bear witness to the *one holy Church*;
- the social fermentation provoked by the accession of the popular masses to public life and awareness, a grand spectacle made tragic by the perversion of communism, including in its denunciation of Christian ignorance and light-heartedness not only the numerous problems of practical morality raised by this, but the great problem of a new Christianity in gestation, a Mystical Body in which work will have its spiritual status and humanity its human condition between wealth and poverty;
- and, in the midst of all this, the Church Militant, finding a new youth in this new world, through a new means of conquest, in which the laity participate in the hierarchical apostolate, bringing the witness and life of the Christian into this environment: an ongoing incarnation in which every layer of human society, by trade and class, will be assumed by those institutions which are the specialist movements, the typical structure of this new Christendom.

So many theological 'scenes' to be played out, for the doctrine of grace, of the incarnation, of redemption, expressly promulgated elsewhere and described by papal encyclicals. They are poor theologians who are buried in their expensive texts and scholastic disputations, not open to these visions, not only the pious fervour of their hearts but formally in their study: theological data at full capacity, in the *presence* of the Spirit.

The '*Unam Sanctam*' series seeks to record, develop and construct a section of this theological data in practice. The ecclesiological categories in which we live, at least in current teaching, remain in sympathy with the treatises of the seventeenth-century 'controversialists', masterpieces of anti-Protestant polemic, but rooted in points of conflict and built according to opportunities which are now largely out of date both in the Church and in the wider human context. More than ever, perhaps, the Church is now working for Catholicity and unity.[7]

In the last few years, Le Saulchoir has had the joy and grace of regularly receiving Young Christian Worker chaplains and activists, who have made this House – wholly concerned with books and timeless theology – one of their most loved and secure spiritual places. For the 'theologians' this spontaneous encounter with the Young Christian Workers and their equivalents has been an immeasurable criteria. Here, they see the witness of Christian authenticity and the supernatural vitality of their strictly theological work.

Their doctrinal and apostolic communion with their brothers involved with the people, whether by their works or their publications (the publications of the 'Juvisy Dominicans', so-called for their former home, among others), are of the same calibre and analogous value. Plato's contemplative did not give up his faith on his return to the City; the theologian, doubly so, must bear his light in the midst of the world, and he can do it without despairing of contemplation. The division of work requires it to be shared, but neither spiritual solidarities nor the identity of different formations are diminished because of this. The difficult task of daily seeing and judging world events in the light of Christianity can only be undertaken with a faith which is rooted in theological knowledge. It is pleasing for us to recognize in such an enterprise, through moving contingencies and against the worst calumnies, the intrepid nature of our father St Dominic and the clear-sightedness of our master St Thomas.

Twentieth-century Christianity, like that of the thirteenth century, is a magnificent place in which to work at theology.

Theological reason

This, then, is the law of theological knowledge and consequently the reason for the cycle of positive disciplines which it employs in its service: the revealed data trumps all. It is not the only dialectic primacy of a statement, but a *presence*, with the inexhaustible realism and the silent insistence that the word implies, for the gaze which has consented. It is here that we can now 'build'.

Now we are at the decisive step. The theologian is the person who dares to speak the Word of God in human terms. Having heard this Word, she owns it, or, more precisely, it owns her, to the point that she thinks through it and in it, that she thinks it. The gift

---

[7] It is in this very perspective and through the obvious requirement of the theological methodology that, in the cycle of study, we dissociate the treaty of the Church itself and the question of the Church as witness to and deposit of Revelation. The former is a problem of credibility, of the authoritarian presentation and transmission of faith in an external institution, the latter the permanent 'mystery of Christ' in his mystical body. The former is a chapter of *De revelatione*, the latter an immediate consequence of the incarnation of Christ and his major grace: here the *De Ecclesia* finds its place. To locate this study as 'apologetics' is to entirely distort the axis of the theological intelligibility of the Church, which is one of the most infuriating imbalances of modern teaching. In the plentiful order of study laid out for the *De Ecclesia* in the *ratio studiorum* we end up in reality with an obliteration of the supernatural sense of the Church. In 1905, Fr Lemonnyer addressed a note to the Order's Commission of studies criticizing this theoretical and pedagogical confusion.

of God is a gift to the extent that it becomes human property: faith is a *habitus*. It is not an extraordinary charism, held out of our human way of thinking by its transcendence; it is an incarnation of the divine truth in the very fabric of our mind and spirit. It is not pure confidence – Luther's *fiducia* – but a 'virtue', embedded in us as a power is embedded in a nature. Faith resides *in* reason, thus empowered to *theo-logein* (speak of God). It is not that the 'old person' leaves behind his impotence before the mystery of God, but that the theologian is the 'new person'. Working out the content of faith in a rational, academic manner does not stop him being this 'new person', but, on the contrary, completes it. By begetting theology, faith is in the very logic of its perfection.

Thus logic follows its course. In accordance with the expected discernments and with the necessary discretion, all the techniques of reason will be deployed within and to the benefit of the mystical perception of the believer. This includes conceptual divisions, myriad analyses and judgements, definitions and divisions, comparisons and classifications, inferences, reasoning in search of an explanation, finally, or above all, deduction, for even though deduction is a characteristic tool of science, where the process of rationalization reaches its proper effectiveness. So many signs of weakness, of course, but also significant rational intrepidity: the 'theological conclusion' encompasses this defect and this boldness. It is a dialectic of the faith in which its power triumphs over its weakness. That same law which a moment ago made us call for the incarnation of the word of God in human words in the course of history now presses us to accept in totality the rule of knowledge which that incarnation implies: theology is in solidarity with the theandric mystery of the word of God, the Word made flesh. Only here can it find such an audacious confidence in the coherence of faith and reason.

Thus we believe, with St Thomas, in theological reason and in the science of theology. *Intellectus fidei*, in the fullest sense of the words, against the opposing but symmetrical attitudes of the 'positives' and the 'mystics', both of whom have misgivings about that reason making itself at home in faith, about that 'scholasticism' definitively constructed on confusing revelation with theology. After what we have said about the transcendence of the word of God and the supernatural nature of faith, there is no need to defend ourselves from a similar confusion. Yet having denounced this confusion, we hold firm to the homogeneity of theological science with revealed data. The introduction of rational statements in the working out of faith is not the corruption which some mean. Founded in the unity of a faith in which the transcendence of the divine word and human realism are in solidarity, we reject any rupture between *mysticism* and *theology*, just as we do between *positive* and *speculative*. We do not give in to the failings of various seventeenth-century Thomists who believed they had to build a *theologia mystica* by extrapolating from speculative theology. This is how they first lost sight of the religious sense of theology, just as elsewhere the same scholars abandoned to the so-called positive theology that permanent return to revelation, which is the only way theological science can renew its religious vigour. Thus the preface of one of Thomas's most famous commentators, who ingenuously admits this breakdown. All our conviction and effort goes to encountering those

> who dream of distinguishing two areas in theology: one which purely intellectual and scholastic, bristling with formulas which religious life can perfectly well

ignore; the other positive and mystical in which supernatural needs, working on the data of revelation authentically recognized thanks to positive theology, will build a dogmatism which eventually is religious, a sort of mystical theology which does not have to take any account of scholastic theology. (A. Gardeil)

Theology, faith working towards theological understanding, is truly and properly a factor of the spiritual life. We cannot do theology by adding 'corollaries of piety' to abstract theses, cut off from their objective and subjective *data*, but rather in holding firm to the profound unity of the theological order.

Theological science, then, is not made up of a collection of 'opinions', more or less external and indifferent to the data of revelation, which can be chosen at whim, once orthodoxy is secure. This would be a pitiful agreement between legalistic faith and the vacuity of the mind. No! – reason, theological reason, is here with all its resources, including the power to conclude. This is why philosophy and philosophies – organized reason – have played such a major role in the history of Christian thought, theology and spirituality. Those who doubt scholastic 'rationalism' need only look at the life and work of Clement of Alexandria, Origen, Dionysius, Augustine, Anselm, Bonaventure, Aquinas, Scotus. It is true that in order to study the history of spirituality, there are some who wish to purge – as they say – these masters of their philosophy, remove the Platonic or Aristotelian contamination from their Christian purity. It is always the same error, in which theology, because of its conceptualism, is external to faith, conceptualizing without faith; but rather than being its result, this is the incarnation of that faith in the human mind.

Likewise there is a *science* of Christian perfection, in which moral theology itself properly consists. It is not a collection of questions of conscience, raised in reference to teachings and resolved according to degrees of probability extrinsic to the adduced authorities. This is soulless legalism without 'reason' from which spiritual theologians, indeed, all good Christians, immediately veer away.

Thus we give ourselves with a religious complacency to the deduction of the divine attributes – to building a treatise on the Trinity starting with the idea of procession – to the knowledge of a sacramental regimen which uses typically human actions in its effective symbolism – to the moral analysis of the supernatural life of grace which the theological virtues and the gifts of the Spirit make intelligible according to the psychological economy of the human person and so on. What a marvel of the divine light which takes possession of the mind to this extent. It is not the embrace of a dialectic scaffold, but an interior arming which faith itself creates in all its divine and human intellectual health: in communion with the science of God, it dares to seek the 'reasons' for the works of God, and thus to gain an understanding of his mystery. *Fides quaerens intellectum*.

If this is the interiority of reason in theology, its great work is singularly narrowed down when it becomes but a defence of dogmas, establishing its rational values as exterior buttresses. The nineteenth century gave way to this increase in apologetics, too often the price of theology's internal poverty. Against this extremism, we would like to think that reason is fertile for sacred doctrine, the maker of sacred doctrine; there is no need to dogmatize in an untimely manner to appreciate the 'Christian' structure and quality of the *theological* concepts of sacrament, instrumental causality, the person, generation, habitus, gifts and so on.

We believe in theological science. We even believe in theological systems. For here, as elsewhere, science tends towards systematizing, in witness to its success (and its failure) in capturing the *data* which it claims to know. In addition, if it is true that the mind's inadequacy for the *data* is at the origin of the 'system', for its advantage and its relativism, there is no field where systematizing would have greater raison d'être than theology, since human understanding is radically, permanently, inadequate for the *data*.

Hence Fr Gardeil's insistence on distinguishing between theological science and theological systems; it is the crucial point of his methodology. It is also the pivot around which the theologian's discretion is shown, at the junction between her two convictions and her two fervours: the primacy of data and speculative construction. It is still the believer who is working, and this work remains highly qualified religiously, in religious understanding; it is not some vain game trying to give a reason for the efficacy of the sacraments through a theory of instrumental causality; neither is it a gratuitous hypothesis which seeks to organize all theological data around the notion of being, or of goodness. It is good, solid work, the work of truth. But the believer knows that his faith no longer works except and according to rational choices: speculative tools have become the decisive factors of this understanding, to the extent that their conclusions are now but the fragile human context of the mystery, a refraction of faith in independent thought.

At the very moment where she gives in to this curiosity, the theologian feels she is free with regard to it and, while deducing for her benefit, does not agree to commit the word of God to this. From this, with regard to the philosophies which she makes use of, that freedom of pace with which she chooses in a system which suits her, an element distends, going as far as modifying the extension and understanding of the most defined concepts, complicating another. It is an intellectual pragmatism which would shock philosophy, but which here witnesses to a faith which is in control of its tools. Thus we are very sensitive to the difference which exists, in their very being, between a philosophical elaboration, pedagogy or culture and a theological argument or construction. A theologian may describe himself as Aristotelian, and may truly be so, through his choices about the psychology of the mind or the metaphysical primacy of being; but he is only this thanks to a spiritual assumption outside of the Aristotelian system, on the one hand, and, on the other, on the condition of a constant openness to other philosophical systems and mindsets.

To note this relativism in the construction of theology, however, is in no way to lapse into eclecticism or to see in the rivalry between theological 'schools' simply a somewhat belligerent salvation from free opinions which correct each other to the advantage of dogma which goes beyond them. We believe in theological reason, while eclecticism is its defeat. The relativism of systems is perfectly translated by their unequal comprehensibility, and therefore truth, whether they coordinate the whole data less well or whether their construction is less organic; whether they pursue this from limited or unpolished perceptions. There are so many theological 'errors' and not just unlikely opinions. The divine truth of faith may not be compromised by these systematic disqualifications; however, it is only affirmed in its human influence to the extent of the system it claims to express: universality, coherence and its principal perceptions give the Thomist system its privileged place. We are Thomists, by reason; even, we might say, by nature, born in St Thomas through our Dominican vocation.

Yet in the end, theological systems are only the expression of spirituality; this is their interest and their greatness. Astonishing as it is to have such theological divergences in the unity of dogma, it is even more astonishing to see a single Christian faith give rise to such a variety of spiritualities. The greatness and truth of Bonaventurian or Scotist Augustinianism are wholly within the spiritual experience of St Francis, which was the heart and soul of his sons; the greatness and truth of Molinism find their spiritual experience in St Ignatius's *Exercises*. One does not pick a system for the logical coherence of its construction or the likelihood of its conclusions; one finds oneself within it, as though born to it, by the guiding intuition with which one lives one's spiritual life, with the system of understanding that includes. A theology worthy of its name is a spirituality which has found rational tools appropriate to its religious experience. It was not by chance that St Thomas joined the Order of St Dominic; it was with no incoherent grace that the Order of St Dominic received Thomas of Aquinas. The institution and the doctrine are closely linked, in the inspiration they both held in a new age, in contemplation which, together, guaranteed fervour, methodology, purity, freedom of mind.

If this is where we belong, it is clear that the theology of St Thomas, by its very interiority, does not compromise the virginity of the word of God, which remains clear of any human weight in its gratuitous revelation. The systems can be true in theological science; they do not engage dogma. There was no worse disgrace for Thomism, whose whole native effort was to found a status of human understanding in Christianity, than to be treated as 'orthodoxy'.

Given our understanding of faith, of its absolute supernatural nature and its radical independence, we sense better than others, at the heart of this faith, both in its artless belonging and in its mystical contemplation, that kind of resistance to systematization which constrains the theologian to not 'settle' in the results of his dialectic but to control himself unceasingly with fear and humility. It is through a mistaken appearance that theology *puts an end to some types of science*; it is not more open, more desirous of progress, more tormented by spiritual purification. We believe with all our hearts in the progress of theology, from fervour as much as from the faith which gives rise to it. But this progress is not in exploiting an inherited system, in the proliferation of new conclusions to the extreme ends of a more subtle dialectic; it has its source in the most secret theological work, from where that insatiable appetite of faith rises in the permanent fruitfulness of the data, which aims at nothing more than the beatific vision – not any other conclusion. The normal place of *invention*, always at work in secular constructions, is therefore both scientifically and religiously that contemplative perception to which the unceasing return to the data gives an ever-new gaze and which arduously underlies the hope of this vision.

For the theologian, therefore, contemplation is not a summit reached here and there through a sudden burst of fervour, which is beyond study, as though escaping its object and method. It is theology's normal place, integral, where scientific organization and innovative invention can be held together in a unique fruitfulness. The simple unity of theology, where the Aristotelian categories of speculation and praxis no longer overlap: from one end to the other of its trajectory, it is some impression of divine science (*quaedam impressio divinae scientiae*). In the exercise of the theological virtue of faith, St Thomas identifies sacred doctrine and the contemplative life. This is enough for us to not reduce contemplation to spiritual exercises and not to treat the spiritual life and theology as two different things. This is the very status of the Order of St Dominic, and its authentic expression is given to us in the sanctity and teaching of St Thomas Aquinas.

From here, in theology in progress, this kind of disinterestedness, this spiritual freedom towards the most appropriate tools, this casual ease in the most engaging encounters with philosophies and cultures, this constant creation within its most integral bodies, this new life in the old man, this boldness in rational joy of the light of faith. Theology is audacious, because, in the self-forgetfulness of contemplation, it is pure; it can have every boldness as long as it is pure – the science of the children of God.

2

'Conversion and grace in Aquinas'

'Conclusion'. *Conversion et grâce chez S. Thomas d'Aquin. Étude historique.* Théologie I (Paris: Aubier, 1944), 211–24.

Henri Bouillard SJ

The almost inevitable default position of the manuals shows theology as a ready-made science, with unchanging ideas, timeless problems and definitive arguments. It is as though it is a discipline given as a one-off, which may be discovered simply through turning the pages of a book. Even more erudite works sometimes leave the same impression. While the authors know that theology has not always existed in its current state in the knowledge of theologians, they imply, at least unconsciously, that it was already given as such in the field of eternal truths and that discursive intelligence simply had to discover it and reconstruct it bit by bit.

A historical study, on the other hand, reveals the extent to which theology is linked to time and to the development of the human mind. It demonstrates what is contingent in theology: relativity of ideas, development of problems, provisional obscuring of certain important truths. We have pointed to this throughout our work. In concluding, we may be permitted to revisit our principal observations and to briefly indicate their importance.

St Thomas has a surprise in store for anyone who comes across him having reverently encountered so-called Thomist theology in a modern manual or textbook. In his works, one expects to read the same problems and answers, and find identical ideas under common terms such as grace, divine aid, conversion and preparation for justification. But we soon observe that, interpreted through this lens, some texts seem contradictory or erroneous. If the reader perseveres in believing that St Thomas's thought was coherent and orthodox, but wishes to take this into consideration, she will spend some time as a philologist and historian. In the text she will note definitions, things to be discerned here and there in addition to the problems which interest her, those which Thomas asked. She will compare Thomas with his contemporaries and predecessors, and will thus discover a living system, but one which is different from what she expected.

Throughout this work, we have observed the extent to which Thomas's theology differs from modern theology in ideas and in the way in which it raises and deals with problems. We have noted how it is dependent on its time, its environment and its author's personal tendencies. What is probably most striking is the Aristotelian mark. Modern theology has, of course, partially retained this but has also thrown much out. St Thomas received many ideas from his predecessors which were shaped according to Aristotle's models and categories. The needs of his time, and his personal genius, led him to emphasize these characteristics and to develop systematically his theology according to the schemes and categories of the *Physics* and the *Metaphysics*.

Thus Thomas conceives of grace as a form; in other words, not only as an inherent quality, but as a principle of operation leading the soul to produce certain determined actions. Free will, in relation to this, is matter. Form and matter together produce the meritorious act. Justification is the movement towards this form, in other words, a generation. In this role it requires preparation, because a form may only be received in predisposed matter. The disposition is said to be ultimate or remote, according to whether or not it coincides with the arrival of a new form. Given that the will is capable of sudden returns, it can suddenly reach its remote disposition. Only necessary and only sufficient, this constitutes the disposition-type. Therefore preparation for grace does not initially describe acts prior to justification but those which coincide with it; in short, preparation is synonymous with cooperation.

The divine movement does not exactly describe what modern theology understands by actual grace. It is not a support whose effect is to gradually increase powers to be able to produce a supernatural act. It is simply the movement of the prime mover, necessary for every form in order that it should produce its act. It does not increase power, it sets it in motion, and makes it pass to action. It is free, when the form which it makes act is an infused habitus. According to the works of Thomas's early teaching, which he later abandoned, it is still free even when it makes a natural action distantly ordained to salvation.

Through these examples, and through others which we may also recall, we see that the ideas used by St Thomas are simply Aristotelian ideas applied to theology. In this sense, they are very different from the theological ideas used by the Church Fathers or even by theologians in our day. For St Augustine in particular, grace is not a form added to free will, to make it produce meritorious acts; it is the 'delight' (*delectatio*) which liberates free will from its servitude to sin. There are not two kinds of grace, one habitus, the other movement, but a single grace, charity poured out into hearts by the Holy Spirit, which makes the human person participate in divine nature and accomplish good. Modern theologians have kept the notion of grace-form or grace-habitus. But generally they no longer allow that an infused habitus is necessary for the production of a supernatural action, for instance, that an act of faith should be impossible without the habitus of faith. Even without a habitus, actual grace can bring about a supernatural action. In addition it is not understood in the same way as it was by St Thomas. Generally an actual grace rising to natural competition is opposed, while St Thomas only named a single motion. We have stopped rigorously tracing the process of justification onto Aristotle's notion of generation. Remote disposition no longer passes for disposition-type. Preparation for grace is no longer synonymous with cooperation: it regularly describes actions prior to justification by which one is disposed to justification.

These differences in notions regulate differences in problems and solutions. It was ever thus, to a greater or lesser degree – but more so in the Middle Ages than in our days. The historical and introspective methods currently in favour lead us at every moment to go beyond the ideas we start from. Medieval theologians, who began from analysis of ideas and definitions which they received as 'authorities', relied upon these notions even when their thought led them to go far beyond the ideas.[1] Most of the time, these notions regulated the questions. For instance, the problem of preparation for grace is only raised in a theology where grace is conceived of as a form in the Aristotelian sense. St Thomas himself said that one cannot prepare oneself for grace understood as a motion. Preparation for grace is necessary because, according to Aristotle, a form can only be received in a substance which is ready to receive it; hence we note that, before the introduction of Aristotelianism, theologians did not discuss preparation for grace. There was the question of conversion, of the 'beginnings of faith' (*initium fidei*), of the cooperation of free will and grace; and there was the pastoral problem of preparation for baptism; but strictly speaking there was no problem of preparation for grace.

The Thomist conception of the relationship between habitual grace and remote disposition may also be explained by the use of Aristotelian systems. The act of faith and act of love by which we convert is at the same time the remote disposition to sanctifying grace and the effect of that grace. Here, Thomas was doing no more than applying the systems of his generation. The change which disposes the subject to receive a new form must end in a remote disposition, which is only remote because it is dependent on the new form. The process of change does not end before generation but in it and through it. This presupposes that the form in which it ends is essentially a principle of operation, whose first action is to create the ultimate disposition for its reception. The influence of Nominalism and the development of ideas in physics meant that, from the sixteenth century onwards, Thomists themselves admitted that this theory was difficult to understand; many, on the pretext of interpreting it, abandoned it. They no longer saw that it was self-evident in an Aristotelian thought world.

The medieval idea of grace also explains some solutions which are surprising to us. In his early works, St Thomas roundly declares that the human person can prepare himself for sanctifying grace through free will, without grace. He wished to exclude a grace which would be another habitus or another form, for this idea was so strongly imposed on his mind by his environment. He went as far as to say that it is not necessary that actions through which a person prepares herself for grace go beyond human nature. Here again, Thomas's mind is dominated by the idea that, in order to go beyond nature, an action must proceed from a superadded form; but it is not necessary that the preparatory action for grace goes beyond nature, since, in relation to grace, it plays the role of simple matter. Thus St Thomas's position is regulated by the Aristotelian schemes which were the models for the ideas he had received from his predecessors.

When he discovered the existence of semi-Pelagianism and then the necessity of emphasizing the divine initiative in conversion, he once again had recourse to an

---

[1] See O. Lottin, 'La théorie du libre arbiter depuis S. Anselme jusqu'à S. Thomas d'Aquin', *Revue Thomiste*, 1927–9, 158.

Aristotelian idea to understand it. The discovery of the *Liber de Bona Fortuna* gave him precisely the idea of God's interior movement necessary for every act of the will. This is how he understood the grace which Augustine described as necessary for the *initium fidei*.

We can now see the extent to which St Thomas understood and expressed Christian truth according to the ideas and systems borrowed from Aristotle. He followed the fashions of his day. If we compare his theory to that of the Fathers, or of modern theology, which is nonetheless subject to his influence, we notice what is contingent in the concepts and systems in which the divine Word is successively incarnate.

Of course we do not mean to deny the doctrinal continuity which links St Thomas to the Fathers and our contemporaries to St Thomas. If we do not emphasize this, it is because it is so obvious and it has often been drawn out. In a historical study, on the other hand, it is useful to draw out the dissimilarities which have often been less commented on.

By going beyond St Thomas to his predecessors and successors, our study has enabled us to discern the origin of several theological ideas and to follow their development over a relatively lengthy period. This is a further example of the contingency we have discussed, all the more interesting as it implies the complementary aspect. The history of these ideas is dominated by a constant fundamental statement: justification is a free gift from God, it is by grace that the human person leaves sin and accomplishes good. This thesis constitutes what we may call an invariant. We still find it in developing notions and systems. What is more, it is this which requires the use of new ideas and schemas, in order to maintain its integrity.

The theologians of the twelfth century, preoccupied as they were with defining and classifying their ideas, asked a question which does not appear to have bothered St Augustine. In Peter Lombard's time, they asked whether grace (then identified with virtue) was a quality or a movement of the soul. The supporters of the former justified it as follows: if grace is a movement of the soul, it comes from free will; and if it comes even partially from free will it is not produced in us by God alone without us. This opinion won the day. It was therefore the desire to safeguard the gratuity of justification which led theologians of that time to understand grace as a quality. Given their systems and ways of thinking, they could hardly do anything else.

A little later, the same idea was clarified in an Aristotelian fashion. Alan of Lille related it to the idea of habitus. Philip the Chancellor defined it as a form, which would become the classical understanding in the thirteenth century.

Since it was understood that divine grace moved the human person to do good, a question arose: If grace is a form, that is, an accident of the soul, how can it move the soul? Can an accident move the being which supports it? The reply was hesitant until the point when Albert the Great reasoned as follows. Grace is a habitus. Now, a habitus, like a nature, inclines us to action, just as weight inclines the body forwards. Thus sanctifying grace moves the soul. Free will behaves towards grace like a material element, which it establishes both in its being and in its operation. The primacy of form over matter defines the primacy of grace in relation to free will.

As grace is properly considered to be a form, a habitus which the person receives only with preparation, it was difficult to understand how this preparation could itself be dependent on grace. As the ultimate disposition was made to depend on justification, there was no difficulty with it. But what about remote disposition? For modern theologians this takes place under the influence of a supernatural movement, actual grace. In the first half of the thirteenth century, this idea had not yet developed. Some imagined that to prepare for grace, the person needed further habitus which were given freely by God. We can see the strength of the current which led minds to understand grace as a quality. Another line of theologians, who also accepted this understanding of grace, stated that one could prepare oneself for justification without grace (in other words, without a habitus added to nature), but not without God, the principal agent and first cause of all good. This thesis raised a difficulty. Since the influence of God is general, exercised on all beings in view of their action, how can we call this grace? Albert the Great replied that it is because, in the person, grace orders to sanctifying grace.

St Thomas speaks about the movement of the prime mover rather than about divine influence. He distinguishes a double grace: one form or habitus, the other movement. But he does not oppose two kinds of movement, one natural and the other supernatural. He only knows of the universal movement of God, without which no form could produce its action. He considers it to be free, in its true sense, when it is in relationship with sanctifying grace and the infused virtues. According to the *Summa Theologiae*, at least, this movement is only preparatory for justification if it actuates an infused habitus or implies its infusion. The habitus implied in perfect preparation is sanctifying grace; imperfect preparation implies at least a habitus of faith which is formless. The divine movement does not prepare for justification and is only properly gratuitous to the extent that it implies one or other of these habitus. It is only in this sense that it is called special. Whether the abstraction comes from its relationship to grace-form or to the habitus of faith, it is only the general or universal movement.

The theologians of the twelfth and thirteenth centuries established an internal and necessary link between the affirmation of a gratuitous justification and the notion of grace understood as a quality and form in addition to nature. From the fourteenth century, Scotist voluntarism and then Nominalism broke this connection. It was admitted that, if God justifies us in fact by habitual grace, he could also have judged us favourably without grace. In the second third of the sixteenth century, one of St Thomas's disciples, Francesco da Vitoria, while admitting the existence of infused habitus, could no longer see the reason why theologians in the thirteenth century had understood these as absolutely necessary to reaffirm the gratuity of justification. Since this logical connection had been broken, the gratuity of the divine movement could no longer be defined in relation to infused habitus. Theologians were therefore led to distinguish between two kinds of divine movement: the 'generalized' (*auxilium generale*) and the 'specific' (*auxilium speciale*) aid. For Gregory of Rimini and Francesco da Vitoria, grace was first and foremost 'the specialized aid of God' (*auxilium Dei speciale*). They attributed an active role to grace which in St Thomas had been the infused habitus. Grace-form was not rejected but relegated to second place.

Later still, as theologians were increasingly defining the gratuity of grace by opposing it to a hypothetical pure nature, the aspect of grace which they most emphasized was the *elevation* of pure nature to the power of accomplishing supernatural actions. Actual *elevating* grace would regularly be placed in opposition to so-called *natural* grace.

Can we now see how the same concern to affirm that our justification comes from God and is absolutely gratuitous later gave birth to different ideas and systems? Grace-quality, divine movement, 'specialized aid of God' (*auxilium Dei speciale*), and elevating actual grace were each conceived in their day to express the gratuity of the divine gift. To maintain the purity of an absolute statement in new intellectual contexts, theologians spontaneously expressed it in new ways. When the mind develops, an unchanging truth can only be maintained thanks to a simultaneous and correlative development of all ideas, holding them in the same relationship. A theology which is not up to date is a false theology.

The history of theology therefore shows us the permanence of divine truth at the same time as it reveals to us what is contingent in the ideas and systems through which we receive this truth. Christian truth never subsists in a pure state. We should not understand this to mean that it presents itself fatally mixed in with error, but rather that it is always embedded in contingent ideas and schemes which determine its rational structure. It can only free itself from one system of ideas by moving to another. For example, if we give up making the ultimate disposition dependent on habitual grace, we need to attach it to divine movement. But then divine movement must take on the qualitative value which is included in habitual grace. Instead of conceiving of divine movement as the actuation of a form, we must substitute the idea of elevating movement. A new concept has been introduced, which will govern the organization of a new system. Divine truth is never accessible outside of all contingent ideas: this is the law of the incarnation.

Yet history does not lead to relativism. It enables us to grasp an absolute within theological evolution: not an absolute of representation but an absolute of statement. If ideas, methods and systems change with time, the statements they contain remain, even though they are expressed in other categories. What is more, it is these statements themselves which, in order to keep their meaning in a new intellectual universe, determine new ideas, methods and systems which correspond to this universe. If it were otherwise, ancient formulas would lose their initial meaning while subsisting all the while. The mind which receives a formula seeks to connect this to the collection of concepts it holds, in order to understand it. It interprets this formula according to what it knows; it reconstructs it according to personal schemas. This is the only way it can understand a new formula. So surely we can see that if the mind unconsciously modifies an idea or a scheme in one or more correlating formulas, all the other formulas must correlatively be modified in order that statements retain their meaning. Moving from one mind to another, markedly different, a statement moves from one system to another. This is what we noted in medieval theology on preparation for grace.

History therefore shows both the relativity of ideas and schemes in which theology is embodied and the permanent statement which governs them. It makes known the temporal condition of theology and at the same time offers the eyes of faith the absolute statement of the divine Word who became incarnate.

To remove any doubt, let us note that the absolute statements which we are opposing to contingent representations do not only include defined dogma, in other words, propositions canonized by the Church, but also everything which is explicitly or implicitly contained in Scripture and Tradition. They also include the invariant or absolute of the human mind, the first principles and the acquired truths, which are necessary to think about dogma. We oppose this group of invariants to whatever is contingent in theological concepts. It is vital to understand that these invariants do not subsist *alongside* and independently of contingent concepts. They necessarily are conceived and express themselves *in themselves*. But when the new concepts change, they contain the same absolute relationships and the same eternal statements.

One might ask whether it is still possible to consider the ideas implicit in conciliar definitions to be contingent? Would that not compromise the unreformable nature of these definitions? For instance, in its teaching on justification, the Council of Trent used the idea of formal cause.[2] Has Trent thus hallowed this use and conferred a definitive character to the idea of grace-form? In no way! It was certainly not the Council's intention to canonize an Aristotelian notion or even a theological idea understood under Aristotle's influence. The Council simply sought to state, against the Protestants, that justification is an interior renewal, not solely the imputing of the merits of Christ, the remission of sins, or God's favour. To this end it used ideas common to the theology of its time. But we can substitute these ideas with others without changing the meaning of the teaching. The proof is in the fact that the Council itself used many more similar ideas drawn from the Scriptures.

Our work enables us to reveal yet another contingent aspect of theology. Not only do ideas and schemes appear, disappear and change, but thanks to external circumstances, it can happen that certain important truths are temporarily obscured, or given less attention. We have demonstrated that, from the twelfth century until the second third of the sixteenth century, theologians appear not to have known about the Second Council of Orange, at which the semi-Pelagians were condemned. Most of them did not even know about the existence of semi-Pelagianism. Of all those studied and cited in our work, only St Thomas – from the *Summa Contra Gentiles* onwards – and Gregory of Rimini had even a rudimentary knowledge of it. The conditions in which ancient texts were transmitted and the working methods adopted explain this lack of knowledge; nonetheless, medieval theology suffered from this lacuna. Catholics sometimes, Protestants often, have criticized medieval theology's semi-Pelagian tendencies. Loofs has described the teaching of Alexander of Hales, St Bonaventure and St Albert the Great as neo-semi-Pelagian;[3] and even the Nominalist school appears to him to be neo-Pelagian.[4] Stufler reckoned that, in his early works, St Thomas

---

[2] The causes of this justification are ... the one formal cause is the justness of God: not that by which he himself is just, but that by which he makes us just and endowed with which we are renewed in the spirit of our mind, and are not merely considered to be just but we are truly named and are just ... in the process of justification, together with the forgiveness of sins a person receives ... faith, hope, and charity.
Council of Trent, Session 6 cap.7 (Tanner, *Decrees*, II.673).

[3] F. Loofs, *Leitfaden zum Studium der Dogmengeschichte*, 4th edn (Halle: Niemeyer, 1906), 544–8.
[4] Ibid., 612–13.

remained silent in particular about texts which criticized semi-Pelagian errors.[5] These judgements are too strong. Not one of the orthodox theologians of the Middle Ages taught the need for grace and its primacy in the work of salvation. But they also held firm to maintaining the dignity, freedoms and responsibility of the human person; they emphasized the necessity of human cooperation. They said that in meritorious actions, nature or free will provided the substance of the act, while grace procured what was meritorious. This way of using the matter-form schema might appear to make grace an accessory, superfluously added to nature which was sufficient on its own. Theologians therefore encouraged the later misunderstandings of their interpreters. Yet it should also be acknowledged that their ideas could lead to semi-Pelagianism and even to Pelagianism. But most of them were unaware of this, because they did not know enough about the history of dogma. Without exception, they were unaware of the existence of semi-Pelagianism, and so did not always express themselves with the exactitude and precision we would wish on the subject of preparation for grace. Their attention had not been drawn to an important point of doctrine, which was not given the desired emphasis. While they were not wrong on the dogma of grace, many of them had not grasped its range. Thus theology suffered from ignorance due to external circumstances; we still see theology, to a certain extent, subject to the contingencies of history, although the instinct of faith has always maintained the essential statements.

Theology is thus linked to time and to history and also exposed to their risks and susceptible to their progress.

When we study medieval theology, not to find the permanent truths of faith writ large there but with the intention of following the twists and turns of thought in detail, we cannot avoid noticing the distance which separates that thought from our own. In the rich inheritance which it has left us lie outdated explanations, old-fashioned schemes and dead ideas. In their time, they served to hand on the mystery and, to that extent, are venerable. But, like a tool which is too old or an unfashionable piece of clothing, they hamper the progress of theological reflection. They stop those who no longer understand them from grasping the exact significance of Christian doctrine. By giving up Aristotelian physics, modern thought has abandoned the ideas, schemas and dialectical oppositions which only made sense within it. In order for theology to continue to offer meaning to the mind, and to be able to make it fertile and progress, it too must give up these ideas. Unfortunately, it is not always easy to dissociate them without error from the absolute truths which they cover. In this regard, historical theology is an indispensable methodology. It shows us the origin of ideas. It demonstrates how such an idea was introduced to respond to a problem which we have moved beyond today. It makes us participate in their alliances and dissociations. Demonstrating both their raisons d'être and their contingency, it frees us from these without compromising the truth. For it helps us to see the permanent statements which their birth and development sought to maintain. Thus anyone who considers theology to be a living thought, as an active and personal knowledge of the divine mystery, cannot but have recourse to history.

---

[5] J. Stufler, 'Die entferte Vorbereitung auf die Rechtfertigung nach dem hl. Thomas', *Zeitschrift für Katholische Theologie* 47 (1923), 180.

3

'The analogy of truth. A philosopher's reflection on a theological controversy'

'L'analogie de la vérité. Réflexion d'un philosophe sur une controverse théologique', *Recherches de science religieuse* 34/2 (1947), 129–41.

Jean-Marie Le Blond SJ

The question of the relationship between historical theology and scholastic theology, which has suddenly become a shrill controversy, calls to mind a more general philosophical problem: that of the relationship between truth and history. This leads us to reflect once again on the nature of truth. This short note does not claim to bring entirely new solutions to this age-old problem; on the contrary, its aim is to draw attention to elementary points, which we believe all can accept and which should warn us against hasty judgements and summary condemnations.

The thesis of the analogy of being is fundamental to St Thomas's ontology. Sketched out in Platonic participation, it had already been taught by Aristotle, at least in terms of substance and accident. St Thomas extended it to the Creator and to every creature and placed it at the foundation of his metaphysics as well as his noetics. Following this thesis, only the perfect and simple Being is the unreserved being, the absolute Being; all others are only beings, or simply *are*, in relation to this pure existence. They maintain a relationship of resemblance with this existence, in a proportionality in which the relationship between essence and existence imitates divine simplicity in a deficient, but real, way. This relationship of dependency in proportion, or attribution – the term is not particularly important – is the relationship of every being to God, who grants it its reality. These are the elementary propositions, familiar even to the philosophical novice, on which we need not dwell.

It is as elementary as the doctrine of the *Transcendentals*: the True, the Good, the One have the same extent as Being and they are at heart the very being of its relationship with intelligence, appetite, self-possession; consequently, these transcendentals, equal to being, possess all the properties of being, including, primarily, analogy. There is therefore an absolute goodness, which is identified with the absolute Being, an absolute unity, which is divine simplicity, an absolute and subsistent truth.

We should emphasize this latter point, for it seems that the force of polemic risks leaving this in the dark. The thesis of the analogy of truth, in fact, does not in any way impose itself on the thesis of the analogy of being. Truth is not univocal;[1] we have said that there is a subsistent truth which is absolute, which is God himself in his simplicity, God as he knows himself and knows all things in himself. The counterargument, on which no Christian philosopher can cast doubt, is as follows. No one will deny it, but we do not always draw out the full consequences of this: all other truths are complex and deficient; they imitate simple truth, without being able to equal it in their multiplicity; they are, in a word, truths which are *analogous* to the first Truth. This is a doctrine which must be maintained when faced with univocity, which is frequent among philosophers and which is the permanent temptation of human reason, which would happily take itself to be absolute reason.

But we must clarify the meaning as follows. It seems that sometimes we confuse the proclamation of the imperfect and analogous nature of human sciences with the denial of its nature as a truth. In reality, to state that our human truths are analogous does not in any way lead us to deny that they are really and properly truths, just as finite beings, analogous to the first Being, are really and properly beings.

To say that a truth or truths as understood and expressed by humanity are analogous is to affirm first of all that they bear a relationship to God. If a being is only constituted as such by its relationship with pure Existence, a truth is likewise only a truth in function of the subsistent Truth. Our human truths are true because, in their multiplicity, and through their assembly of concepts and judgements, they bear the shadow of divine simplicity; unity, not simplicity, which characterizes our judgements and expresses the relationship of an object to a subject, an essence to an existence, a quality to a substance.

They are still true – and this is perhaps the most important point – because, in grasping the whole unity of concepts and judgements, the mind sees its tendency towards the absolute. The position of the absolute, the existence of the unlimited action, is in effect implicit in every judgement by the use of the verb 'to be', whether it is 'copulative' or 'existential'.[2] This position of the absolute, which gives our true statements precisely their proper nature, constitutes the *form* of our knowledge, in an affirmation which extends to the infinite and whose various representations bear limiting *matter*. It unveils the ideal and the strength of the mind in this fundamental, implicit affirmation of the absolute which sustains all its actions. It is the identical twin of the Thomist thesis of the limitless-ness of the action and its reception in power.

---

[1] Cf *De Veritate* I.iv.c; II.xi. There are many others which are equally obvious.

[2] The Augustinian school emphasized this point and used it as the foundation of the ontological argument. It was also admitted by St Thomas, who integrated it into a number of fundamental truths. By proclaiming the analogy as the origin of the concept of being, St Thomas in fact means that this notion includes the absolute (Ia.2.a.1 ad 1us).

Editor's note: the verb 'to be' may be used to express existence ('I think, therefore I am') or to describe the subject of the verb ('God is good'), when it is 'copulative'.

In this sense, human science seems by design to be a relation of the absolute, and it is this which makes the most humble of our judgements, on the most ephemeral of events and the most contingent of subjects, into unreformed truths: it is simply and in a certain way absolutely true that it rained today at a particular time, or that I was cold at a certain point. In thinking about these events, the person has related them to absolute truth and therefore has put them in the absolute.[3]

To acknowledge this point makes us reaffirm that absolute aspect of our true statements. At the same time, to safeguard the transcendence of divine truth and to avoid any danger of ontologism or proud rationalism, it forces us here on earth to maintain an unbreachable divide between our human judgements and systematizations – even if we are talking about the clearest and best constructed system – and subsistent Truth. Only the latter can be absolutely absolute, imperfectible, because it is perfect. The best human system, on the other hand, will never be the *best possible*, than which it cannot be thought to be more true (*quo verior cogitari nequit*), which, in the order of truth just as in the order of perfection or of being, remains the divine prerogative.[4] It is simply the best *in fact*, always separated by a chasm from the simple intuition which is God's possession and which he alone can communicate in a participation of his being. What is more, to talk about an absolute or unique system appears unreasonable. The Thomist synthesis itself, a certain synthesis, consecrated for the use the Church makes of it, prescribed by the Church for the formation of its clergy and in any case singularly open, cannot be equalled to the subsistent Truth and does not convey all its treasure. In fact in the Middle Ages, other syntheses were aligned to it, alongside it, underneath it: those of St Bonaventure, of Blessed Duns Scotus, of Francisco Suàrez: perhaps less firm, less well constructed, but complementary rather than opposed; they too are part of the Christian treasury and express aspects of it which Thomism does not ignore but emphasizes less.[5] In future, other attempts might be ranged alongside the

---

[3] Even in false statements, the question of truth – the position of the absolute – is mentioned: even though it is false, an erroneous statement is an effort towards the truth. We can apply what St Thomas says about sin and its 'positivity' to the error (cf. IaIIae. 85.5.ad3; see too IaIIae. 72.1.ad 2; IaIIae 75.1,c; IIaIIae.10.5.ad1; *De Veritate* 28.6.c; *De Malo* 2.a.1 ad4; a.12.ad 2; a.2 ad.10).

[4] One should therefore not hesitate to speak about degrees of truth, in the same way as we speak about degrees of being. Theology acknowledges this, even while attaching great importance to the *note* with which the theologian qualifies dogmatic formulas, theological conclusions and hypotheses. We believe that a tendency to ignore these notes, to put theological conclusions on the same level as revealed dogma, and to attribute the same value – sometimes even a greater value – to religion's 'scientific formulas' than to its presentation through the Gospel or dogma mistakes this theological attitude, at the same time as it ignores the philosophical doctrine we recall here on the analogy of truth.

[5] Of course in certain points these systems are opposed to and contradict one another – for instance, St Thomas uses analogy of being, Duns Scotus, univocity. But we must be careful of confusing such systematic oppositions with contradictions of fact. 'Caesar has been assassinated; Caesar has not been assassinated.' One of these statements is simply true, the other simply false. This is not the case for most philosophical statements which are built into systems and can only be fully understood within this context. Further, despite the words, these contradictions themselves may often be reduced to differences in a point of view, just like today's discussions where we are opposed to one another without having made an effort to understand. Thus Duns Scotus's univocity is not exactly what St Thomas denied. One could of course opt for Thomas's doctrine, judging that Thomas's perspective would be deeper and fuller; but the univocity we negate in this case would not be, strictly speaking, univocity in Thomas's sense. We refer to Gilson's wonderful studies on the starting point of Duns

Thomist synthesis, which will continue the asymptomatic human effort to approach the absolute, by which we hope to be possessed in our other life. However powerful it is, Thomism always remains a system, a unified multiplicity, irreducibly other from absolute simplicity. It relates to this, imitates it in a perfect fashion, but not in a simply perfect fashion; it must remain different.

This seems to us to be a truth of common sense. It is also the expression of that profound truth that the absolute nature of our truths comes to them not so much as representations to which they are applied, but as a statement itself. These representations cannot entirely hold it in their limits, but the statement goes beyond them as far as the absolute. The reflection on the absolute nature of our truths thus leads us to find their origins in the design of the mind itself rather than in the limited representations which are enlightened by this design, which we meet on our path.[6]

Relative to the absolute and consequently distinct from the absolute, human truth, on the other hand, is relative to the many and to change. A relationship is always defined by two terms and, just as the finished being is constituted both by the act of existence and by the limit which this act receives and defines, so human truth, while a truth, remains human and implies human limitations, such as the splitting inherent in our thought which occurs by building and dividing the systems which various languages impose and which do not remain totally external to thought itself. More generally, in a well-chosen word loved by our times, the human *situation*.

The truth we are capable of here on earth is thus a composite truth, which results from the encounter between two elements. On the one hand, the design of the absolute, the more or less implicit position of the existence of that absolute. This is the positive element which gives truth its proper character and imprints it with the image of subsistent Truth. On the other hand, the concrete situation in time and space, a limiting and restrictive element which, in human truth, explains the human character, not the character of truth. This is the truth which we can attain in our present state, an effort towards the absolute, an affirmation of that absolute, but the effort and affirmation of a human person, limited by the human condition, with all its inheritance, placed in an environment, coming into the history of the world and its ideas at a particular moment.

According to this second aspect, the study of human truths is clearly linked to the knowledge of history, and it is not distasteful to speak of successive aspects of the truth, developing in time. To place a philosophical author in his spatial and temporal context, to seek to resurrect the precise manner in which problems were posed for him, to try to enter his concrete psychology which is of course of its time, is therefore not the fantasy of a mind which is more curious about humanity than about objective truth; it is the necessary counterpart of and complement to this objective study. In other words, integral philosophical and theological study cannot be reduced to pure logical study, which would be situated outside of time. To be real and concrete, and to avoid

Scotus's metaphysics. The author's solid Thomism did not prevent him from doing justice to Duns Scotus; *understanding* the latter while preferring Thomas, he resisted simplistic condemnations.

[6] It is clear that the truth of a statement is immediately dependent on the nature of the subject and the object united in it. But the object and the subject are united by the mind in its tendency towards the absolute; without the mind, there would, of course, be no truth.

a dangerous simplification, to grasp the human truth following all the aspects which contribute to determining it, this study must take account of psychology and history. The clear and absolutely legitimate distinction between logical truth and psychological or historical truth does not need to be pushed until they are totally separate, but an appropriate and conscientious methodology is required to unite the logical perspective of 'right' to the psychological and historical perspective of 'fact', in an effort which is clearly difficult to maintain but which shows itself to be fruitful and which is always necessary.

Actuality thus contributes to the definition of truth, not in the sense chosen by some contemporary existentialists, for whom it contributes a decisive or even unique element and for whom it is enough to condemn a system by declaring it to be out of touch, or to crown another by proclaiming it to be on-trend. Actuality, on the contrary, as we have just seen, is no more than the limiting and negative condition which is part of human truths. But negative and limiting as it is, it is nonetheless the real condition of these truths, and it is impossible to truly know them without considering their actuality. Each period of history, each school, each person has their original way of leaning towards the absolute and of making out its image. These tendencies and images converge and are analogous but remain differentiated by their starting points.

This is true even of St Thomas's system, which cannot be abstracted from its time, in the way that some divine words can. Thomas was in a context and in order to fully grasp him we must reconstruct that actuality. The relatively backward state of our knowledge of St Thomas stems from our attempts to place him above and outside of time as a result of either clumsiness or excessive veneration. 'So little have we read the literature of theological treatises published since the sixteenth century, that we have been unable to be struck by the place they give to discussions *"de mente sancti Thomae"*', wrote de Guibert.

> And if, looking closely, we seek to follow the development of these discussions through three centuries of plentiful theological work, we will be no less struck by the lack of progress made on most of these points. We unerringly continue to approach these very texts, each one emphasising and exploiting the text which they prefer and finding an explanation for those which bother them.[7]

It is true that during the last twenty years the objective and precise knowledge of Thomas's Thomism has progressed; this progress is due precisely to the effort of historical masters who have undertaken the difficult work of perusing medieval literature which has then shed light on the *situation* of St Thomas in history, which has not always been given due consideration.[8] This work has really only just begun: Gilson recently acknowledged that we still know so little about the Latin and Arab authors whom we need to study in order to situate that dialogue with his contemporaries,

---

[7] J. de Guibert, *Les doublets de saint Thomas d'Aquin* (Paris: Beauchesne, 1926), 20. Fr de Guibert finds the reason for this trampling in the absence of a historical method for the study of the Angelic Doctor's texts.

[8] Here we should mention in particular Gilson's wonderful work, as well as that of Chenu, Théry, Mandonnet, van Steenberghen, Grabmann, Ehrle and many others.

which has such importance in St Thomas. Nonetheless this research has enabled us not only to follow the work of the Angelic Doctor but also to catch a glimpse of his mind and his methodology, which are each singularly flexible and innovative. Gilson, in a phrase we would not personally have chosen, but whose paradoxical turn grabs the attention, even went as far as to state that Thomism is 'the only Modernist attempt which ever succeeded'. It is clear, in any case, that St Thomas, motivated both by his concern for souls and by his desire for the truth, was possessed by a healthy taste for current trends. In the face of the defiant conservatism of the Augustinians of the thirteenth century, he did not hesitate to use a philosopher who was as compromised and as compromising as Aristotle. He kept up to date with all the tendencies of his time and reading the *Summa Contra Gentiles* alone is enough to show with what care and even sympathy he studied the Arabic philosophers. It would of course be rash to claim Thomas's innovative attitude as authority for a new 'Modernist attempt' every ten or fifteen years; but it is equally rash and incorrect to cheapen this system to attach ourselves only to its letter. This would be a substantial infidelity to Thomism itself as well as an error about the nature of human truth.

Faced with this analogy, this convergence and this difference in human truths, one might perhaps be tempted to try to set aside the *invariant* that they contain, which is the basis of their similarities, at least in the doctrines which are drawn from them in a loyal effort and firm intelligence.[9] But to claim that this constitutes an *absolute* and *complete* system would be to forget the human condition and to radically misunderstand the elementary law of analogy, which is precisely that it cannot be reduced on the one hand to univocity and to equivocation on the other. A resemblance – and it is not necessary to be a philosopher to be aware of this – cannot be cut up into a partial identity and total difference of other parts, but it is precisely a *resemblance*, a negation of identity and relationship by itself. It draws itself out of a group, a group of relationships which cannot be fragmented without losing the resemblance. This is the clear meaning of the Thomist theory of analogy of proportionality. In terms of our knowledge, we can say that it is a bronze coin, of real but low value; we would be pursuing a chimera by trying to exchange the coin for the piece of gold which it represents. The piece of gold, which synthesizes all wealth in itself, can only be acquired if God distributes it, by communicating directly with us.

In this claim to constitute an objective doctrine which would reunite in itself the eternal acquisitions of all the philosophies, we can of course recognize a trace of the superior vocation of the human mind to knowledge without shadow. Yet, because of the lack of patience and submission to the human condition which it demonstrates, we can also question whether this tendency does not cover an unconscious bias, even among outstanding Christians, towards the hidden influence of modern rationalism. This was dominated by Descartes's mathematical dreams; and we know what it led to with Spinoza and what the risks of this attempt towards univocity are. Goodwill and literary fidelity to certain texts of St Thomas, even while not neglecting their spirit, is not enough to protect us against these risks.

---

[9] We should emphasize that we are talking about philosophical systems, not statements about facts.

In drawing to a close these basic but necessary reflections (especially in our times) on the nature of truth, it will be understood in what sense the classical definition of the truth 'as an adequacy of the mind and thing' continues to be important. There cannot be any question of a total adequacy, but only a certain assimilation which always leaves a certain amount of ignorance: 'We do not know everything about anything.'[10] Only God's knowledge is absolute and reaches beings absolutely whatever they are, in their very existence. Our knowledge is abstractive and always misses some aspect of the beings which we know; it does not become an untruth by this but remains incomplete, not only in the sense that it does not know something about the object but also in the sense that it does not perfectly grasp what it knows, precisely since it abstracts it and considers it apart from the whole.

It is likely that the Thomist theory of the concept seems, in abstraction, to imply a true intuition of essence, derived from the material conditions which limit its understanding in the thing itself; but with regard to that theory 'rightly' on knowledge, we must bring the multiple testimonies to the modesty of St Thomas on knowledge as we practise it ourselves. In fact, not only did St Thomas emphasize our powerlessness in reaching the mind, which we only grasp through the heterogeneous symbols we are able to sense; not only did he firmly underline the imperfection and analogical nature of our knowledge of the soul and of God, in reaction to Augustinianism (this being one of the major characteristics of Thomist psychology, to which the Cartesian 'angelism' is opposed); but in addition, with regard to sentient beings themselves, St Thomas repeatedly stated that if by right, in abstraction, the mind attained the nature of things and enjoyed a sort of intuition of essences, in fact the specific, substantial differences remained unknown to us.[11] It follows from this humble statement, very different from the serene dogmatism of some contemporary scholastics, that most of our concepts have their roots, not in an intuition, properly called, of nature but in a group of systems, a collection of perceptible representations whose division enables us to establish a sort of provisional label by which we can designate their quiddity. In this case, the *quiddity*, as the name implies, designates rather the interrogation about a substance more than its true understanding: the existence of this substance is raised without its nature having to be grasped.[12] From here comes the precarious, reformable nature which is attached to many of our definitions, and their link, which most often has not been entirely broken with either metaphor or with the extrinsic processes of classification.[13] Because of this loyal statement of the conditions in which we exercise our efforts towards knowledge, we acknowledge St Thomas himself to be both a philosopher of depth and a philosopher of common sense.

---

[10] Cf *De Veritate* II.1.
[11] Cf., for example, *ST* Ia.29.1.ad 3 – this is not an isolated text in Thomas's work.
[12] According to Thomas, this is about specific quiddity and not about more general concepts. But – precisely because they are more general – these concepts do not show the formal, decisive element, the specific difference of the beings which we know.
[13] It is noteworthy that Aristotle recognizes the precarious and almost conjectural nature of the methods which he proposes to reach his definitions. In the final analysis, they only procure a *pistis* [belief] not a science; yet these definitions are the principles of our science: by admitting that we are gifted with the intuition of a nature, nature only enters into science to the extent that it is formulated in discourse and expressed by a definition.

If we were to simply forget this doctrine of analogy it would have serious consequences. If by some mishap Christian philosophers should let themselves slide into this, our contact with the modern world would definitely risk being broken in a definitive fashion, leading to a complete breakdown in communion between the thought of seminarians and that of the rest of humanity.

A similar attitude would go against the deepest directions and desires of the Church, which seeks to adapt not only to the language but also to the mindset of people who are far distant and is not afraid of seeing its theology translated not only into foreign words but also into foreign concepts. It is ready, without wishing to impose a terminology and thought which would repel them, to receive our separated brethren from the Eastern Churches and from the United Kingdom and America. It is no less anxious to adapt to changes in time than to the distances in space.

But these points go beyond the field of philosophy. It remains the case – and this is, probably, the most important – that in this very field a similar narrowness would unleash an error against truth. It would mark the misunderstanding of analogy, of the transcendence of divine truth and the proper nature of human understanding; it would be the sign of the hidden, but very real, victory of Cartesian rationalism and Spinozan univocity, whatever venerable vestment they are dressed up in. Perhaps a theologian could demonstrate the intrusion of this rationalism into certain theories of quasi-natural faith, where human logic leaves almost nothing to grace. In any case, it is seen in the confusion which some people wish to establish between the absolute and the univocal, between the relative and the analogy. This is a grave danger for Christian philosophy and is profoundly opposed to the spirit of St Thomas. Truth has an absolute character, but it is not univocal. Our human truths, which are not purely relative, are only analogous to the divine truth.

4

'Supernatural and superadded'

'Surnaturel et Surajouté', *Surnaturel. Études historiques* (Paris: Aubier-Montaigne, 1946), 375–94.

Henri de Lubac SJ

A further attribute [to supernatural] was introduced to the theology of grace, one destined for an increasing success and which would profoundly influence doctrine. This epithet was 'superadded' (*superadditus*). We must briefly recap its history, for this explains both, on the one hand, the long-standing, instinctive resistance to the introduction of *supernaturalis* and, later, how its meaning became established.

In the modern theology of grace, it is almost axiomatic that humanity, deprived through sin of the supernatural gifts with which the Creator had adorned it in its original state, differs from humanity conceived in the state of pure nature 'as though despoiled to nakedness' (*tamquam spoliatus a nudo*). Evoked by the parable of the Good Samaritan as commented in Christian antiquity, the metaphor would receive an increasingly precise meaning as *superadditus* found itself more and more used in the theology of the 'supernatural', and only the first part of the full adage, 'despoiled of grace, wounded in nature' (*spoliatus gratuitis, vulneratus in naturalibus*), tended to be retained. God had 'superadded' a certain number of gifts (sanctifying grace and preternatural gifts) to human nature in Adam, with the aim of preparing him to obtain a supernatural end, which itself was 'superadded'. Stripped of these gifts by sin, as of clothing or ornament, humanity found itself returned to the nudity of its essential nature: *homo nudatus*.

But this metaphor of stripping back did not stand out from the first. It had to fight for a long time against the opposing metaphor. This is what the consideration of the very word *superadditus* shows us.

The word is often found in John Scotus Eriugena, but far from using it to describe a supernatural object, in his works, by contrast, it always describes the consequences of sin. Eriugena distinguishes between humanity in its initial condition, that is, as it would have been if it had had to remain innocent, and the person as sin made him, that is, in reality as God created him in anticipation of that sin. In both cases it is the same nature, simultaneously spiritual and corporal, but the 'simple, true, and natural' body in which the pure human essence consisted in the Creator's first thought has had an exterior and material body 'superadded' to it, including the division of sexes and what should really be called a changing and corruptible garment.[1] Through this body and its uncouth attributes, God punished humanity for its sin, but more than that, he enabled humanity to expiate that sin.[2] 'Superadded to nature' – John Scotus most often wrote *superadditum*, sometimes *superadjectum* (further added)[3] or *supermachinatum* (further devised)[4] – such a body is almost 'outside of nature';[5] it is even 'against nature', if we envisage it in its effects, particularly in the concupiscence which makes us similar to animals.[6]

Now, the doctrine that John Scotus expounds here is, like many others, not unique to him. It reproduces the teaching of St Gregory of Nyssa, and the words he uses are themselves a precise translation of Gregory's own words, 'kindred with the irrational ... was added',[7] in which we recognize the Stoic language used by Cicero.[8] Gregory adds that '"God created man in the image of God"; then he adds the peculiar attributes of human nature, male and female',[9] while in his *On the soul and the resurrection* he adds, 'when we have cast off that dead unsightly tunic' so shall we cast off 'the accretions' of the passions.[10] For what is natural to humanity is 'a life similar to divine nature', while 'sensory life' was 'superadded' to humanity.[11]

These formulas, and others like them, summarize in word and image the interpretation of numerous authors, both Latin and Greek, of the verse in which God gives Adam and Eve animal skins to wear as they leave paradise (Gen. 3.21).[12] Whether these tunics consisted of the body itself – as Clement of Alexandria explains to Julian Cassian, leader of the Docetists,[13] and which Origen borrowed, according to St Epiphanus's accusations[14] – or whether, more subtly, being only flesh 'uncouth, mortal, recalcitrant'[15] with the 'carnal thoughts' which accompany it,[16] it remains the case that 'superadded' was ascribed to humanity after the sin. We are now covered by a 'leprosy' of which we must be purified,[17] with 'mud' which we must wash off,[18] with a 'filthy garment'[19] which we must remove to achieve salvation. If we wish 'to

---

[1] John Scotus Eriugena, *De divisione naturae* II.2; IV.20 (*PL* 122.802A; 803A).
[2] Ibid., II.10,12; (*PL*122. 538A-B) IV.5 (760B), 12 (799–800), 13 (802C).
[3] Ibid., IV.12 (*PL* 122.801 C and 802A).
[4] Ibid.
[5] Ibid.
[6] Ibid., V.7 (*PL* 122.874–875).
[7] Gregory of Nyssa, *On the Making of Man*, 16 (*PG* 44.181C); *NPNF* Second Series V.
[8] *De finibus bonorum et malorum* III.
[9] Gregory of Nyssa, *On the Making of Man*, 16 (*PG* 44.185A); *NPNF* Second Series V.
[10] Gregory of Nyssa, *On the Soul and the Resurrection* (*PG* 46.149A; 148D).
[11] Gregory of Nyssa, *On the Soul and the Resurrection* (*PG* 46.149A; 148D), *Homily I* (*PG* 44.624B); this idea may be seen in Athanasius, *In psalmum* 50.7 and in Philo, *De mundi opificio* 46.
[12] Eriugena, *De divisione naturae* II.26 (*PL* 122 583–4); IV.20 (*PL* 122.836-7).
[13] *Stromata*.III.14.
[14] *Letter to St John of Jerusalem*, trans. Jerome (*PG* 43.385–387).
[15] Gregory of Nazianzen, *Discourse* 44.8 (*PG* 36.655A).
[16] Gregory of Nyssa, *On Virginity* 12 (*PG* 46 376B).
[17] Eriugena, *De divisione naturae* V.6 (*PL* 122.874A).
[18] Gregory of Nyssa, *On Virginity* (*PG* 46.372C).
[19] Zach. 3.3; Origen, *Homilies on Luke* 14.

rediscover our natural state', 'to restore in us the hidden image of God', 'to return to the Paradise where Paul heard ineffable words', we must 'leave all foreign elements behind' as we strip ourselves of these skins which are our 'carnal filth' and our passions.[20] Before sin, Adam and Eve were naked.[21] When the soul has rediscovered that nudity of its essence in the purity of its first condition, made in the image of God, a mirror of divinity, it will be able to see God. Thus, says St John Climacus, it can 'sing to the Lord the triumphal hymn of purity'.[22] 'Purity' and 'perfection' match one another.[23] The process of deification is a process of simplification. The entirety of the Saviour's work has no other end than to assure this. This is expressed in the West, for instance, in the Mozarabic liturgy, in a preface for the Feast of the Circumcision:

> We, leaving those skins by which Adam, destined for death, was unwillingly cast out of Paradise, so that the virtue of continence should be set aside not by means of the skin of the body but the covering of confusion, having been freed from carnal desires, from which the corruption of the transgressor has been eliminated.[24]

We find the same way of speaking in the East, in, for instance, Constantine the Deacon's *In Praise of All the Martyrs*,

> We knew that you were the Lord Christ and we all stripped off our uncouth tunics which had been ripped by whips and swords. And now today we are once more dressed in our former and beautiful nudity, which does not cause us to blush.[25]

Two biblical memories thus gave rise to two opposing images: the man robbed on the way to Jericho and the tunics of skin given to those exiled from Paradise. On the one hand it is the order of grace which is 'superadded'; on the other, the order of sin. Of course, in this order of images there is no point talking about logical contradictions, any more than the two opposing metaphors contradict one another in the way they condense two representations of the mystical life: the two words 'ecstasy' and 'instasis', 'entry' and 'exit' of the Song of Songs.[26] Here it is not strictly speaking a question of doctrine. It is no less true that we are dealing in some ways with two systems of representation, themselves signs of two currents of thought, two conceptions of the supernatural life which were long opposed to one another. While the concept expressed in the allusion to 'animal skins' initially seems to have triumphed, this is because it converged with Platonic views which themselves were familiar to many Christian writers. Origen implicitly recognizes this when he writes in the *Contra Celsum*,

---

[20] Gregory of Nyssa (*PG* 46.101D, 372D, 374, 420C).
[21] Gen. 2.25. Eriugena *De divisione naturae* IV.19 (*PL* 122.835A).
[22] John Climacus, *Ladder of Paradise* (*PG* 88.900B).
[23] Origen, *De Principiis* I.3.8.
[24] *PL* 85.221.
[25] Constantine the Deacon, In Praise of all the martyrs, 35. (*PG* 88.520A); cf. Eriugena *De divisione naturae* IV.20 (*PL* 122.836–7).
[26] Cf. Gregory of Nyssa *On the Song of Songs* 12 (*PG* 44.1024D-1025A).

And the expulsion of the man and the woman from paradise, and their being clothed with tunics of skins (which God, because of the transgression of men, made for all who had sinned), contain a certain secret and mystical doctrine (transcending that of Plato) of the soul's losing its wings and being borne downwards to earth, until it can lay hold of some stable resting-place.[27]

More precisely, the Biblical narrative encountered the Hellenistic understanding of the descent of the soul through the celestial spheres. As the conjunction of two world views became ever more intermingled, it seemed ever more normal to interpret the *expulsion* from Paradise as a *fall* because in Hellenistic cosmology Paradise was often located in the third heavens. Falling from planet to planet towards the earth, the soul, in Hellenistic thought, wove an ever tighter net around itself; it put on a series of material layers and more and more earthly passions, a growing burden of impurity, which, if one day it were to be saved, it would have to strip off in reverse order as it returned upwards. Like Adam and Eve, chased out of Paradise and crossing the threshold guarded by the Cherub, it passed through the gates of heaven equipped with ferocious guardians. The divine spark was obscured, buried beneath an ever-thicker layer, a true 'tunic of ignorance'[28] in proportion to how far it was from the Home from which it had detached itself. Of course this schema was found in all the religious philosophies of the period, including the mystery religions such as the cults of Isis and Mithra, while also being used by the neo-Platonists, particularly Proclus[29] and Olympiodorus the Younger.[30] The Gnostics of every school received and adapted it, or rather drowned the Christian mystery in it. Faithful to their custom of mixing dogmas and pagan myths, they often returned to the story of the animal skins.

It might be said that this coming together was necessary. On both sides, in fact, it was often the same word: *chitōn* (tunic). According to the elderly Empedocles, the celestial being was enclosed in a tunic.[31] Plutarch would say that nature envelops souls in a fleshly tunic foreign to them.[32] It is therefore not surprising that, according to St Irenaeus[33] and Tertullian,[34] the Valentinians explained that the *chitōn dermatinos* ('fleshly tunic') was none other than material, feeling flesh, coming to super-add itself to a body whose essence was more refined, to make an earthly being. Theodotus likewise taught that, 'Adam was clothed by the fourth man, that is, the earthly man: it is this that we should understand by the animal skin.'[35] It is by an identical process of descent and gradual dulling that the Saviour eventually donned our flesh to effect our salvation.[36] According to Theodotus, who here links the memory of Genesis to a

---

[27] Origen, *Contra Celsum* IV.40. ANF IV.516.
[28] *Poimandres* 7.2; cf. Plotinus, *Enneads* 3, 6, 5; Philo, *Allegories of the Sacred Laws*, 2.65.
[29] Proclus, *Elements of Theology*, 9.
[30] Olympiodorus the Younger, *Commentary on Plato's Phaedro*.
[31] Empedocles, *Fragment*, 126.
[32] Plutarch, *De esu carnium*, 2.
[33] Irenaeus, *Adversus Haereses* I.5.5. (PG 7.500–501).
[34] Tertullian, *Adversus Valentinianos*, 24.
[35] Cf. Clement of Alexandria, *Excerpta ex Theodoto*, 55.
[36] Cf. Irenaeus, *Adv. Haereses* I.2.6; I.12.4. (PG 7.465 and 576). Christ's descent via the spheres was a theme preached by the Gnostics.

text from Leviticus, the souls of the elect will follow their Saviour upwards through the seven heavens, successively stripping themselves of everything which obstructs the spirit.[37]

As in many other areas, the Gnostic heresy granted the theology of the Fathers something which they could only purify and filter to let it enter into the orthodox synthesis. Origen, for instance, said that after this life, 'souls, if they are pure and not weighted down by the leaden mass of wickedness, will rise through the air towards the zone of the purest, most ethereal of bodies, abandoning the heavy bodies of this world and their filth.'[38] Even more freely or, we might say, poetically, Gregory of Nyssa would show the Word descending in search of the lost sheep, in other words, humanity, and donning the natures of the various spheres which he encountered in the course of his descent, to the extent that the angels charged with guarding the earth did not recognize him on his arrival.[39]

On the other hand, he applied the text from the Song of Songs, 'the guards took off my garment' to describe the ascent of the soul using the image of the Spouse. Already the souls had stripped off the first garments in the initial stages of its ascent:

How did it still have a robe when the city guards had stripped it off? Because having rejected the former tunic and stripped off all veils, she surpassed herself in purity, to the extent that the former purity, compared to the current, seemed to her to be a garment once again. Thus the rising towards God always makes everything one had seem impenetrable once one has discovered it.[40]

However, even used with discretion and stripped of any precise cosmological allusion, the metaphor of stripping off retained a certain flavour of dualistic spiritualism alongside a mysticism of pantheistic tendencies from encounters with Platonism and Hellenism. It was, therefore, not without dangers – the danger of the doctrine of the *nous*, of which it is an example. But among the authors attached to the Church's tradition, the balance would find itself restored in some ways by the idea of another garment, that of total purity, light, glory, which it is necessary to don after having rejected the first in order to participate in the salvation promised by Christ. It was not enough to put away the old man: as Paul also taught, one had to put on the new man. This was how it was explained to those who came to request baptism: 'You, O Catechumen, are outside paradise, you share the exile of Adam, our first father … Now the gate opens: strip off the old man like a dirty garment, receive the garment of incorruptibility which Christ offers you.'[41] Is this not what passages such as the verse from Ecclesiastes, 'At all times, dress in white' (Eccl. 9.8),[42] or that verse from the Psalms, 'dressed as though in a garment of light', mean?[43] Or, as we read in Isaiah, 'He

---

[37] Cf. Clement of Alexandria, *Excerpta ex Theodoto*, 27, 58.
[38] Origen, *Contra Celsum*, VII.5; cf. *Periarchon* II.11.
[39] Gregory of Nyssa, *On the Ascension of Christ* (PG 46.693C).
[40] Song 5.7; Gregory of Nyssa *Homilies on the Song of Songs* 12 (PG 44.1029B).
[41] Gregory of Nyssa, PG 46.420C.
[42] Cf. Theophilus, *Paschal Letter*.
[43] Peter Chrysologos, *Sermon* 82 (PL 52.432A).

has clothed me in garments of salvation, he has wrapped me in a cloak of saving justice' (Isa. 61.10), or Ecclesiasticus 'He has covered him in a garment of glory' (Eccl. 15.5; *Vulg.*). The angel in Zechariah ordered Joshua to 'take off his dirty clothes' and then said, 'I have taken your guilt away' and dressed him in festal robes (Zech. 3.4). Finally, the gospel parables mention the wedding garment required by those who are invited to the feast, and the tunic and slippers the father has brought for the prodigal son on his return.[44] Paul, too, spoke of this mysterious garment to the Corinthians (2 Cor. 5.3), and it was he who made a symbol of the white robe donned by the newly baptized, these 'lambs', praised earlier by the Psalmist.[45]

Thus in both Scripture and Liturgy, this is not just a matter of a simple stripping down, or of its opposite, but of an exchange. The author of 4 Ezra already understood this.[46] This was also the habitual thought of the Fathers. In the divine Passover which opens the great nuptial chamber to us,[47] the garment of sin must be replaced by the garment of justice.[48] Having rejected the mortal tunic, to reach salvation humanity must once again put on the garment of immortality lost through Adam's sin.[49] To have the right to enter the festal hall, we must exchange 'the ignominious fig-leaves' with 'a garment of light', a 'holy', 'divine' garment, 'created according to God' and 'made of light and air' for the purity of our behaviour.[50] We must receive the mantle of the Spirit,[51] and that royal purple which is Christ, 'our honour and our ornament'.[52] The Mozarabic Missal, which we saw celebrated spiritual nakedness, also praises the infant human Christ at Christmas.[53] On Easter Sunday, Rupert of Deutz shows us Jesus Christ, our great high priest, leaving the sordid garments of our mortality and in exchange putting on the new glory of the resurrection and immortality, applying Isaiah's words to the Church.[54]

We see the truth expressed in all these texts where the subject is exchange. Their meaning is often more than moral: humanity is not truly spiritual and only reaches perfection through an entirely gratuitous participation in the unique *Pneuma*.[55] The *nous* is not divine through itself, and it is not enough that it again becomes in fact what it is by right in nature. Like a precious pearl found in mud,[56] once it is returned to its

---

[44] Tertullian, *De pudicita* 9.11; Gregory of Nyssa (*PG* 44.1143A-B).
[45] Hilary, *Tractatus in psalmos* (Ps. 64). For a description of the baptismal rites, see Cyril of Jerusalem, *Second Mystagogical Catechesis* (*PG* 33 1077-1084). In *Kingdom of the divine lovers*, Ruysbroeck describes baptism as 'The soul receiving the garment of innocence, in other words, being robed in the death and merits of Christ' (ch. 2).
[46] 4 Ezra 2, 38, 45; cf. Rev. 19.8; Gregory of Nyssa, *On the Soul and Resurrection* (*PG* 44.103A).
[47] Psuedo-Chrysostom, *In Pascha* 6.5 (*PG* 59, 745).
[48] Cf. Hilary, *In Mathaeum* 26.2 (*PL* 9.1056D); Jerome, *In Isaiam* (*PL* 24.603C); Theodulfus of Orleans, *De ordine baptismi* 14 (*PL* 105.233-234).
[49] Philip of Harveng, *De salute primi hominis* 23 (*PL* 203.615).
[50] Cyril of Jerusalem (*PG* 33.361A, 341A); Gregory of Nyssa (*PG*44.409C; 1184-1185; *PG* 46.108A).
[51] Hilary, *In Matthaeum* 22.7 (*PL* 9.1044B).
[52] Gregory of Nazianzen, *Discourse* 40 (*PG* 35.561B); Gregory of Nyssa (*PG* 44.1003D-1004A).
[53] *Benedictio* (*PL* 85.189).
[54] Rupert of Deutz (*PL* 167.324Aff; cf. *PL*167.1352D).
[55] There is a further doctrine which is analogous to what we have just examined in Hellenistic gnosis and in neo-Platonism; cf. Dodds, *Proclus, Elements of Theology* (London: Clarendon Press, 1933), 313-21. But these 'luminous tunics' and 'astral bodies' cannot really be compared to the new clothing which is Christ or God's Spirit.
[56] Pseudo-Chrysostom, *margaritēs Borborō phuromenos* (*PG* 61.744).

purity and its initial brilliance, the divine image must again achieve divine resemblance. If something of this resemblance has been given to the first man, if he was created in grace, then it will be true to say that sin has removed this from him. Thus we find ourselves following the line of the second metaphor, the opposite of the first. It appears that Origen is its author, in his exegesis of the parable of the Good Samaritan. His allegorical interpretation is found virtually unchanged in all commentators, whether Latin or Greek, on the third Gospel:

> Wounds are disobedience and sins. Man is stripped of his garments, that is, he loses incorruptibility and immortality, and that he is despoiled of all virtue. He who is left half-dead for death has won part of his human nature.[57]

This image of a stripping by sin is also found in St Cyril of Alexandria,[58] in a homily by Pseudo-Chrysostom for Pentecost Sunday,[59] in St Augustine[60] and in Pseudo-Eucherius's commentary on Genesis, where Adam and Eve are described as 'knowing their misery being deprived of grace'.[61] In an address on the life-giving cross, St Germanus of Constantinople made the first man say, 'I was stripped, I who was master of my house, and I remained bare of my garments of light',[62] and Simon the New Theologian shows him stripped for the glory of God and the Holy Spirit.[63] Nevertheless, it is appropriate to note that the two texts which mention the Gospel of the Good Samaritan, garments ripped off and injuries inflicted, are generally considered to be two equivalent images, complementing one another to translate the same fact. This appears clearly in St Ambrose's commentary and that of St Jerome. Humanity is stripped and thus finds itself injured.[64] We are not initially injured, as we would naturally think in a straightforward account: 'not wounded, though nude'.[65] In reality, in our authors' view, Adam did not lose some extrinsic gift through sin but, as it were, a part of his very nature: the gifts which he had received from the Creator raised him above the rest of nature, that is, above all creation, but they were interior to his proper spiritual nature.[66] Thus we can say that 'falling he was wounded and deprived of all the natural gifts granted to him'[67] or even, 'innocence lost, nudity was almost the natural clothing'.[68]

The second metaphor thus does not really approach that of *supperadditus* as it would be known in later theology; nowhere is it the required correlative, although this

---

[57] Origen, *In Lucam* Hom. 34.
[58] Cyril of Alexandria, *In Joannem* I (PG 73.160B).
[59] Ps-Chrysostom, *Homily for Pentecost* (PG 61.744).
[60] Augustine, *City of God* XIV.17 (PL 41.426); *Confessions* XIII.9 (PL 33.848).
[61] Pseudo-Eucherius (PL 50.9, 12B).
[62] Germanus of Constantinople (PG 98.228D).
[63] *Address* 3 (PG 120.332C).
[64] Ambrose, *In Lucam* VII.73 (PL 15.1718B).
[65] Jerome, *Letter* 64.5.
[66] Andrew of Crete, *On Human Life and the Dead* (PG 97.1269B); Gregory of Nyssa, *On Virginity* (PG 46.372C).
[67] Eriugena, *De divisione naturae* IV.15 (PL 122.811C).
[68] Helinandus, *Sermon* 23 (PL 214.675).

is not entirely absent in the ancient period. We can read this in Didymus the Blind's commentary on Psalm 17:

> Some perhaps believe that it is a pure pleonasm to say, 'In hearing his ear heard me'. Does the person who hears not always hear through the ear? Yet the superfluous superadded mention of the ear is not in vain, since all those who hear God do not do so simply by using human and mortal listening, but thanks to the divine ear which is superadded to them; he has thus added an ear to me to hear.[69]

But such language remains exceptional and should not force the meaning. It would only become popular much later. Among the Byzantines, Simon the New Theologian would write, alluding to St Paul's *superindui* ('I have also put on'), that the baptized put on the tunic of the spirit of uncorruptibility as 'from above'.[70] Among the Latins, it was not until the thirteenth century that the metaphor entered theological language and met with success.

We now turn to how it was introduced and its precise meaning and usage. It is quite natural to say that the accident is 'superadded' to the essence, or the *habitus* to the faculty, or the form to the matter. Thus Abelard, writing about the formation of the person, wrote, 'where something would come from matter, it is said correctly to be form, added on to be formed' (*ubi de materia aliquid fit forma ei superaddita formari proprie dicitur*).[71] Having noted that 'power adds above substance …', Richard Kilwardby asked whether, in addition, the free will which is a habitus 'adds something above nature and the natural powers of the soul'.[72] A little later, Gondissalvus explained that the substance is 'quanta' not by itself but 'by the quantity which is superadded' and that the essence of the soul is disposed by the power 'as it is superadded through the accident'.[73] Alexander's *Summa* describes beatitude as 'there is substantial beatitude in eternal joy, and accidental or superadded beatitude in eternal joy'.[74] Now, these pairs of concepts were in frequent usage in Aristotelian philosophy, and so the word *superadditus* would become frequent in the language of the scholastics. St Bonaventure, writing about angels, would therefore speak of the *habitus* 'superadded [to them] by nature'[75] and said about the Trinity that, according to our way of understanding, 'it adds supernature to the person'.[76] Nothing here touches on the order of grace, and the very word *gratia* which sometimes appears in the context was far from always describing something supernatural, as Bonaventure noted elsewhere.[77]

At the same time, if we distinguish two kinds of activity in humanity – first a 'natural' or necessary activity and then a moral activity, an exercise of free will and a source of merit – we can say that they constitute two orders, the second of which is 'superadded'

---

[69] Didymus the Blind, *Commentary on Psalm 17* (*PG* 39.1264C-D).
[70] Didymus the Blind, *Address 19* (*PG* 120.414D).
[71] *Expositio in Hexaemeron* (*PL* 178.774D).
[72] *In Sent.*
[73] *Quaestiones disputate* 10.
[74] *Tertia pars* 12.2.
[75] *In 2 Sent.* D.3 P2.
[76] *In 1 Sent.* D.34.q.1.
[77] *In 1 Sent.* D.4.a.1.q.2, *ad objecta*.

to the first. In relation to the genus of nature, in effect, the genus of morality is a 'second being'.[78] It is in this sense that Peter of Tarentaise wrote, 'morality, which is founded on [super] nature'.[79] Here there is nothing left of 'supernature': what is said of 'morals' is also said of 'artificial things'.[80] Blessed Aelred, considering the two orders of things which are but one in God but which are distinguished in the creature, that is, 'nature' and 'virtue', said that the second is superadded to the first in the human person;[81] and St Bernard, distinguishing between several degrees of freedom, assimilated the first degree, the inalienable levelling of all spiritual beings, to nature itself, the image of divinity and, on the contrary, recognized in the two following degrees a superadded accident 'the accidental and similar divine power and wisdom'.[82]

However, there are close links between the order of grace and the order of morality. Each together indissolubly constitutes the order of 'resemblance'. The free act, moral and meritorious, depends on grace; from this come the paired expressions, such as 'good moral or grace', which are found especially in the writings of the early Franciscan theologians,[83] or the definition of 'virtues' such as 'good grace'.[84] 'Good grace and virtue', as Albert the Great said.[85] In addition, this grace, which, with the virtues it gives rise to, forms an 'accidental gift',[86] was itself influenced in theology by Aristotelianism, thought of according to the categories of accident and *habitus*. Finally, if there were a more precise question of Christ's grace, coming to repair primitive 'nature', it appeared as a second grace, given after the event, with an eye to replacing and even surpassing the first. Thus there were three reasons to use the description *superaddita*, as Hugh of St Victor had already noted.[87]

According to one of William of Auxerre's definitions, grace must be defined as 'habitus superadded to nature', and in a formula which recalls Hugh of St Victor, 'supernature is merited'.[88] According to Eudes Rigaud, the 'gift', to the extent that we see it as something superior to simply virtue, is a 'habitus superadded to virtue to ensure good deeds'.[89] And if, whether in an angel itself or in an innocent man, we try to distinguish, with the dual moral and natural actions, the dual grace which each procures, we can say with Peter of Cells, in a formula like those mentioned above, that 'God superadded second grace to first grace'.[90] Stephen Langton distinguished between two kinds of nature: on the one hand, the very powers of the soul, and on the other, the virtues. Both are gratuitous, but while the former are only a given grace, the latter constitute an added grace,[91] which of course means that the person may be indefinitely

---

[78] Roger Marston, *De statu naturae lapsae* q.2.
[79] *In 2 Sent.* D.40.q.2.a.2.
[80] Ibid.
[81] *Sermones de oneribus*, 8 (*PL* 195.391C).
[82] *De gratia et libero arbitrio*, ix.
[83] E.g. Alexander of Hales, *Questions inédites*.
[84] Anonymous *Summa* of Basle.
[85] *Summa theologiae* 2a Paes. Tr.4.q.14.m.4.a.2. ad objecta.
[86] Rupert of Deutz (*PL* 167.261D).
[87] *De sacramentis* 1.I (*PL* 176.274B).
[88] *Summa aurea* 1.2.tr.II.
[89] *In 3 Sent.* D.34.
[90] *Liber de panibus* i.
[91] See Englehardt, *Beiträge*, vol. 30, p. 461.

content with the former, as though the latter were simply an optional decoration. St Bonaventure talked about 'superadded grace' (*gratia superaddita*), 'which converts the soul to God by the habit of virtue'.[92] For St Albert the Great, while the divine 'image' resides properly in the natural powers of the reasonable soul, the 'resemblance' indicates a conformity in grace, 'which is considered in addition as if it were the quality of nature' (*quae superducitur naturae sicut qualitas*).[93] St Thomas's habitual language can be explained in the same way; for instance, when he says that the 'light of grace' is 'superadded nature' or a 'gift of superadded nature', it is because he sees in it a 'form' or a 'habitus'.[94]

In all this, while formally it is about grace, nothing is applied to the supernatural order as such, defined by the ultimate end. This may be said to be 'supernatural', at least in passing and with some distinctions. 'The vision of the divine essence is said to be the supernatural end, not because it can in any way be desired naturally, but because it cannot reach one solely through nature (*sed quia non potest ad ipsum ex solis naturae principiis pervenire*).'[95] This is even more the case since God himself is a 'supernatural good',[96] a 'good beyond nature'.[97] But 'superadded' is never used: such language would have no meaning to the thirteenth-century mind. Whatever 'superadded' is, it is but the collection of means destined to achieve this end.[98] This is the original justice, or the gift which produces it.[99] 'Justice, by the grace of Adam was added to the natural principles' (*Justitia ex gratia Adae fuit addita super principia naturalia*),[100] 'in addition to the faculties of natural principles'.[101] It is grace. It is glory itself but always on condition that they are understood from a very clear position, not as included in the final end of spiritual nature but in their particular reality, as distinct from that end, like means, 'dispositions' which are able to procure it. This, for example, is the 'light of glory', not 'beatitude' or the 'vision of God'. St Thomas expresses himself very clearly on the matter in the *Contra Gentes*.[102]

Gradually, however, due to the structural analogy between the two words, and also their joint use to describe the same realities, the two adjectives *superadditum* and *supernaturale* tended to become interchangeable. The means, being homogenous to the ends, were supernatural as well as superadded: the end thus risked appearing superadded as well as supernatural. The day would even come where the former of these words would be given as the definition of the second. That day, for a whole school – and almost all the Schools – *supernaturale* would be *superadditum naturae* (supernatural would be superadded to nature), not only in the sense of 'a good superadded to the

---

[92] *In 2 Sent.*, prologue.
[93] *Summa theologiae* P.2. tr.12.q.71.
[94] *S.T.*IaIIae.109.1.
[95] Sylvester of Ferrara, commenting on St Thomas, *CG* 3.51.
[96] Giles of Rome, *Super 2 Sent.* D.22.q.2.a.1.
[97] Bonaventure, *In 2 Sent.* D.29.q.2.ad.4.
[98] See Anselm's *Sentences*.
[99] Richard of Middleton, *In 2 Sent.* D.30.a.3.q.1.
[100] Peter of Tarantaise, *In 2 Sent.* D.32.q.2.a.3.
[101] Thomas, *In 2 Sent.* D.19.q.1.a.2.
[102] Thomas, *CG* 50.3.c.150, 153.

natural good' but in the sense of 'finality superadded to natural finality'. For many this would be the basic meaning of the word, a meaning which, acting as a reference for particular meanings, would ensure the unity of the idea. But under the appearance of an entirely natural and innocent development, a sort of revolution had been carried out in the understanding of humanity and its relationship to God.

5

'Current trends in religious thought'

'Les orientations présentes de la pensée religieuse', *Études* 249 (1946), 5–21.

Jean Daniélou SJ

The problems of theology and philosophy of religion, which in days gone by seemed to be the privilege of an elite group of initiates, are now reaching an ever-wider audience. The success of series such as '*Théologie*' or '*Unam Sanctam*', the founding of journals such as *Dieu vivant* or *Maison-Dieu*, and the development of university-level centres for religious studies aimed at the laity, such as the *Centre universitaire catholique* or the *Conférences du couvent de Saint-Jacques*, are significant indicators of this. There are multiple causes, but allow us to indicate the two main ones. First, the renewal of Christian life among elites and the demand for more substantial doctrinal and spiritual nourishment than is normally available. Second, the virulence of contemporary forms of atheism, which challenge not particular aspects of Christianity but rather its whole world view and which requires Christians to be much more aware of the originality of their doctrine.

Now, we should state at the very beginning – all the more since we shall note below that the future is full of promise – that this great demand by minds and souls for a living Christian intellectual thought is made more acute, decisively this time, by the fact that contemporary theological, apologetic or exegetical teaching is often insufficient. If we enquire whether theology is present in the intellectual world, it is most likely because it has been absent from it. Fr de Montcheuil, in one of his classes at the *Institut catholique*, noted that 'by handling the most valuable and the most contemporary of truths, theology gives an impression of being absent and unreal.'[1] It is not that theology should adapt to current trends but – and this is vital – it must respond to the needs of the living souls of our day. As de Montcheuil added, 'When we ask theology to renew itself, we are not asking it to express itself in a new philosophy, but to assimilate the spiritual experience from which that philosophy has sprung.'

---

[1] Translator's note: Daniélou fails to give any reference to his citations from de Montcheuil.

The sense of the rupture between theology and life was once felt sharply by the generation in which the movement known as Modernism was born. As with every religious crisis, what is debatable in Modernism is not the problem it raised, but the answer which it provided, for the problem it raised was real enough. Modernism bears witness to the dual defect of the religious thought of its time, which seems at first glance to be contradictory: on the one hand the loss of any sense of the transcendence of God by a rationalized theology which treated God as yet another object of thought; on the other hand, the mummification of a thought which remained fixed in its scholastic forms and had lost contact with developments in philosophy and science. But, in wanting to react to the first, Modernism fell into agnosticism; and in seeking to remedy the second, it ended up misusing critical exegesis. Thus, as is so often the case, by its very excesses, it hindered rather than helped the renewal of religious thought. Rather than renewal, it brought about a hardening. Faced with the danger of agnosticism, neo-Thomism also blamed theological rationalism. What is more, the excessive criticisms, of Loisy in particular, created an atmosphere of suspicion around biblical studies which has only begun to lift following the recent Encyclical on Sacred Scripture.[2] It must be said that this atmosphere of fear and constant danger of denunciation paralysed the work of Christian researchers; many of those who have been the Church's credit since the start of the century have been more or less suspect in their lifetimes, and the most regrettable misunderstandings between Christian elites and the hierarchy are far from being completely resolved.

In truth, such temporary severity was needed to respond to the dangers of Modernism. Neo-Thomism and the Biblical Commission were the protective railings. But it is clear that protective railings are not responses. Again, I turn to de Montcheuil, who wrote that 'Modernism will not be liquidated until we have a theological methodology which satisfies the demands from which Modernism was born.' This is simply because Modernism itself was no more than the unfortunate expression of authentic demands. We should add a further aspiration, which perfectly describes the present moment. Theoretical speculation which is separated from action and not engaged with life has had its time. It is a commonplace among otherwise antagonistic philosophies, such as Marxism or Existentialism, that thinkers should be engaged. The same tendency may be found within Christian thought.

Thus contemporary theology is faced with a triple demand. First, it must treat God as God, not as an object, but as the Subject *par excellence*, who is manifest when and how he wishes; and consequently it must be penetrated by a religious mindset. Second, it must respond to the experiences of the contemporary soul and take account of the new dimensions which science and literature have given to space and time, which literature and philosophy have given to society and the soul. Finally, it must be a concrete attitude to existence, a response which engages the whole person, the interior light of an action in which life is played out in its entirety. Theology will only be alive when it responds to these requirements. The following pages will seek to show how what is now taking shape allows us hope now and for the future, and that theological

---

[2] Translator's note: Daniélou refers here to Pius XII's encyclical letter *Divino Afflante Spiritu*, 'on Promoting Biblical Studies', published in 1943.

thought is in the process of once more taking its place in intellectual life and becoming present again to our times.

The return to the sources

The first characteristic which marks contemporary religious thought is its contact with the essential sources: the Bible, the Church Fathers, the liturgy. Of course, in theory, this contact has never been lost. But in the thirteenth century, theology, which until then had essentially been commentary on the Bible, constituted itself as an independent area of academic study. At the time, such independence was a factor of progress. But the result was a gradual rupture between exegesis and theology, each discipline developing according to its own methodology, and a gradual drying up of theology. Among other things, Protestantism brought about a violent return to the Bible, in contrast to a purely scholastic theology.

The last fifty years have seen the first phase of restoring the Bible to its central place in Christian thought. First of all, Catholic scholarship had to come up to speed with developments in various areas of biblical studies, archaeology, philology and literary criticism. Much work has been accomplished in this field. In the past, Lagrange or de Grandmaison; today Coppens, Podechard or Robert are among the great names. But now that this preparatory work – which must continue – has been completed, there is a second stage to cover, which is for theological thought to benefit from this rediscovery of the Bible. For while the Bible is a collection of historical documents of inestimable value, which must be studied as such, it is even more the Word of God addressed to us, which contains teaching for men and women of today.

This work of biblical theology is currently at the heart of research and is very advanced in terms of the New Testament. The impetus has come from the work of the 'Form History' Protestant school: Bultmann, Dibelius, Cullmann, Schmidt, etc. Applying the processes of phenomenology to exegesis, they then applied their efforts to analysing the content of the major religious categories of Scripture. Works such as Kittel's *Logos* or Schmidt's *Kingdom of God* have enriched theology. Catholic study has begun on the same path with works such as Cerfaux's *The Church in the Theology of St Paul*. This is a fruitful trend which communicates theology and exegesis while taking inspiration from contemporary philosophical methods.

The question of the Old Testament is more delicate. Here we are in a paradoxical situation. On the one hand, the Church offers us this as food for the soul in the liturgy. On the other, its literal meaning, even according to the teaching of Christ himself, is partially obsolete. This paradox has been resolved by the use of the liturgy and the Fathers, who encourage us to search for figures of Christ in the Old Testament, helping us to better understand 'its unfathomable depths.' As the Basel exegete Vischer has rightly said, 'The Old Testament shows us *what* Christ is, the New Testament *who* he is.'

The problem today is thus to rediscover what was fruitful in the methodology of the Fathers, which alone can prevent the Old Testament from becoming an archaeological curiosity and allow it to become food for the soul. However, this attempt comes up against the suspicions of some supporters of academic exegesis, who, rightly content that they have won the battle against reactionary exegesis and restored to the academy its right to study Scripture, fear that this return to the Fathers marks a step backwards and the easy option. But clearly there is no question of this. We are required to seek to rediscover, in relation to the developments of contemporary scholarship, an interpretation which restores to the Old Testament its prophetic and figurative nature which is a major part of its interest to us. The question of figurative exegesis, which is one of the liveliest in current theology, will probably, in the years to come, be an opportunity for courteous and fruitful confrontations between academic and theological exegetes, whose contributions are equally needed. From these confrontations we may expect the development of a new theology of prophecy, in other words, the relationship of the Old Testament to the New, an idea called to play a key role in tomorrow's theology.

The return to the Scriptures has been accompanied by a noteworthy renewal of patristic theology. This is hardly surprising when we recall that the work of the Fathers is largely a vast commentary on the Holy Scripture, which, from Hippolytus of Rome to Bernard of Clairvaux, constitutes the proper field of Christian thought. Over the centuries, it has been applied to establish correspondences between the Old Testament, the New Testament, liturgy, spirituality and eschatology: a marvellous scholarship in which the whole of Christian thought found its unity and to which we have lost the key. This patristic renewal is expressed in numerous studies dedicated to the Church Fathers, in particular in the '*Théologie*' series, in which Gregory of Nyssa, Clement of Alexandria and Augustine have each been the subject of important works, and in the '*Sources chrétiennes*' series, which publishes translations of the works of the Fathers with substantial introductions.

This renewal of patristic studies is not new. Already at the start of the century a series of translations, edited by Hemmer and Lejay, appeared.[3] But if we compare the '*Pères apostoliques*' with the '*Sources chrétiennes*' we see that they come from different mindsets. For Hemmer-Lejay, it was above all about publishing historical documents, which bore witness to ancient faith. The more recent series suggests that we may demand more of the Fathers. They are not only true witnesses of how things once were but also more contemporary food for the people of today, because in them we are rediscovering precisely a certain number of categories which are part of contemporary thought and which scholastic theology had forgotten.

First of all we should note the idea of history. Contemporary philosophical work, from Hegel to Marx to Bergson, has put history at the centre of modern thought. Now, the idea of history is foreign to Thomism, despite the fact that the great patristic systems turned on history. For Irenaeus, Origen or Gregory of Nyssa, Christianity was not only a doctrine but also a history, the history of the gradual 'economy' through which God, taking humanity in its primitive state, gradually allowed it to mature following the stages marked by the major biblical eras, through a teaching full of mercy, until humanity was able to receive the Incarnate Word. One of the noteworthy books of our times, de Lubac's *Catholicisme*, has contributed to re-establishing the link between the

---

[3] Translator's note: Hippolyte Hemmer (1864–1945) and Paul Lejay (1861–1920) edited the ten-volume '*Pères apostoliques*' (1904–1927), which offered the Greek text of key Apostolic-era writings, including apocryphal gospels, with translation into French.

historical vision of the Fathers and the vision of our contemporaries. The Norwegian theologian Molland noted that the idea of the 'figure' worked for the Church Fathers in the same way that 'evolution' does for our contemporaries: it enables us to think historically.

There is a further aspect of patristic theology which makes it contemporary. One of the characteristics of contemporary religious life is that the problem of salvation is focused much less on the individual, as in the West since St Augustine, than on the communal. What gives the person of today the spiritual shock which pushes conversion is less, 'how do I save my soul', and more 'I must save the souls of my brothers and sisters'. The success of *Action Catholique* is due to its understanding of this. This is the same vision as that of the Greek Fathers, for whom salvation is above all envisaged as the salvation of humanity, conceived of as a single reality, which Christ has penetrated with divine life and which is now saved in itself. From this comes the contemplative optimism which characterizes this thought, and which Russian Orthodoxy has inherited. The return to the dogma of the Mystical Body has led to a new emphasis on patristic texts in which this doctrine shines out from every page. We should note that there is a danger in this tendency, that of misunderstanding the tragedy of personal destiny and neglecting the interior life. But it is also a considerable broadening out and a path towards the forgetting of the self which is indeed the key to the Kingdom.

Finally, to the biblical and patristic streams, we must add the liturgical. This is the third source to which theological contemplation comes for nourishment, rediscovering liturgical archaeology, like biblical archaeology, the contemplation of hidden realities behind sacramental signs. Here again, the contemporary renewal is a return to the primitive tradition, in which liturgy was understood not only from the perspective of its efficaciousness but also from the perspective of teaching, since it is an efficacious sign and efficacious primarily in what it signifies. Alongside commentaries on Scripture, written to give its spiritual sense, the Fathers wrote commentaries on liturgical rites, called mystagogies, which were designed to give their hidden meaning. The incomparable masterworks remain the *Mystagogical Catechesis* of Cyril of Jerusalem, Ambrose's *Treatise on the Mysteries* and Pseudo-Dionysius's *Ecclesiastical Hierarchies*. Louis Bouyer has just brought this genre to life again with his beautiful book, *The Mystery of Easter*.

It is noteworthy that, within the liturgical movement, we have found the same development as in the biblical movement. Here, as there, the primary work needed was archaeological. This is what characterized the two main branches of the liturgical movement, Solesmes, drawn to medieval liturgy and the perfection of Gregorian chant, and Baumstark's, studying comparative liturgy. But today, now that the place of the liturgy has been restored to the Christian life, we may begin to draw out its mindset and find its thought. This plan, which was indeed that of Dom Guéranger, as Olivier Rousseau's wonderful work shows in his *History of the Liturgical Movement*, has been taken up by the contemporary school of Maria Laach and its main leader, Dom Odo Casel. Here liturgy has become the location of the human encounter with the Mystery of God, made more present through worship, without losing anything of his numinousness. This theology of the mystery of worship is one of the sources of contemporary theology. It shows more clearly what Otto's research demonstrated and incorporated into orthodox theology.

In addition, in the liturgical movement we may also rediscover one of the traits of contemporary thought which we have already indicated, the concern of being in touch with life. The effort to place the liturgy within reach of the faithful, begun by men such as Fr Remillieux and Fr Doncoeur, is now poured out into great accomplishments such as Fr Duployé's *Centre de Pastorale liturgique*, the *Maison-Dieu* journal and the '*Lex Orandi*' series. At a time when the desire for temporal incarnation is among the most pressing of concerns of the Christian laity, risking drawing a certain moralism with it, the liturgical movement maintains contact with Christianity's mystery and its sacred aspect.

Philosophical influences

While current theological thought once more plunges its roots into the solid and nourishing soil of the Bible, the Fathers and the liturgy, if it is to be a living theology it must still enrich itself via contact with contemporary thought. Theology's proper function, like the angels on Jacob's ladder, is to ascend and descend between time and eternity, and to knit ever new links between them. Thus the human universe, which a Nietzsche, a Kierkegaard or a Dostoevsky has discovered, the material universe which opens the depths of the earth's history or the starry heavens to us, forces theological thought to expand in a similar way. Here the temptation would be that laziness which makes us take the garment of truth for truth itself, and because the words of Christ are not mentioned, persuade us that we can manage without changing the ways in which we have expressed it.

Yet the main currents of thought are precisely part of this dual widening of our vision. Marxism, heir to scientific philosophy, of which it is the most recent systematization, enriching Darwin's biological evolutionism with a sociological evolutionism and the vulgar materialism of Hegelian dialectic, represents a broadening of our view of the outside world. It corresponds to that discovery of the immensity of space and time in which the destinies of the individual and even of the human species seem to be simply tiny events. It is expressed in faith in a general sense of progress, in which humanity's greatness is to know how to submit and to lose interest in one's own destiny.

Faced with this abyss in the universe, existential philosophy opened a further abyss, deeper yet, which is the abyss of humanity. More aware of the absurdity of a world in which everything apparently contradicts the wishes of the human person and her progress towards a better future, it places all reality in human freedom. But through a merciless analysis, whose initial examples are to be found in Pascal, and which has been deepened over the last century by all the great authors, it shows the insufficiency of all the realities suggested by this freedom, detecting in it the presence of an infinity which denounces all the finite consolations through which we seek to slake our thirst. Faced with this desert-like world, the person is driven to despair. In the tragic sentiment of this transcendence in relation to everything around us, she can find a proud and bitter satisfaction, taking herself for God; thus is the attitude of a Nietzsche or a Sartre.

Defying appearances to the contrary, one may also depend through faith on the word of Christ, as do Kierkegaard, Barth, Gabriel Marcel and Max Scheler. In any case, it is the infinite nature of human freedom which is the central grasp of this thought.

To the twin abysses of historicity and subjectivity, we should add the general perception of coexistence according to which each of our lives has an effect on the lives of others, common in Marxism and Existentialism. These abysses thus oblige theological thought to expand. It is clear that scholastic theology is foreign to these categories. The world of scholasticism is the unchanging one of Greek thought, its mission to incarnate the Christian message therein. This understanding maintains a permanent and always valuable truth at least as it consists in affirming that the decision of human freedom or the transformation by humanity of its living conditions is not an absolute beginning by which humanity creates itself but the response to a call from God, whose expression is the world of essences. Furthermore, it makes no room for history; on the other hand, placing reality in essences rather than in subjects means it ignores the dramatic world of persons, concrete universals which transcend all essences and are only distinguished by their existence, that is, not according to the intelligible and intellectual understanding but according to value and love or hate.

Now, theology has begun to align itself to these aspects of modern thought, first of all in the field of history. This is thanks to the work of Teilhard de Chardin, who dealt audaciously with the problem and forced Christian thought to take account of the perspectives opened up by evolution. Questionable as some of his views may be, his work has been an agent of fermentation, hidden yet active, whose influences on the theology of our time will have been considerable. And the broad outlines of his thought, according to which history gradually rises from the world of life to the world of thought, from the world of thought to the world of Christ and which is close to the views of the Fathers, remain to be grasped.

In fact it is an uncontrollable demand of Christian faith that history should have a meaning, that time is not the reflection of eternity which it is for Platonism but a growth in which succession itself is a progress in the strongest meaning of the term, that is, acquiring value. And, in this sense, we must challenge the deformation of Christianity by Gnosticism, as we find it even among some Fathers of the Church, where Redemption seems to be presented as having the sole object of bringing humanity back to its primitive state, so that it appears as though it would have been better if nothing had happened and everything had remained in its primitive unchanging state. Already in the second century, St Irenaeus denounced this static conception and affirmed both the religious value of history and the fundamental goodness of creation.

This optimistic perspective must be complemented by another, that of original sin, which has an equally uncontrollable demand on Christian thought. Original sin consists of three essential facts: that humanity before Christ was under sin; that human freedom brings with it responsibility for that sin; and that humanity is united in sin. Now, here Christian thought will find its echo not in Marxism but in our other contemporary current of thought, Existentialism. We should not forget, of course, that for its founder, Kierkegaard, original sin, in its most theological sense, plays a key role. It is the theme of one of his main works, *The Concept of Anxiety*. Transposed into a secularized world and now only the expression of the absurdity of this world, it is the same data which we find among contemporary existentialists: Simone de Beauvoir could put *Original Sin* on the cover of her latest novel. It is remarkable that the dogma of original sin places us precisely in the presence of these two abysses – the abyss of history and the goodness of the world, and the abyss of freedom and the absurdity of the world – which are precisely, as we saw above, those which Marxism and Existentialism open before us. We see how the Christian mystery is the locus for the ultimate expression of the conflict of modern, and thus, so that theology may be present to its time, it suffices to respond to all demands and to hold on simultaneously to Irenaeus and Augustine, Teilhard and Kierkegaard.

This is not the only aspect by which Existentialism affects Christian thought. It is useful to note that the current of thought which was born with Kierkegaard is a reaction against the way in which the theology of his own time rationalized the Christian mystery. He affirmed the mystery of the personal God, hidden in the shadows which cannot be broken and entered into by anyone, who only reveals himself through love, against a theology which treated God as an object. Thus he reminded the theologian of the attitude of reverence with which she must approach the mystery which she wishes to scrutinize and which, by definition, escapes her grasp. Here we find one of the characteristics of the theological renewal, that sense of the mystery of God, which restores apophatic theology (*via negativa*) to its rightful place and which may be seen simultaneously in an Orthodox theologian such as Lossky, a Protestant theologian such as Barth or a Catholic theologian such as Castel.

A final trait of Existentialism should be noted. Alongside a doctrine, it presents a method which is characterized by the fact that rather than demonstrating the links between ideas, as Aristotelian logic or Hegelian dialectic do, it insists on their irreducibility. This was the phenomenological route by which Otto demonstrated the irreducibility of the category of the sacred, by which Scheler definitively characterized the Christian *agape* as Freudian or scientist and by which Gabriel Marcel defined faith and hope. I need not show how this method, even incomplete, is valuable for the demonstration of the originality of religious categories against attempts of reduction which are the foundation of sociological or psychoanalytical interpretations of religion. This methodology must now become the basis of every theology which is founded on descriptions of concrete religious realities, whose links it will then determine.

Contact with life

Renewed by the deepest sources of religious life, given life through its contact with currents in contemporary thought, in order to live, theology must also respond to a third demand: it must take account of the needs of souls, be given life by a spirit of the apostolate, be wholly engaged in the work of the construction of the Body of Christ. Here again, it rediscovers the attitude of contemporary thinkers. 'Until now, philosophy has only interpreted the world; now it must transform it', wrote Marx, in his *Theses on Feuerbach*. In our world, it is impossible to separate thought and life; a thought which is not first and foremost a witness seems to be an undefinable quantity.

Today's people, living in the world, will demand that theology explain the meaning of their life. It is no longer possible, as in the past, to dissociate theology from spirituality. Theology was on a speculative, timeless plain; spirituality too often consisted in practical advice separated from the vision of the spiritual director. A strong trait of contemporary thought is the attempt to join theology and asceticism together again, as in the time of the Church Fathers, so that they may complement one another. The success of spiritual authors who are also filled with doctrine, such as Gregory of Nyssa or Cardinal de Bérulle, is characteristic of this, as is the success of works of religious anthropology such as Jean Mouroux's work *Sens chrétien de l'homme*.

This constitution of spiritual theology, which seeks to study our condition as children of God and particularly to define the vocation of the Christian laity, is developed on three principal axes. First, the realm of individual conduct. Many Christians feel a salutary inferiority complex before some forms of heroism inspired by current doctrines. This is the drama expressed in the books of Coudenhove-Kalergy. From this comes the concern, in the face of the Nietzschean exaltation of risk and the dangerous life, of presenting a heroic Christianity which exalts all the forces of humanity. This is the spirit which guides the meditation which Marcel Légault brought together in his volume, before being inspired by the very adventure of existence. It is also the inspiration of Emmanuel Mounier in his *Affrontement chrétien*. He asks whether 'Christianity is a pseudonym for the coalition of the weak and the fearful? A virile renaissance seems if not a substance, at least the necessary preface to a spiritual renewal.'

Another current emphasizes charity above all, as the substance of the Good News. It is liberally expressed in the spiritual literature created by the movements of Catholic Action, and particularly the Young Christian Workers. In a recent survey by *Vie Spirituelle* on the type of holiness towards which we are drawn, a female activist from Catholic Action wrote in summary of many other responses that 'a characteristic of modern saints is charity as love for our neighbour'. It is very clear that this is emphasizing an essential aspect of Christianity. However, it is noteworthy how often this current, like the previous one, puts the emphasis on the *human* aspect of holiness and that its essentially theocentric nature is left in the dark. This becomes a serious problem when, as sometimes happens, these views are accompanied by a critique of traditional spirituality and the life of union with God. This is the case for Nygren, for instance, who presents an entirely Protestant critique of mysticism. Some Catholics are not exempt from a similar complaint. This way leads to a considerable impoverishing of religious values and a return to a sort of moralism.

In the second case, the demands of souls have led to a considerable deepening of theology and spirituality of marriage. Here there has been a flourishing of works which have been published in the last decade. It is notable that what marks the better among them is precisely the concern to not only bring practical advice but to found this on a sacramental theology and the religious value the sacrament gives the person. This is the doctrine which inspires works as *Le mariage comme vie consacrée* by Rochelle, Hildebrand's *Le mariage*, Evdokimoff's *Le sacrement de l'amour* and magazines such as *L'Anneau d'or* and *Famille et Chrétienté*. This theology has benefitted from recent studies on the philosophy of love, such as those of Scheler and his disciples. Here again, these efforts are not to be exaggerated. But it is incontestable that theological reflection has greatly helped many Christian homes to deepen their spiritual life.

Finally, theological reflection must be exercised to enlighten Christians at the level of their temporal, and particularly their political, action. It is certain that the events of the last few years posed serious problems for numerous Christians for whom temporal engagement was imposed as an indefensible demand and who reflected on the significance of this demand. Here again, traditional spirituality, aimed at the clergy, had few answers for the lay conscience, and they had the feeling of being more or less abandoned by the Church in the face of sometimes outrageous options which their conscience forced them to take. Fr de Montcheuil dealt with these serious questions in his little book, *L'Église et le monde actuel*.

Here the theologian seems to have a dual role. On the one hand, he must give value to all human reality. And in this regard there is something entirely legitimate in the current reaction against a depreciation in temporal values which is not in the spirit of Catholicism. This depreciation, as Fr Féret noted in a recent article,[4] has often arisen from confusion between the spiritual and the theological perspectives, between St John of the Cross and St Thomas Aquinas. The depreciation of creatures, legitimate from the spiritual perspective, which places itself at a practical and pedagogical point, becomes illegitimate when it is transformed into a theological judgement.

But equally the theologian must situate values in a global vision of the Christian person and consequently clearly show the primacy of the new creation operated in humanity by grace, which spreads through the theological virtues, principles of familiarity with God and supernatural charity with men. Now, it is very clear that this supernatural life cannot develop without mortification, that the mystery of the Christian person, like that of Christ, is that mystery of death and resurrection. This is doubtless the aspect which most risks being misunderstood today. The recent survey by *Vie spirituelle* mentioned above gives sometimes concerning testimony to this.

At the same time as it deepens the mystery of personal holiness, Christian thought must be open to universalist perspectives. All the great currents of thought which confront each other in today's world have a cosmic aspect. Too often Christianity, which is by definition Catholic, has a narrow character and does not dare to place itself in wide perspectives. In particular, we need to get used to the thought that Christianity, which was initially expressed in Graeco-Roman culture, is called to be incarnate in the other great world cultures, of India, China and Africa. We must even go as far as to say that this is the means, not of a progress of Revelation, which ended with Christ, but of a progress of dogma, the forms of each mentality enabling an emphasis on new aspects of the inexhaustible richness of Christ.

It is this new path of theology which the great pioneers of contemporary missionary thought, such as Fr Lebbe in China, Fr Aupaiais in Africa and Fr Monchanin in India, have opened up. The first two have died, while the third is currently in India completing his work on the incarnation of Christianity in Hindu thought. In their ploughing a whole missionary theology has been used, which has established its own ways of expression. In particular, we are familiar with the works of Fr Pierre Charles

---

[4] Henri-Marie Féret, 'Pour un renouveau du sens chrétien de l'homme', *Vie spirituelle* 304 (1946), 163.

and the Louvain school. The '*La Sphère et la Croix*' series, to be published this year by Éditions du Seuil, will be inspired by the same perspectives and will seek to express a specifically missionary theology and spirituality. Here again, we note the effort to go beyond the anecdotal level which too often restricted missionary writings in the past in order to deal with the problem in its theological reality.

These are the broad outlines of the task currently offered to Christian thought. It must be said that the hour is decisive. Earlier generations accumulated materials; now we must build. For this we need people who can join a profound sense of the Christian tradition to a life of contemplation which gives them an understanding of the mystery of Christ, an acute sense of the needs of their time and a burning love for the souls of their brothers – people who are all the more free with regard to the whole of humanity, to whom they will be ever more closely linked by the interior link of the Spirit.

6

Anon. 'Response to "The sources of Theology"'

'La théologie et ses sources. *Réponse*'. *Recherches de Science Religieuse* 33 (1946), 385–401.

A couple of months or so ago, an offprint of '*Études critiques*' from a forthcoming issue of the *Revue Thomiste* was sent to us, which includes an unexpected indictment of a number of Jesuit theologians. Most of us, convinced that such disputes are usually vanity exercises, would have preferred to remain silent, but authoritative voices persuaded us to respond. Each one of us is perfectly aware that his work is debatable and wishes only to take advantage of the critique, severe though it may be, levelled against us. We also know that several of our publications raise serious questions, whose facts are nonetheless essential for all, and which we make no claim to solve alone. But this article is something else entirely. The reader, we believe, will see that complaint is not unfounded; and if she is unaware of the general situation, she will also understand that it is opportune.

May God ensure that this matter is soon closed and that all in the Church may devote themselves unanimously to these more arduous but magnificent tasks to which the Sovereign Pontiff recently urged us, *to the greater glory of God and the building up of the Church*.

20 November 1946.

Fr Labourdette does not wish one to profess 'the essential historical relativism of every human expression of divine truths'. He does not want Christian thought to have a 'bad shame of its past'. He does not want 'theological wisdom to be borne away on the flotsam of impermanence'. He does not want the historical method to be weighed down by a 'pseudo-philosophy', which 'replaces the metaphysical notion of speculative truth with the more modest notion of historical truth'. He does not want 'a perpetual overhaul of our concepts of God' to be carried out on the pretext of criticizing 'historical progress'. He does not want a 'nominalist philosophy' which, through a real 'caricature of the life of the spirit', would profess that 'our reason ... only directly reaches these concepts, and these concepts are empty abstractions, logical frameworks whose value is entirely pragmatic.' He does not want the statement 'the divine message is also addressed to our understanding' to be denied. He does not wish to subscribe to 'the complete emptying of the idea of speculative truth'. He does not want it to be said that truth is 'inaccessible' to us nor that our mind can be denied the power of grasping truth, 'in the most certain of its notions, a timeless truth'. He does not want metaphysics and theology to be judged in the last resort as 'categories of aesthetics'. He does not want 'something other than a teaching which awakes in us the sense of the beautiful or introduces us to an incommunicable experience' to be expected. Finally, he does not want the fact that 'in the field of knowledge there are definitive acquisitions' to be questioned.

How right Fr Labourdette is! It goes without saying that we do not want this any more than he does. No one is entitled to suspect us of seeking these things, and Fr Labourdette himself does not cite a single word of ours which would lead him to think this. Thus, while we are happy to state that we are in full agreement with him on these matters, we remain astonished that he invites us to explain ourselves. Yet he is careful – and we thank him for this – to clarify that he does not attribute the 'theory' he is battling to us, that his anathemata are not directed against us but only 'opportunistic', that his analysis 'goes beyond' our thought and that he has been careful to 'try us for our tendencies'. The trial is not, in our eyes, limited to that, and any reader will doubtless see that we are on trial without being accused.

As it would never occur to us to question the good faith or benevolence of the author, we are forced to seek an explanation for this strange phenomenon. It resides, we believe, in his methodology.

There are of course many erroneous paths and this methodology brings together a number of them. The first is a preoccupation of the mind. Our author is affected by serious anxiety. A monster heresy has risen up before his face, whose signs he cannot now stop himself from finding everywhere. If, as may be deduced from his words, this monster is real today, why not describe it properly? And why not attack it, rather than harassing poor passers-by who, he acknowledges, are just there 'opportunistically'. In other words, why not bring his criticism to bear on works where the doctrine which he denounces so clearly and precisely is professed, rather than spreading suspicion lightly over a whole series of other writings?

In any case, these works are not part of a whole. Whether books or journal articles, they are written by a range of authors, have various natures and have been published in different times and circumstances. Thus the second defect of Labourdette's methodology – to try to offer a commentary on some works by using others, without taking the trouble to analyse a single one. Hence to understand the hidden meaning of innocent translations of the Fathers, he must interpret them according to a collection of historical studies. This series in turn can only reveal an essential characteristic of its spirit thanks to a preface in another work, written by another author, published by a different publishing house. And all these works on history, doctrine or translation are, according to Labourdette, due to a 'general plan' that this or that article or review helps to reveal. We do not dispute the fact that fraternal links, a common vocation, shared masters and shared apostolic concerns exist among us, which could give the impression of a family of thought. The solidarity among us which is assumed is no less illusory: although none of us is independent of our shared history in our work, we are aware of many differences, often profound, between us in methodology and thought.

Only an error of perspective could allow our critic to attribute so clumsily to all of us what he wrongly thought he had discovered among us.

This methodology of a 'general presentation', similar to the 'synthetic picture', takes us into the third area of misunderstanding, where, despite everything, nothing appears to Labourdette to be reprehensible, aside from the 'background thoughts'. Here we find him not only on the slope but already in the pit of the most obvious subjectivism! Once such an understanding is accepted, how can we be surprised that he sniffs out danger from the most innocent statement, and thus unconsciously encourages the thought that any correct thought arises at the least from a 'tendency' to error?

Let us now offer some examples of the results.

The '*Sources chrétiennes*' series gives translations of the Greek Fathers. Fr Labourdette presents this in such a way that he is able to conclude that 'in truth, the whole problem of theology and its claim to set itself up as *an intellectual discipline proper*, is found here'. If only this were the case – for with but a little ingenuity any problem can be presented as global. But it seems to us more objective to observe that that 'here' must be taken in its most obvious sense, describing the page of the *Revue Thomiste* on which it appears, without any relationship to our 'sources'. Our critic has quite simply projected the problem which is the ordinary object of his personal concerns and work onto the '*Sources chrétiennes*'.

In a brief preface, a recent work recalls the – very banal – distinction between dogma and theology, and without any pretence at originality. Commentary:

> we would like the progress of theology not to be assimilated to the progress of dogma: the differences are only too obvious. But how can we not see that the reasons by which we fight the assurance of theological progress to the benefit of a perpetual rejuvenation of our ideas about God, according to the diversity of time and cultures, would retain all their value to restore the progress of dogma itself to proportions unacceptable to the Church?

Which reader would not think that this 'one' is the author in sight? Yet it is nothing of the sort, and even the most discerning detective would find none of the 'reasons' in this work which 'one' attributes to it. In the same place, we read, 'How can we admit that nothing remains of the heights reached by the mind in days gone by?' Who, we wonder, has ever asked that such a thing should be admitted? What can Labourdette even be alluding to? But this is not all. One of the essential ideas of the work in question is that it returns us to the teaching of St Thomas (whether well or poorly understood is another matter) outside of the multiple complications and deformations of modern times. This book, we are told, published in the '*Théologie*' series, 'emphasizes its nature of reaction against St Thomas speculatively drawn up theology'.

In the preface to another work, another author, to temper some naive fads, wrote, 'Every "adaptation" to contemporary taste will end in the same way, and theology will no more escape this universal law than architecture.' One might suppose that our critic recognizes such a wise suggestion. Not at all! This comparison, on such a well-defined point as architecture, indicates to him an entire erroneous system, which destroys every truth! Yet nothing in his criticism demonstrates that he has read a single line of the work itself.[1] He is further distressed by the words 'The same applies to St Thomas', on the same page. Yet this should reassure him. A moment ago he feared that an exaltation of the Fathers could only be to the detriment of the great Doctor. And now here he is saying, in the same words, that these texts cannot be 'pastiches' through an over-literal imitation or a fantastical 'adaptation'. He does not wish to see any text buried but, on the contrary, warns against treatments which would end in texts being buried. Is this not what more than one fervent Thomist says today, in another 'style'? On both sides, let us acknowledge the same love for the Tradition, the same desire to be firmly supported by it. Here however is something more daring, perhaps arising from a more acute feeling of the problems which our age poses, a more victorious confidence in the eternal youth of the Church.

A further example. In a very general article, whose expressions were sometimes a little hasty, one of us, reviewing the main contemporary currents of thought at the very heart of Christianity, symbolized the two most opposed currents using the names of Fr Teilhard de Chardin and Kierkegaard. In the words of our critic this became, 'thanks to the efforts of Fr Teilhard de Chardin, appends the benefits of Marxist, existentialist, and other thought-systems'. Do the worst 'betrayals' of translators ever get this far?

One can see from these examples that while one might well be blamed for 'replac[ing] the metaphysical idea of speculative truth by the more modest concept of historical truth', a more attentive respect for the humble historical truth, or a little more objectivity from the reader, could have avoided such efforts expended by those who most jealously guard the speculative truth.

However, the most usual process to which we have recourse, which is the weft of this whole 'critical study', is that of 'overshooting'. It is stated, we have said so. But is the author truly aware of what this is in reality? Has he noticed that these 'overshootings' are giants' steps and not on the road but on the cliffs alongside it? He thinks this is a way to make a 'tendency' stand out. This reminds us of an anecdote. 'Unhappy fellow', a wise man once said to his friend in difficult circumstances,

> unhappy fellow, beware of proclaiming that there are three persons in one God so carelessly! With but a slight exaggeration, it will be said that you are saying there are four. And by speaking about three, are you not only in fact demonstrating a slight tendency to suggest that there are four? Just say that there are two persons: that is incontestable, and in that absolutely central position, which reassures everyone, you will have the advantage of not moving towards the extremity of truth – the point which is so close to error.

From a practical perspective, it was not too badly argued. And we should hardly have remembered this anecdote had we been party to Fr Labourdette's process of reasoning. We are spoken of with certainty. (*Securi loquebamur.*) Alas, how can one ever be certain one is right? We could, against the historical evidence, have denied that there is any element of relativity in the life of the human mind down the ages; against

---

[1] However in another passage he warns us that 'on another occasion' he will tell us exactly what he thinks.

all rational evidence, we could have denied that there is any element of relativity in human knowledge in general. Or at least we could have not mentioned it, not even in fact dared to state the facts which might lead one to such a conclusion. We could have been content to state, as is certain and apparent in what we have written, that truth remains unchanging down the centuries and that our understanding is not cut off from the absolute. But would we have covered the subjects we have done? We say this: each of us deserves the accusation of relativism as much as the statement that there are three persons in God deserves the accusation of tending towards stating that there are four.

These comments introduce us to a fundamental debate which we do not wish to evade. We know what our Institution's particular rules and the Church's general directives are in this area. We fully intend to remain actively faithful to the demands of both, each according to the obligations of his particular situation. But Fr Labourdette's demands seem to us far from simply coinciding with these rules and directives. He also seems to have forgotten that the methods of history are not those of a dogmatic treatise and that research is not carried out in the same way as teaching. Hence the misunderstandings which lead him to speak about 'relativism'.

This relativism, which Labourdette's pen constantly references, is presented under a dual aspect: the historical and the doctrinal. Now, we believe that this is how we can also discover the dual historical and doctrinal illusion thanks to which Labourdette thinks he is correct to mention when discussing us, albeit without formally crediting us.

First, this is a curious philosophy of the history of theology. Fr Labourdette informs us that he has 'no disdain' for the first twelve centuries of Christian thought. We are happy to believe him. However, he seems to only appreciate them once the Thomist synthesis has drained them of any substance. Since this synthesis 'represents that truly *scientific* status of Christian thought', why linger on its prescientific state? So many specialists are dedicated to its study, reconstructing this prehistory, in order to show how, gradually, through a thousand and one trials and errors, the definitive synthesis was prepared – all well and good. But let us not pretend that even today, seeking intellectual nourishment easily assimilated from those distant days would demonstrate a sort of 'clear depreciation' of the efforts which followed. As for the later centuries, there is no room to ignore them, which would be to deprive oneself of 'beautiful and authentic progress', but it must be clearly understood that this progress does not in any way include even the slightest overhaul. The synthesis, he says, is definitive; its categories are all eternal; thus, it can be a question merely of adding some embellishments or drawing some consequences.

We hasten to add that such a conception is attenuated here and there by much more reasonable statements, where, for instance, there is only the question of ensuring the perennial nature of the 'major teachings' of the theological knowledge developed in the Middle Ages. This is almost contradicted by a statement, which we believe we are correct to attribute to the same author, since it appears in a recent volume of the *Revue Thomiste*,[2] which in the most rigorous terms gives an account of the criticism

---

[2] After a series of aphorisms which, he tells us, 'too many minds inspired by sincere faith' would raise doubts about, he adds, 'what was true still remains. What is false today was always false. What is incomplete must be completed.' He continues, 'The life of a doctrine is not the destruction of its animating principles, of course, but the growth of the truth which it expresses, the ongoing

addressed to us. In particular, it explains the sort of scandal arising from the start at the thought that, unlike the '*Collection Budé*' for classical texts, we might somehow try to give life to the writings of Christian antiquity; that, rather than seeing them as purely 'historical documents', only to be used by experts or the curious, we would be unafraid to make them available to the intelligent general reader; that rather than always treating them simply as objects from the outside we might in some way try to give the reader an awareness of the fraternal links which, down so many centuries and despite such dramatic changes in mindsets, make the thought which they transmit to us and the thought we live today an expression of a single faith; finally, that we should go so far as to state that in some ways (and only in some ways), the Church Fathers can sometimes seem closer to us than later theologians. Such a 'mindset' seems most worrying; can such an 'intention' be compatible with 'honest work'?

Yet we shall continue to think that the progress of theology is not as straightforward as might be supposed; that it is in no way absolute. In the long chain of tradition, what follows does not annul what has gone before. To assimilate the nutritious and substantive is not to exhaust it. One may state this without any lack of respect for St Thomas, without any 'depreciation' of his work and his eminent place, just as believing in later progress which is not simply an addition is not in any way to deny its grandeur or solidity. The very nature of scientific systematization which we rightly lend the Tradition (we may be somewhat exaggerating) fatally draws in particular choices, particular 'partialities', which its greatest admirers and the most fervent faithful would have no difficulty recognizing; likewise the simple fact that it was developed in a particular century. For example, why be so outraged when we say that, in historical terms, tradition lacks a certain sense of history, as though this were not the case – with some nuances – of the whole of medieval thought in its most wonderful flourishing! This observation has been made hundreds of times for a long time, but does not in any way indicate that this thought is 'exhausted', as we have been made to say, neither that one cannot find in it any principle or 'marker' for new building, but which shows that it needs to 'expand' to remain a living theology.

More generally, a 'rigorous scientific expression of Christian thought working on the truths of faith' inevitably leaves many more concrete elements outside it, which it does not contradict. Consequently one may – and to fully embrace Catholic

---

elimination of the slag and waste, the modification of certain forms of expression.' Does this not go at least as far as the 'cloak of comparison' which one of us is accused of, interpreted in a way opposed to its clear meaning? (There is no question of rejecting the traditional notion of common good like an outdated garment but, on the contrary, of emphasizing it, as the whole work makes clear.) An earlier article in the same journal (December 1939, p. 793) commented about the doctrine of marriage as follows: 'It seems to me that in this area of theology, as in many others, fidelity to the most essential thought of St Thomas enables us to overshoot his formulas to the point of appearing to change them.' These are perhaps liberal or over-complacent formulas, for any innovation seen to be useful may be given the label 'Thomist'. Yet if others do so, with more timidity, as one of us has done by a simple statement of a particular notion completely engaged in a clearly academic context; or if they honestly state something which has been found to be modified in the Thomism of history, then the whole truth collapses, and belief in truth! We must state clearly that what is missing from such rigorous judgement is rigorous thought. Note too that there is something arbitrary about claiming a rigorously academic technique and a perpetual openness and extreme plasticity at the same time for the same theory.

tradition, must – draw on other resources, without in any way contesting or rejecting the necessity of this tradition. Is it not a law of the mind that it truly progresses and deepens its knowledge only through a rhythm which periodically draws it back to the origins of its thought, not by an indefinite reflection or a forced march always going from consequence to consequence? This still applies, and perhaps above all for theological reflection. Thus the more we exalt St Thomas, the less we have to fear that a direct appeal to the sources on which he himself drew is wrong: on the contrary, this is a condition of understanding him better, deepening our knowledge of him, better discerning in him those 'truths' promised to marvellous developments.

If we may be permitted a comparison here, which is in no way harmful to Thomas: no one would dare to say that the riches of Scripture have passed into the definitions of faith and current teaching of the Church, and thus there is no need to return to it. Well perhaps, in extreme circumstances. Yet who would not immediately see the fault of such denial? And does the Church itself not commit us to study the Holy Scriptures ever more, without exception for even those passages on which it has pronounced? The Fathers do not have the same authority, of course; they are secondary sources, derived, in no way sufficient, and yet they still play an important role; they have not only played this role in the past but continue to do so in the present. They are not sources in the restricted sense of literary history, but living, flowing sources.

When complaints are made that some studies are less interested in the 'objective signified' of the thought which they analyse than in the 'subjective life' that this thought demonstrates, a historical relativism, which is calamitous to the very idea of truth, is being attacked. What studies and thoughts are these? We are not told.[3] We find only a footnote in support of this new cycle of accusations, a short account in which the relationships between schools of theology and schools of spirituality are questioned, as though the latter were simply a case of empirical psychology! And once again, thanks to this confusion, the 'overshooting' phenomenon comes into play, which brings down on us a glittering tirade in which the author's virtuosity finds a place to call on 'the Freudian doctrine of the dream' and the 'psychoanalytic method'! And, we are told, this is simply an 'enlightening bringing together'. As he seeks to reassure us that he is not really assimilating the 'form of reflection', and that we are fighting the 'technique' of psychoanalysis, what are we complaining about?

There remains the question of doctrinal relativism, taken on its own and no longer in its application to the history of theology. Here the complaint may be summarized in a single word: anti-intellectualism. (The development of this subject, following M. Benda, of the 'powerful push forward of irrational philosophies' and their 'culture of equivalence' introduces a moment of humour to this complaint.) In response, let us try to give rather more intellectual clarity than we find in the accusation. The word is in fact full of equivocation. Two adjectival forms correspond to the noun: anti-intellectual and anti-intellectualist. The anti-intellectual is against intelligence: none of

---

[3] Although why one would not be interested in the 'subjective life' we cannot see. Nothing forces us to always discuss timeless truth. One can believe in many things without recalling them in every circumstance and without making them the particular focus of one's studies. And what is more, is it really possible to not take account of that 'subjective life' if we wish to truly reconstruct a way of thinking?

us accepts being described as such and, once again, it would be difficult to show that we are this. Anti-intellectualist is against intellectualism, and here the question becomes more complex, and it is important to distinguish between the two.

In theology there can be a certain intellectualism against which we are quick to take a stand. This is a position which tends to make Christian revelation the communication of a system of ideas, while it is first and foremost, and always will be, the manifestation of a Person, the Truth in Person. Christ is at one and the same time the bearer and the object of the divine message. The Word of God, in its unique and definitive fullness, is the Word made flesh. It does not follow from this that revelation may not express itself in concepts, that the passing of time does not oblige this conceptual expression to clarify and gain depth, or that one should not expect only a pragmatic kind of help from this, without the value of truth as truth. To those who, thanks to some scruple or poorly drawn out reflection, are inclined to doubt the human mind's capacity for the truth, the Incarnation of the Word rather brings new reasons for confidence. But it follows from this that Catholic truth will always overflow its conceptual expression, and even more so its scientific formulation into an organized system.[4] This is what Christian thinkers in all ages have sensed instinctively. This is what enabled Bonaventure and Thomas, without renouncing their differences, to understand one another by something other than a pure spirit of charity. We do not wish to insinuate that our critic would contest these things. But we believe that he has not given them the full consideration they deserve. In addition to purely philosophical reasons of order, they commit him to show himself more conciliatory towards other forms of thought than his own without thus believing that he is betraying truth. They would make him more able to understand the price the Church attaches to the freedom of theological schools within the one orthodoxy. They would prevent him from giving into any kind of temptation to monopolise the truth, in its content and its very form, and to impose on everyone a particular conception in the name of faith. In theology more than in other disciplines, we should fear greatly that 'intellectualist' deformation which takes a system to be *the* truth and, what is more, which conceives the truth to be a system. We know excellent Thomists, close to us and far from us, who are perfectly able to keep themselves from these dangers. In this we believe them to be more truly Thomist than others; in any case, more truly theologians.

If one understood intellectualism to be precisely a certain conception of things, 'a doctrine which puts all the value and intensity of life, and the very essence of good, identical to being, in the act of intelligence, the rest only being good through participation' (Rousselot), such a conception is clearly debatable; perhaps it over-systematizes the thought of St Thomas, but from the perspective of faith we shall

---

[4] Is it not also a fact that, in their successive appearance, theological systems and dogmatic treatises themselves, as soon as they take on a certain depth, are always more or less linked in their structure to a range of mindsets? Yet for all this they still reach the same objective truth, but each only expresses a single aspect at heart, and together they do not exhaust. Thus – a classic example – theories of redemption, conceived as Christ's victory over the devil, or as an expiatory sacrifice, or satisfaction. These aspects are not mutually exclusive, and we can hold onto all of them, but no more than they are organized in a logical and scientific whole. Should we close our eyes to this evidence to avoid relativism or subjectivism?

not raise any objection against this in principle. (And yet there are so many ways to understand 'the act of intelligence'!) We should doubtless each have slightly different reactions to this and we do not imagine that Fr Labourdette wishes to examine us on this point. However we grant him that several of us, who came young to St Thomas and partly under the influence of Fr Rousselot, were once enthusiastic about some aspects of Thomist intellectualism as he presented it to us and that we continue to admire the vigour with which he made it his own.

The very way in which it has been conducted means that this whole discussion is built on false foundations. Despite our efforts to introduce a little logic and clarity, we sense that we have not been successful. Perhaps we were wrong to not restrict ourselves to a straightforward denial. Elementary and close to common sense as the reflections above are, what will be made of them if they are treated in the same way as our earlier writings? In the light of a certain reading, all good sense becomes mad, all truth a lie, the most simple statement suddenly appears to conceal chasms of shadowy complications. Yet how can such a discussion not be sterile? We find ourselves confronted with entirely negative criticisms without any contribution to any of the problems we have raised, without research into a better solution, with almost nothing to feed a true exchange.[5] No account is given of the facts which are raised. Of each work cited, only the characteristic which it is thought might contribute to an imagined erroneous system is referenced. We are constantly made to look as though we are opposed to general statements which in fact we consent to. When detail is required, it is in disputation over words where it seems a moment's attention could have spared us.[6] A constant accusation of heterodoxy is advanced, semi-withdrawn, then reiterated. We would not have replied, had some concurrent signals not indicated a non-imaginary, wider 'design'. The unusual way in which this declaration of war has been released has already given us food for thought. Given that there are some very detailed echoes of conversations, correspondence, unrest which come not, we are clear, from the same author but from the same circles and related groups, we fear that while the dark days of Modernism are, thank God, now long gone, the dark days of *intégrisme* are only too close to returning.

It is true that our critic does not take us to be pernicious. He does not attribute to us a formal intention of destroying dogmas. But who does he take us for – not to mention our censors and superiors, without whom we cannot publish a word – if he thinks we are all so blind that we cannot see that we are destroying them? The accusation is too strong, and the range of those it attacks too wide, for us not to feel that we have the right to ask him whether he has reflected on this. It is also true that he deals considerately with the 'esteem' he has for our projects, the 'sympathy' for our 'aims', and perhaps he

---

[5] We shall nonetheless continue, over the coming year, to attempt to publish our positive contribution to the examination of live problems, particularly the relationships between theology and history in the pages of the *Recherches* and elsewhere.

[6] We may have read somewhere that we should 'treat God as God, not as an object, but as the Subject *par excellence*, who is manifest when and how he wishes'. The author of this statement is reminded of the 'notion of the object' of 'theological language' to the extent of explaining to him, with supporting texts, that the word 'object', *'objectum'* is used by the [First] Vatican Council to describe the mysteries of faith. And yet surely everyone can see that the word is not being used in the same way in the two instances!

will take advantage of this to be surprised in turn at our reaction. Of course we are aware of and most grateful for his esteem. We would like to see in that the beginnings of a better understanding in the future. But the accusation remains. We are summoned to the witness stand, and the smile the judge gives us from his dais does not in any way reduce the force of his judgements. We hope we may say to him that a journal is not a court and its editor no judge. At the very least he can do no useful work in such a role. We would like to hope that he will acknowledge this and that it will now be possible for us to work in collaboration with him, without prejudice to our legitimate difficulties and without excluding this shared effort of suing for peace, in the service of the same truth. There are too many heresies in the world, they are too real, there are too many fatal and virulent errors for us to be able to dwell further on disputes of another age. Fr Labourdette may be assured that we no more want to see the spirit of Christianity fall into 'a spirit of abandonment' than he does; we do not wish to yield in any way to him in doctrinal vigilance: we believe we have all demonstrated this on more than one occasion. We aspire only to be his associates in the defence of the faith, from whichever angle it appears to be threatened. But we also believe that, here as elsewhere, the best defence consists above all in a positive contribution. We try to do only our little bit. We cannot all be all things [to all men]. (*Non omnia possumus omnes.*) We do not understand this as quantity, but we know that a single man, a single school, a single country, a single Religious Order cannot itself provide all the notes which will go to compose the Church's great concerto. May he and his imitators also do their work in this way, may they do better and greater things than us: we shall rejoice as we have already rejoiced about this in other circumstances. In particular, may they give us more and more of those works which are so sought after which contribute to make St Thomas better known in his writings and in his thought. We shall not wait to applaud them for expressing the same opinions and perspectives as we do: without yielding to the relativism which they rightly condemn, our sense of the Church's greatness and universality is strong enough to allow that there are many differences, even intellectual ones, within it, and we shall never allow the frontiers of orthodoxy to be reduced to those of our personal thought in its most systematic expression. We believe that to do so would make us not more intrepid, but blasphemous. The first rigour in dogmatics is a rigour against oneself.

Part Two

Attacks on 'the new theology'

Introduction

7 Pietro Parente, 'New tendencies in theology'

Pietro Parente (1891–1986) was an Italian priest and theologian, who taught at both the Pontifical Urbanianum and Pontifical Lateran universities in Rome. He was also a well-known neo-Thomist who promoted and defended the neo-scholastic method. In 1942, he penned this brief article for *L'Osservatore Romano* in which he justified the placing of Chenu's *Le Saulchoir: Une école de théologie* and Louis Charlier's (1898–1981) *Essai sur le problème théologique* on the Index of Prohibited Books.

8 Réginald Garrigou-Lagrange, 'Where is "new theology" going?'

The Dominican Réginald Garrigou-Lagrange (1877–1964) has been called the 'doyen' or 'dean' of twentieth-century Thomism. Professor of Theology from 1909 until 1959, and holder of the first Chair of Spirituality from 1919 at the Pontifical University of St Thomas (the 'Angelicum') in Rome, this 'sacred monster of Thomism' was the arch-defender of the neo-Thomist methodology.[1] Following his early studies in the Dominican novitiate at Flavigny, he was sent to study at the Sorbonne, where he came into contact with, among others, Loisy, Blondel, Bergson and Durkheim – all of whom he regarded with suspicion at best.

Having completed his studies at Fribourg, he taught first at Le Saulchoir – the Dominican House of Studies newly refounded in Belgium after the expulsion of Religious – before moving to Rome where he spent the rest of his life. Here he was a popular teacher of both theology and spirituality, an expert on John of the Cross as well as mystical and ascetic theology, and supervisor to many doctoral students, including Marie-Dominique Chenu and, in the 1940s, one Karol Wojtyła, whose doctoral thesis was on spirituality and faith in St John of the Cross.

---

[1] See Richard Peddicord, *The Sacred Monster of Thomism: An Introduction to the Life and Legacy of Réginald Garrigou-Lagrange OP* (South Bend, IN: St Austin's Press, 2005).

Garrigou-Lagrange had a horror of Modernism: this article ends with the assertion that '"new theology" is returning to Modernism'. Bouillard, de Lubac and, implicitly, in the 'circulated papers' he refers to, their elder and influential confreres, Pierre Rousselot and Teilhard de Chardin, are all clearly in his sights as the 'new Modernists'. At stake here are two questions: first, the neo-Scholastic method itself, which relies on Aquinas's theology and philosophy; second, the immutability of truth.

9   Marie-Michel Labourdette, 'Theology and its sources'

10   Marie-Michel Labourdette and Marie-Joseph Nicolas, 'The analogy of truth and the unity of the methodological method'

The Toulouse Dominicans, Marie-Michel Labourdette (1908–1990) and Marie-Joseph Nicolas (1906–1999), were absolutely opposed to the 'new theology'. Labourdette, professed in 1926, was appointed editor of the *Revue Thomiste* in 1936 and also taught at the Institut catholique de Toulouse until the 1970s, when his neo-scholastic approach fell out of favour in the post-Vatican II Church. His contemporary and confrere Nicolas was the Provincial of the Toulouse Dominicans between 1946 and 1957, and also taught at the Institut catholique de Toulouse.

These two articles, along with Daniélou's 'Current trends', mark the apogee of the debate between the Toulouse Dominicans and the Fourvière Jesuits during the 1940s about the nature of theology, played out in the various theology journals run by each house. Labourdette's article had Daniélou's article firmly in its sights, alongside Bouillard's *Conversion et grâce*, and the two Fourvière series, '*Sources chrétiennes*' and '*Théologie*'. The Jesuits, led by de Lubac, responded to Labourdette; Labourdette and Nicolas then joined forces to write the lengthy 'response' to the Jesuit 'response'.

These two articles represent a struggle, as the Toulousains saw it, for the very soul of theology: Is theology an eternal science, whose truths, like God, are unchanging; or must it respond to the needs of the world, not by changing, denying or ignoring those truths but by expressing them in ways more accessible to contemporary culture? The battle finally came to an end, as recorded above, when Nicolas travelled to Lyon.

7

'New tendencies in theology'

'Nuove tendenze theologiche', *L'Osservatore Romano*, 9–10 February 1942, 1.

Pietro Parente

At the beginning of our century the Modernist heresy led to a general confusion in the field of the sacred disciplines. A virulent attack was launched on traditional scholastic theology, strengthened by the heritage of St Thomas and of his great commentators. It showed no respect for scholastic theology's predominantly speculative nature; it ridiculed its syllogistic forms, its methodology, its abstract nature; it accused it of being defective in its criticality, historical documentation and precise exegesis of the sources. Finally, scholastic rigour was blamed for the acquiescence and suffocation of religious vitality. The echo of the invective of Laberthonnière, Loisy and Le Roy against scholasticism and in particular Thomism has not yet spent itself.

The encyclical *Pascendi* struck down Modernism, and Pius X's successors have repeatedly called lost souls back to the safety of the teaching of St Thomas. Not a few Catholic teachers, who firmly hold to traditional positions, have risen up to defend these positions from modern attacks, whose methodologies and criteria are more responsive to the changing demands of the times. In this way new forms and new tendencies arise to deal with theological questions, assailing divine revelation and thus dogma.

But work in such a delicate field has been and remains an opportunity for academic accidents for those who, even with good intentions, dedicate themselves to it without watchful caution. A regrettable example of such an incident is the recent decree from the Holy Office that placed two books which deal with the nature and methodology of theology on the index. They are two short works, one by Fr Chenu (*Une École de Théologie: Le Saulchoir*, 1937), the other by Fr Charlier (*Essai sur le problème théologique*, 1938), which reveal two souls burning with the new methods and the new currents of theological thinking, which have their beginnings in the Modernist lobby.

Chenu and Charlier, two academics who are part of a well-known seedbed of culture, in which the names of Gardeil, Lemonnyer and Mandonnet gloriously resound, have doubtless written with the best of intentions. But their lively temperament, love of novelty and the almost juvenile audacity of a full frontal attack on the traditional systems have pushed them to stake out a reform of theology which, while not short of good observations and some correct highlights, is yet unfortunately infected with many dangerous principles, which lend themselves to real deviation from orthodox doctrine.

The Holy Office decree is not surprising for anyone who has read the two books carefully; indeed, they have already been criticized by capable theologians such as Boyer and Gagnebet. The two works demonstrate a pronounced shared affinity and a substantial commonality of ideas and attitude. Fr Charlier follows the riskiness of certain of Chenu's original theories and goes even further. Both bring discredit on scholastic theology, its speculative nature, its method, the value of its conclusions, which proceed from the data of revelation; this discredit naturally also falls on St Thomas.

When the two authors insist on nature as purely analogical and the relativity of dogmatic formulas sanctified by the ecclesiastical Magisterium, when Charlier affirms that true rational demonstrations cannot take place in theology and that theology must be a contemplation and sense of mystery rather than reason, fitting into the mystical life of the Church, one has the impression of finding oneself faced with a strange evaluation of human reason from the vantage point of sentiment, religious experience, which reminds one of Möhler's theories, later updated and exaggerated by the Modernists.

Chenu and even more so Charlier demonstrate unacceptable ideas about the development of revelation and dogma. For them, the data of revelation is not fixed and immutable, but in continued growth not only in the minds of the faithful who learn it but also intrinsically, in that revelation is almost in action in the living Magisterium of the Church and evolves and grows together with the Church, as though it were not true that revelation was closed with the death of the last Apostle and was entrusted as a sacred deposit to the ecclesial Magisterium, to be guarded faithfully (Vatican I)! Evolution thus is not only suggestive but also an object of dogma, contrary to what the Church teaches in opposition to Modernism (*Pascendi*).

Furthermore in these two works we deplore the evaluation of the positive proof of Scripture and Tradition by theological theses, as well as the strange identification of Tradition (the fount of revelation) with the Magisterium of the Church (custodian and interpreter of the divine Word).

In summary, this *nouvelle théologie*, championed by both clever Fathers, demonstrates an attempt to crudely demolish the now classical system of our school. Neither does it offer materially sound criteria for a reconstruction in harmony with the unavoidable requirements of *perfect orthodoxy*.

Every theologian worthy of the name must not drench himself methodologically in old positions, but can and must be aware of his environment and his time, making the most of the good which may be found *in new ideas and new trends* with the aim of bringing up to date his teaching and his research. But no new tendencies, no critiques, no demands for modern thought may permit the Catholic theologian to damage or to change the principal lines of the immutable truth revealed by God, guarded, interpreted and defined by the infallible Magisterium of the Church, preserved by the Holy Spirit, tempered by the illuminating sense of modernity. Neither a bellicose rebellion against the past, nor a mania for novelty and progress, nor a spirit of adventure, but rather a place where tradition and authority have normative value and right of precedence over individual will and reason.

8

'Where is "new theology" going?'

'La nouvelle theologie où-va-t-elle?' *Angelicum* 23 (1946) 126–45.

Réginald Garrigou-Lagrange OP

In a recent work by Fr Henri Bouillard, *Conversion et grâce chez S. Thomas d'Aquin*, we read, 'When the mind develops, an *unchanging truth* can only be maintained thanks to a simultaneous and correlative development of all ideas, holding them in the same relationship. *A theology which is not up to date is a false theology.*'[1] In the preceding and following pages it is shown that St Thomas's theology is no longer current in several important areas. For instance, St Thomas conceived of sanctifying grace as a *form* (a radical principle of supernatural operations whose immediate principle are the infused virtues and seven gifts [of the Holy Spirit]). 'The ideas used by St Thomas are simply Aristotelian ideas applied to theology.' What follows? 'By giving up Aristotelian physics, modern thought has abandoned the ideas, schemes and dialectical oppositions which only made sense within it.' It has, therefore, abandoned the idea of the forms. How can the reader not conclude that, as St Thomas's theology is no longer current, it is a false theology?

But then why have the popes so often recommended that we follow St Thomas's teaching? How does the Church itself, in canon 1366§2 of the [1917] Code of Canon law, insist that 'the studies of rational philosophy and theology and the instruction of students in these disciplines truly bring the professors to the reason, doctrine, and principles of the Angelic Doctor, which they should hold as sacred'?

What is more, how can '*an unchanging truth*' maintain itself if the two ideas which it brings together by the verb 'to be' are *essentially changing*? An unchanging relationship can only be conceived of if there is something unchanging in the two terms which it unites. Otherwise we might as well say that an iron crampon can immobilize flotsam. Doubtless the two ideas which are united in an unchanging statement are initially confused and then distinct, such as notions of nature, the person, substance, accident, transubstantiation, real presence, sin, original sin, grace and so on. But if what is basic

---

[1] My emphasis.

to these ideas is not unchanging, how can the statement, which unites them through the verb 'to be', be unchanging? How can we maintain that the real presence of the Body of Christ in the Eucharist requires transubstantiation if these ideas are essentially changing? How can we maintain that original sin in us depends on a willing sin by the first man if the notion of original sin is essentially unstable? How can we maintain that particular judgement after death is irrevocable for eternity if these ideas are called to change? And finally, how can we maintain that all these statements are unchangingly *true* if the very notion of truth must change and if we must substitute the traditional definition of truth (conformity of judgement with the external real and its unchanging laws) with that suggested in the last few years by a philosophy of action: conformity of judgement with the demands of action or the human life which is always evolving?

Do dogmatic formulas themselves retain their immutability?

Bouillard responds that the statement expressed in them remains, but adds,

> One might ask whether it is still possible to consider *the ideas* implicit in conciliar definitions to be contingent? Would that not compromise the unreformable nature of these definitions? For instance, in its teaching on justification, the Council of Trent used the idea of *formal cause* (session 6, ch.7, canon 10). Has Trent thus hallowed this use and conferred a definitive character to the idea of grace-form? *In no way!* It was certainly not the Council's intention to canonize an Aristotelian notion or even a theological idea understood under Aristotle's influence. The Council simply sought to state, against the Protestants, that justification is an interior renewal ... To this end it used ideas common to the theology of its time. *But we can substitute these ideas with others without changing the meaning of the teaching.*[2]

No doubt the Council did not canonize the Aristotelian notion of form, with all its relationships with other notions of the Aristotelian system. But it did approve it as a *stable human notion*, in the sense in which we all speak about what formally constitutes a thing (here, justification). In this sense the Council is talking about sanctifying grace as distinct from actual grace, saying that it is a supernatural, infused gift, which inheres in the soul, and through which the person is formally justified (Denzinger 799, 821). If Councils define faith, hope and charity as *permanent infused virtues*, their radical principle (habitual or sanctifying grace) must also be a permanent infused gift and thus distinct from actual grace or from a transitory divine movement.

But how can we maintain *the meaning* of this teaching of the Council of Trent, 'sanctifying grace is the formal cause of justification' if '*we substitute these ideas with*

---

[2] My emphasis. Translator's note: note, too, that Garrigou-Lagrange here does not quote from the conciliar documents, as Bouillard does, but merely gives the reference to Denzinger.

others' to that of the formal cause? I do not say 'if we substitute a verbal equivalence', but, quoting Fr Bouillard, 'if we substitute these ideas with others'.

If it is *other* it is no longer that of the *formal cause*. Thus it is no longer *true* to say with the Council that 'sanctifying grace is the formal cause of justification'. We must be content to say that at the time of the Council of Trent, grace was conceived as the formal cause of justification, but that today we must conceive of it *otherwise*, that this outdated conception is *no longer current* and thus it is *no longer true*, for a doctrine which is no longer current is, or indeed said to be false.[3]

The answer will be that one can substitute *another equivalent notion* for that of the formal cause. This is just a lot of hot air (emphasizing first of all *other[wise]* and then *equivalence*), the more so since this is not just verbal equivalence but a whole *other notion*. What has become of the very *notion of truth*?[4]

This most serious question repeatedly returns: is the conciliar statement maintained as *truth* by conformity with the external truth and its unchanging laws, or by conformity with the demands of human life which are always evolving?

We can see the danger of the new definition of truth, no longer the sufficiency of the thing and the intellect (*adequatio rei et intellectus*) but conformity of the mind and of life (*conformitas mentis et vitae*). When Blondel suggested this substitution in 1906, he could not have foreseen all the consequences in the field of faith. He himself might be appalled, or at least very concerned, by this.[5] Which life are we talking about? It is human life. Thus how can we avoid the Modernist statement, 'truth is no more immutable than humanity, since it has evolved through, in, and with human persons'

---

[3] What is more, it is defined that the infused virtues (and above all theological virtues) from which habitual grace derives are qualities, *permanent principles* of supernatural and meritorious operations; thus the habitual or sanctifying grace (by which we are in a *state* of grace) from which these virtues proceed as though from a root must itself be a *permanent infused quality* and not a motion like actual grace. It was well before St Thomas's time that faith, hope and charity were conceived of as *infused virtues*. What could be clearer? Why waste time on the pretext of moving questions forward, putting the most certain and fundamental truths in doubt? This is an indication of the intellectual disarray of our time.

[4] See Maurice Blondel, *Annales de philosophie chretienne* 15 June 1906, p. 235: 'The abstract and chimeric *adequatio rei et intellectus has been substituted by methodical research into the adequatio realis mentis et vitae.*' It is a great responsibility to call the traditional definition of truth, accepted for centuries in the Church, chimeric, and to speak about *substituting* it with another, in every field, including that of theological faith.

And do his more recent works correct this deviation? We cannot comment. In *L'Etre et les êtres* (1935), he says that '*No intellectual evidence, even that of* absolute principles of the self and those which possess an ontological value, *can be imposed on us with a restricting certainty*' (415). To admit the ontological value of these principles we must have a *free option* as prior to that option their ontological value is only probably. But we must admit them according to the demands of action *scandium conformitatem mentis et vitae*. It cannot be otherwise if we substitute ontology's *philosophy of being* with a *philosophy of action*. Therefore truth is defined, no longer in function of being, but of action. Everything is changed. An error on the first notion of truth brings in its wake error about everything else. See too Blondel's *La Pensée* (1934), I.29, 130-136, 347, 355; II.65ff, 90, 96-196.

[5] Another theologian, cited below, suggests that at the time of the Council of Trent, *transubstantiation* was conceived of as the change, or conversion of the substance of bread into that of the Body of Christ, but that today it is better to conceive of *transubstantiation* without change of substance, but conceiving that the substance of the bread which remains becomes the efficacious sign of the Body of Christ; and then claims to still maintain *the Council's meaning!*

(Denz. §2058).⁶ We can understand why Pius X described the Modernists as those who 'pervert the eternal concept of truth' (Denz. §2080).⁷

It is extremely perilous to say that 'notions change, statements stay the same'. If the very notion of truth can change, statements cannot stay true in the same way, nor according to the same meaning. Thus *the meaning of the Council* is no longer maintained as intended. Unfortunately the new definition of truth is spread among those who forget what Pius X said: 'Further let Professors remember that they cannot set St Thomas aside, especially in metaphysical questions, without grave detriment' (*Pascendi*).⁸ All the more reason to snap one's fingers at any kind of metaphysics or ontology which seeks to substitute the philosophy of being with the phenomenon of becoming or of action.

Is it not the new definition of truth which is to be found behind the new definition of theology? *'Theology is nothing more than a spirituality or a religious experience which has found its intellectual expression.'* And then think of statements such as 'If theology can help us to understand spirituality, spirituality, in many cases, can in turn enlighten our theologians, and oblige us to conceive of different types of theology. ... To every great spirituality corresponds a great theology.' Does this mean that two theologies may be true, even if they are opposed and in *contradiction* about their principal theses? If one maintains the traditional definition of truth, one will answer no. If one adopts the new definition of truth, conceived of not in relationship to being and its unchanging laws but in relationship to diverse religious experiences, one will say yes. This takes us spectacularly close to Modernism.

Readers will recall that on 1 December 1924 the Holy Office condemned twelve statements taken from the philosophy of action. Among them, at number 5, was the new definition of truth:

> Truth is not found in any particular act of the intellect in which 'conformity with the object', as the scholastics say, is held, but is always in the process of becoming and it consists in progressive adequation of the intellect and life [experience], namely in a certain perpetual motion by which the intellect tries to evolve and to explain that which experience equals or action demands. Nevertheless that law states that in every advance there is never anything valid or permanent.

Many today are returning, unaware, to these errors.

But then how can we maintain that sanctifying grace is *essentially supernatural*, *gratuitous*, and in no way due to human nature or to angelic nature? It was clear for St Thomas who, in the light of Revelation, admitted this principle: faculties, the 'habitus' and their acts are specified by their formal object; the formal object of human and angelic understanding is massively inferior to the proper object of divine understanding: *the Deity or the intimate life of God* (*ST* Ia.12 ad 40). But if one completely ignores metaphysics, making do with historical scholarship and psychological introspection,

---

⁶ Translator's note: *Lamentabili* §58.
⁷ Translator's note: Pius X, *Encyclical Letter Pascendi Dominici Gregis*, §13.
⁸ Translator's note: *Pascendi Dominici Gregis*, §45.

Thomas's text becomes unintelligible.⁹ From this perspective, what will be retained of the traditional doctrine on *distinction* which is non-contingent but necessary *to the order of grace and the order of nature*?

Fr Henri de Lubac touches on this in his recent work *Surnaturel. Études historiques* (1946), in which, apropos of the probable sinlessness of angels in the natural order, we read that 'nothing in St Thomas indicates the distinction which a certain number of Thomist theologians would later forge between "God the author of the natural order" and "God the author of the supernatural order" ... as though natural beatitude ... in the case of the angel should have resulted from infallible, unsinning (impeccable) action.' On the contrary, St Thomas often distinguishes the ultimate supernatural end from the ultimate natural end¹⁰ and points out that 'the devil's sin was not in anything which pertains to the natural order, but according to that of the supernatural' [*De Malo* 16.3; Ia.63.1.3]. In this way we lose interest completely in the major pronouncements of St Thomas's philosophical doctrine, that is, the twenty-four Thomist theses approved in 1916 by the Congregation for Studies.¹¹ What is more, Fr Gaston Fesard SJ has discussed the 'blessed numbing which protects the canonised Thomism, which Péguy also described as "entombed", while thought devoted to its contradiction flourishes'.¹²

An April 1946 article in the same journal said that neo-Thomism and the Biblical Commissions' decisions were 'protective railings but no response'. And what is proposed in place of Thomism, as though Leo XIII were mistaken in his encyclical *Aeterni Patris* or as though Pius X, renewing the same recommendation in his encyclical *Pascendi*, were on the wrong track? And where is this new theology, with its new masters as its inspiration, going? Where is it going, if not down the path of scepticism, fantasy and heresy? In a recent speech published in *Osservatore Romano* (19 September 1946), His Holiness Pius XII said, 'Much is said, but the reason insufficiently explored, about the "new theology", which is always moving, always on a journey, but never arrives. If such an opinion is seen to be embraced, what becomes of unchanging and unchangeable Catholic dogma? What becomes of the unity and stability of faith?'

Application of new principles to the doctrines of original sin and the Eucharist

It will certainly be said that we exaggerate, but even a small error on first notions and first principles has incalculable consequences which those who are mistaken

---

⁹ Having reached the centre of his argument, Bouillard claims that Thomas, in *ST* I.IIae.113.a.8 ad 1 '*no longer relies on reciprocal causality*', apropos of the immediate disposition for justification, as he had done in earlier works. On the contrary, as any Thomist knows, it is clear that Thomas is discussing precisely this, which sheds light on the whole question. What is more, and elementary, reciprocal causality is *always* verified when the four causes intervene, that is, in every future. Any student of theology, having heard St Thomas's treatise on grace explicated article by article, considers that this is a truth which may not be ignored.
¹⁰ Cf. Ia.23.ad1; IaIIa.62.ad.1; *de Veritate* 14.ad2.
¹¹ Translator's note: Fergus Kerr lists the theses in 'A Different World: Neo-Scholasticism and Its Discontents', *International Journal of Systematic Theology* 8, no. 2 (2006), 128–48 (132–4).
¹² G. Fessard, *Études* 247 (1945), 269–70.

cannot foresee. The consequences of the new perspectives which we discussed above must therefore go much further than the foresight of the authors we have quoted. It is difficult not to see these consequences in various typed papers which have been circulated, some since 1934, among clergy, seminarians and Catholic intellectuals. In them we have found the most singular statements and denials about original sin and the real presence.

Sometimes the reader is warned about these novelties, for instance, suggesting that such an idea may at first glance appear crazy, but if we look more closely it is not without probability and it is accepted by several. Those with a superficial understanding are taken in, and the formula that 'a doctrine which is not up to date is no longer true' makes further progress. Some are tempted to conclude that 'the doctrine of the eternity of the punishments of hell is no longer current, it would seem, and thus is no longer true'. The Gospel tells us that one day the charity of many will freeze up and they will be seduced by error. Traditional theologians are under a strict obligation of conscience to respond to this, otherwise they are failing gravely in their duty, for which they will have to give account to God.

In the duplicated papers distributed in France over the last few years, at least since 1934, according to those I have, the most fantastical and false doctrines are taught on original sin. In these papers, the act of *Christian faith* is not conceived of as a supernatural and infallible adherence to revealed truths *revealed through the authority of God* but as an adherence by the mind to a general perspective on the universe. It is a perception of what is possible and *most likely* but not demonstrable. Faith becomes a collection of likely opinions. From this point of view Adam appears not to be an individual man from whom the human race descends, but rather a community.

Hence we can no longer see how to maintain the revealed doctrine of original sin as it is explained by St Paul: 'One man's offence brought condemnation on all humanity; and one man's good act has brought justification and life to all humanity. Just as by one man's obedience many were made sinners, so by one man's obedience are many to be made upright' (Rom. 5.18-19 NJB). All the Fathers and the Church, the authoritative interpreter of the Scriptures, in both its ordinary and formal magisterium, have always understood that Adam was an individual person, as Christ later was, not a community.[13] Now we are offered a probability whose meaning contradicts the teaching of the Councils of Orange and Trent (Denz. §175, 789, 791, 793).[14]

What is more, in this new perspective, the incarnation of the Word is to be a moment of universal evolution. The hypothesis of the material evolution of the world is extended into the spiritual realm. The supernatural world is in evolution towards the full coming of Christ.

Inasmuch as it affects the soul, sin is a spiritual thing and thus outside of time. Thus it is unimportant for God whether it took place at the start of human history or during the ages. Original sin is thus no longer a sin in us which derives from a voluntary

---

[13] Cf. M. J. Lagrange OP, *L'Épitre aux Romains*, commentary on ch. 5.
[14] Translator's note: Denzinger paragraphs are as follows: §175 (Council of Orange, canon 2); §789 and §791 (Council of Trent, Session V, ch 2, On original sin); §793 (Council of Trent, Session VI, ch 1, On justification).

misdeed by the first man, but arises from the misdeeds of human persons which have influenced humanity.

We now come to a desire to change not only the way theology is expressed but *its very nature*. Theology is no longer considered from the perspective of infused faith in divine Revelation, interpreted by the Church in its Councils. There is no more question of Councils, as instead we are in the perspective of *biology* completed by the most fantastical wild imaginings which recall those of Hegelian evolution, which itself kept nothing of Christian dogma, bar the name. In this we are following the rationalists and doing what the enemies of faith want, reducing it to constantly changing opinions which no longer have any value. What remains of the word of God given to the world for the salvation of souls?

In the paper entitled 'How I believe' we read,

> If as Christians we want to keep those qualities of Christ which are the foundation of his authority and our adoration, we have nothing more, even nothing other to do than to accept to the very end the most modern ideas about Evolution. Under the combined pressure of Science and Philosophy, the world is ever more central to our experience and to our thought as a system tied to activities gradually rising towards freedom and conscience. The only satisfactory interpretation of this process is to view it as irreversible and convergent. Thus a *universal cosmic centre* is defined before us in which everything comes to an end, in which All is felt, where all is ordered. Well, this is the physical pole of the universal Evolution which, in my opinion, is necessary to locate and recognize *the plenitude of Christ* ... Evolution, discovering the world's summit, makes Christ possible, just as Christ, giving meaning to the world, makes Evolution possible.
>
> I am perfectly well aware that this idea is vertigo-inducing ... but by imagining a similar marvel, I am doing nothing other than transcribing in terms of physical reality the juridical expressions in which the Church deposits its faith ... I have unhesitatingly taken on the only direction which it seems possible to me in order to progress and consequently to save my faith.
>
> Catholicism initially disappointed me with its narrow representations of the world, and its incomprehension of the role of Matter. Now I recognize that after the incarnate God it reveals to me that I can only be saved by being of one body with the universe. And in the same breath my deepest 'pantheist' aspirations are satisfied, reassured, and guided. *The World* around me *becomes divine* ...
>
> A *general convergence of religions* towards a universal-Christ who, at heart, will satisfy them all: this seems to me to be the only possible conversion of the World, and the only one imaginable for a Religion in the future.[15]

Thus it is claimed that the material world has evolved towards the spirit and the world of the spirit will evolve naturally, as it were, towards the supernatural order

---

[15] My emphasis. Similar and equally fantastical ideas may be found in Teilhard de Chardin, 'Vie et planètes', *Études* May 1946, 158–60, 168; 'Un grand événement qui se dessine: le Planétisation humaine', *Cahiers du monde nouveau*, August 1946.

and the fullness of Christ. Thus the Incarnation of the Word, the mystical body, the universal Christ are moments in evolution. From this perspective of a constant progression from the origin, there does not seem to have been a fall at the start of human history, but a constant progression of good which triumphs over evil according to the very laws of evolution. Original sin in this reading is the result of the sins of human persons who have exercised a grim influence over humanity. This is what remains of Christian dogma in this theory, as far from our Creed as it is close to Hegelian evolution.

In this same paper we read that 'I committed myself to the only route in which it seemed to me to be possible *to make progress* and *consequently to save my faith*.' Thus faith itself is only safe *if it progresses*, and it changes so much that we can no longer recognize the faith of the Apostles, the Fathers and the Councils. This is one way of applying the principle of new theology: 'a doctrine which is no longer current is no longer true', and for some it is enough that it is no longer current *in some circles*. Thus we conclude that truth is always in the process of becoming (*in fieri*), never unchanging. It is conformity with judgement, not with being and its necessary laws but with life which is always evolving. We see where those propositions condemned by the Holy Office on 1 December 1924 lead to.

We find a further example of similar deviance in typescript papers on the Real Presence, which have been circulating in recent months among clergy. In them it is said that the true problem of the Real Presence is not that which has been posed until now. 'To all these difficulties the answer given is that we have created them: Christ is *present in the manner of a substance* … This explanation sidesteps the true problem. We should add that in its misleading clarity it suppresses the religious mystery. In truth, there is no longer a mystery there, but only a wonder.' St Thomas was therefore unable to raise and answer the problem of the Real Presence, with his clarity being merely *misleading*. We are told that the new explanation offered 'evidently implies that one substitutes the Cartesian and Spinozan model of thought for the scholastic model'. A little later we read that transubstantiation 'as a word is not without its inconveniences, any more than original sin. It responds to the way in which the scholastics conceived of this transformation and *their conception is unacceptable*.'

Here we are distanced not only from St Thomas but also from the Council of Trent, where transubstantiation is defined as a truth of faith, and 'what the holy catholic church has suitably and properly called this change'.[16] Today these new theologians say that 'this word is not without inconvenience … it responds to an unacceptable conception'.

> In the scholastic perspective where the reality of the thing is 'its substance', the thing will only be able to change if the substance changes … through transubstantiation. In our current perspective … when by virtue of the offering made of them following a ritual determined by Christ *the bread and wine have*

---

[16] Translator's note: Council of Trent, Session XIII, Decree on the most holy sacrament of the Eucharist, ch 4 (Tanner, *Decrees*, II.695).

become the efficacious symbol of Christ's sacrifice and consequently of *his spiritual presence their religious being* not their substance *has changed.*[17]

And the author adds that 'This is what we mean by transubstantiation.' But clearly this is no longer transubstantiation as defined by the Council of Trent (Denz. §884). It is obvious that the introduction of these new notions does not retain the Council's meaning. The bread and wine have become no more than 'the efficacious symbol of the spiritual presence of Christ'. This brings us singularly close to the Modernist position, which does not affirm the Real Presence of the Body of Christ in the Eucharist but which simply says from a practical and religious perspective, behave towards the Eucharist as you would towards the humanity of Christ.

In the same paper, the mystery of the Incarnation is similarly described. 'While Christ is truly God, we cannot say that through him there was a presence of God in the land of Judaea … God was no more present in Palestine than elsewhere. The *efficacious sign* of that divine presence was made manifest in Palestine in the first century of our era; this is as much as we can say.'[18] Finally, it is noted that 'the problem of the causality of the sacraments is a false problem, born of a false way of posing the question'.

We do not believe that the writers we have just discussed abandoned St Thomas's teaching: they have never adhered to it, nor ever understood it correctly. This is distressing and worrying. How can we form anyone but sceptics with such a way of teaching? For nothing firm is offered in replacement for St Thomas's teaching. What is more, it is claimed that they are subject to the Church's supervision, but how?

One theology teacher has written to us:

The debate turns on the very notion of truth, and, without being aware of it, we return to Modernism in thought as in action. The writings which you describe are widely read in France. They exercise a huge influence, on so-so minds it is true, as serious people are not attracted to them. It is necessary to write for those who sincerely wish to be enlightened.

According to some, the Church has only recognized St Thomas's authority in the field of theology and not directly in philosophy. On the contrary, Leo XIII's encyclical *Aeterni Patris* focuses mostly on Thomas's philosophy. Likewise the twenty-four Thomist theses proposed by the Sacred Congregation for Study in 1916 are philosophical and if these major statements of Thomas have no certainty, what value can his theology, which constantly returns to them, have? Finally, as we have already recalled, Pius X wrote, 'We warn the teachers so that they may correctly hold to Aquinas, and equally

---

[17] It is also claimed that 'In scholastic perspectives the notion of the *thing-sign* is lost.' This is not at all the case: for instance, see St Thomas, *ST*, Ia.1.10.

[18] St Thomas clearly distinguishes a three-fold presence of God. First, the general presence of God in every creature which he maintains in existence (*ST* Ia.8.1); second, the special presence of God in the just through grace (*ST* Ia 43.3); third, the presence of the Word in the humanity of Jesus through the hypostatic union. Thus it is clear that after the Incarnation God was more fully present in the land of Judea than elsewhere. But when we think that St Thomas did not even think of raising these questions, we throw ourselves into all sorts of adventures, and we return to modernism in the casual way we have highlighted in these pages.

that abandoning Aquinas, especially in metaphysics, is gravely detrimental. What starts as a small error ends in a major error.'

Where do these tendencies come from? A good judge wrote to me that

> we are reaping the fruits of attendance at university without due caution. Students want to be with the masters of modern thought to convert them, and they then allow themselves be converted. Gradually the masters' ideas, methodology, disdain for scholasticism, historicism, idealism, and all their errors are accepted. While such company is useful for minds which are already formed, it is surely dangerous for others.

Conclusion

Where is new theology going? It is returning to Modernism, because it accepts the proposition of substituting the traditional definition of truth, the sufficiency of the thing and the intellect (*adaequatio rei et intellectus*) as though it were a chimera, with the subjective definition of the sufficiency of the reality of mind and life (*adaequatio realis mentis et vitae*). This is most explicitly stated in the proposition cited above, taken from philosophy of action and condemned by the Holy Office on 1 December 1924.

> Truth is not found in any particular act of the intellect in which 'conformity with the object', as the scholastics say, is held, but is always in the process of becoming and it consists in progressive adequation of the intellect and life [experience], namely in a certain perpetual motion by which the intellect tries to evolve and to explain that which experience equals or action demands. Nevertheless that law states that in every advance there is never anything valid or permanent.

Truth is no longer conformity of judgement with the external reality and its unchanging laws, but conformity of judgements with the demands of action and human life, which are perpetually evolving. The philosophy of being, ontology, is being substituted by the philosophy of action which defines the truth in function of action, no longer in function of truth. And thus we return to the position of the Modernists: 'Truth is no more immutable than the human person, for as with the person, evolves in and through the person' (Denz. §2058), leading Pius X to say that the Modernists 'pervert the eternal notion of truth'(Denz. §2080).

Thus we return to the Modernist position, which was what our Master Fr M. B. Schwalm warned about in his articles in the *Revue Thomiste* of 1896 and 1897 on the philosophy of action, Fr Laberthonnière's moral dogmatism, the contemporary crisis of apologetic, the illusions of idealism and their dangers for the faith. But many thought that Fr Schwalm was exaggerating, and gradually allowed the new definition of truth to be established, and more or less stopped defending the traditional definition of truth: conformity of judgement with the external being and its unchanging laws of non-contradiction, causality and so forth. For them, the truth is not *that which is* but *that which becomes* and is ever-changing.

To stop defending the traditional doctrine of truth and to allow it to be said that it is a *chimera*, that it must be *substituted* with something more vitalist and evolutionist, leads to complete relativism, which is a very grave error. What is more, and this is ignored, this leads to saying what the enemies of the Church wish to hear us say. When we read recent works, we see that they express real satisfaction with this, and that they themselves propose interpretations of our dogmas, whether it is original sin, *cosmic evil*, incarnation, redemption, Eucharist, the final universal reintegration, the *cosmic Christ*, the convergence of all religions towards a universal cosmic centre.

Thus we can understand that, in a recent speech reported by the *Osservatore Romano* (19 September 1946), the Holy Father should, while discussing the new theology, have asked, 'If such an opinion is seen to be embraced, what becomes of immutable Catholic dogma, its unity and stability?'

Yet as Providence only allows evil for a greater good, and as we see an excellent reaction by many against the errors we have just emphasized, we can hope that these deviations will be the occasion for a true doctrinal renewal, by a deeper study of the works of St Thomas, whose value appears ever greater when we compare them to today's intellectual disarray.[19]

---

[19] Of course we allow that *true mystical experience* which proceeds rightly from the gifts of the Holy Spirit, above all from the gift of wisdom *confirms faith*, for it shows us that the revealed mysteries correspond to our deepest aspirations and draw out the highest desires. In the same way, as the Vatican Council said, we can, through the natural light of reason, have *certainty of the existence of God*, author of nature. Except that for this the *principles* of these proofs, particularly that of causality, must be *true by conformity to the extramental ens* and *certain of an objectively sufficient certitude* (prior to the free option of the man of goodwill) and not only a *subjectively sufficient certitude* such as that of the Kantian proof of the existence of God.

Finally the *practical truth* of prudence *in conformity with right intention* presupposes that our intention is *truly right* in relation to the final end of man, and judgement on the end of man must be *true according to the mind in conformity with the extramental reality* (cf. I.IIa 19.3.ad2).

9

'Theology and its sources'

'La théologie et ses sources', *Revue Thomiste* 46/2 (1946), 353–71.

Marie-Michel Labourdette OP

Among the many works which enable Christian thought to be ever more aware of its history and to return to its sources, we find there has been no more interesting enterprise over the last few years than the series begun by Éditions du Cerf, edited by Frs H. de Lubac and J. Daniélou, SJ: the *'Sources chrétiennes'*. Neither is there anything which promises more. The ten volumes published to date already constitute a wonderful work: they offer us translations of works which are particularly representative of the Greek tradition, always accompanied with fulsome and meticulous introductions and thought-provoking notes. Publishing difficulties prevented most of these volumes being accompanied by the original texts, an indispensable addition which must not be delayed![1] A recent circular leads us to hope for great developments which, if they take place, will turn this magnificent undertaking into a unique work which cannot be too highly praised. The collection will extend on the one hand to the sources of Latin Christianity and on the other to some non-Christian works whose importance for the development of theological reflection enables them to be considered as 'sources'. Our account will simply bear on the first ten volumes and the authors they introduce. It is possible that the promised broadening of the project and widening of the editorial team will change these authors and, in balancing them, enrich the shared spirit, already so clearly stated above all in those works whose editors are the very editors of the series.

---

[1] To date we have received the following ten volumes:
Gregory of Nyssa, *Contemplations on the Life of Moses*, intro. and trans. J. Daniélou SJ; Clement of Alexandria, *Protrepticus*, intro. and trans. Cl. Mondésert SJ; Athenagoras, *A Plea for the Christians*, intro. and trans. G. Bardy; Nicolas Cabasilas, *Commentary on the Divine Liturgy*, intro. and trans. S. Salaville AA; Diadocos of Photius, *One Hundred Chapters on Spiritual Perfection*, intro. and trans. E des Places SJ; Gregory of Nyssa, *The Creation of Man*, intro. and trans. J. Laplace SJ, notes J. Daniélou SJ; Origen, *Homelies on Genesis*, intro. H. de Lubac SJ, trans. L Doutreleau SJ; Niketas Stethatos, *Spiritual Paradise*, trans. and comm. Marie Chalendard; Maximus the Confessor, *The Four Centuries on Charity*, intro. and trans. J Pégon SJ; Ignatius of Antioch, *Letters*, intro. and trans. Th. Camelot OP.

Such an undertaking makes us think of what Guillaume Budé's series has done for classical studies. Yet it is different from Budé in two ways. First, there is less of a critical concern. Many of these works are not exactly critical editions, but a meticulous 'working text'. Much as we would want total scientific rigour, we cannot blame the series' founders for this. On the contrary, we are thankful that they did not feel obliged to undertake lengthy scientific work but rather ensured that we can have these precious texts, in very contemporary form, in our hands. The second difference is that the series is clearly guided by an intention which directs the selection of texts and has an immediate action in mind: a shared spirit, which goes alongside certain predetermined theological positions, marks several introductions and commentaries. This spirit and positions, which we shall discuss below, translate into something quite different from the purely historical concern of introducing these ancient authors.[2]

Other journals have described or will describe the technical qualities or faults of these translations; they will appreciate the critical worth of the edited texts and the historical truth of the introductions and the notes. While not disinterested in this perspective, we at the *Revue Thomiste* would like to emphasize the great riches which these texts offer speculative theology. Many are venerable; all express an effort of human reflection on the truths of faith. Thus we shall refer to several of them. This time, in an initial general presentation focusing on the general design of the whole rather than the detail of the published volumes, we would like to deal with some more general problems which seem to us to be important for contemporary theology.

It is important not to separate the '*Sources chrétiennes*' from another series which has just made a striking start at Éditions Montaigne. This is the '*Théologie*' series, edited by the Fourvière Jesuits, and in which Frs de Lubac and Daniélou are so involved that they appear to be its leaders.[3] In the parallelism of the two series there is a similarity of mind about which we must admit we have serious reservations, but which demonstrates a positive and constructive intention, in itself more important than the faults which taint it: that of a theology which is more aware of the richness of its sources, the multiplicity of its historical expressions, the circumstances of its development and the most contemporary and current human realities. We declare that we are in full agreement and sympathy with such an intention.

What strikes us as we read these ancient texts, and which stands out even more clearly in the *Sources chretiénnes* series due to the emphasis in the translators' notes, is that most of our problems may be found in them. These problems, however, are at a

---

[2] Fr Daniélou clearly describes the intention of the new series in opposition to Hemmer and Lejay in his 'Les orientations présentes …', p. 10. This intention, which is well illustrated by his own introduction to the first volume of the series, does not appear in several others, which fortunately have sought only the greatest precision and remain models of sober work which do not have any other intentions guiding them or lying behind them.

[3] The '*Théologie*' series currently comprises eight volumes:

H. Bouillard, *Conversion et grâce chez S. Thomas d'Aquin. Étude historique*; J. Daniélou, *Platonisme et théologie mystique. Essai sur la doctrine spirituelle de saint Grégoire de Nysse*; H. de Lubac, *Corpus Mysticum. L'Eucharistie et l'Église au Moyen-Age*; Cl. Mondésert, *Clément d'Alexandrie. Introduction à sa pensée religieuse à partir de l'Écriture*; G. Fessard, *Autorité et bien commun*; J. Mouroux, *Sens chrétien de l'homme*; M. Pontet, *L'exégèse de saint Augustin prédicateur*; H. de Lubac, *Surnaturel. Études historiques*.

stage where they have yet to be fixed into an over-literal formulation. It is almost banal, and too easy, to note that in many areas the problematic of our theology has become academic, by which I mean that it is something which is learned and often bookbound. It still tends towards reflection and to real solutions, but thought seems to lack some kind of activation, and it is almost weighed down, thinking itself perfected and complete too quickly. And this comment, in my opinion, goes further than Scholastic teaching; there is a certain perfectly authentic and solid manner of asking theological questions, even in reference to their scriptural sources or concerns about contemporary realities. Because the questions themselves are formulated according to traditional categories whose intuitive worth we have not been careful enough to retrieve, we cannot get out of a received problematic. Anyone who has had to teach theology cannot have failed to encounter that intellectual laziness, which prefers a formula to intellectual understanding, quicker to rest on known facts than look towards initial non-perceptions to remake the whole future path of thought in its own image, thanks to fully personal reflection.

This is why, purely from the point of view of speculative theology, it is excellent to encounter an entirely different problematic than that which we are accustomed to encounter. For a theology whose main formulation is Latin, this is the case with the most representative works of the Greek tradition. This desire to 'shock' is surely not absent from the founders of this valuable series, and we thank them for having so quickly offered us such a rich collection to meditate on. We are not among those who think that St Thomas's theological wisdom would shatter under this shock or that it would be dispossessed from the place it has come to hold in the Church if confronted with very different kinds of reflection, which themselves are authentically Christian. We do not believe that such a comparison, were it to be made, necessarily leads to the profession of the essential historical relativism of every human expression of the divine truths, in the sense that (outside formulas of faith, of course) for every human expression of the divine we must look for a truth which is not in conformity with what is really God or supernatural humanity, but a truth of expression and suggestion of the ineffable realities which humanity feels.

In truth, the whole problem of theology and its claim to set itself up as *an intellectual discipline proper* is found here. We have described elsewhere how it seems to us that this problem should be resolved.[4] It is this solution that we are led to compare with one of the principal difficulties it encounters, more in the contemporary 'mentality' than in explicitly formulated theories. In the very position of the problem, we are going beyond the expressions in books which have given rise to this opportunity. It should of course be clearly understood that our exact aim is to shed light, through opposition or solutions; that we try to lead each to its most explicit formula; and that we are not here attributing to anyone the theory which we are fighting. Further, many tendencies seem to converge towards the solution, to the extent that rather than remaining an ideal solution, it receives from this a 'global truth', we think exactly that we shall put on trial

---

[4] 'La Théologie, intelligence de la foi', *Revue Thomiste* 1946/1.

these tendencies giving each what it needs in the absence of formal texts or on the faith of a few lines taken out of context.[5]

Before any criticism we must indicate the great success in our eyes of M. J. Mouroux's book, *Sens chrétien de l'homme*, sixth in the '*Théologie*' series. We do not seek to shield this wonderful book from what we have called the 'spirit' of the series. It is not difficult to demonstrate how it fits into the series and responds to its highest ambitions, but it seems to us that it represents precisely what is excellent in that spirit, without offering any of what might be contested in some of the other works.

Mouroux sought to write neither an erudite book nor a theological essay whose technical character would have made it difficult for those who are not 'members of the guild'. 'This book seeks only to be a testimony', but such modesty should not fool us. It is true that Mouroux's consideration is generally not precisely along the lines of a scientific analysis but rather along the lines of a theology which extends into meditation. According to the author's words, it is a 'lengthy theological reflection'. But this reflection is nourished and, as it were, impregnated with a living grasp of the sources of Christian thought, particularly the Word of God, above all St Paul. Such a hold is impossible without detailed study and deep familiarity.

The analysis of this book would be materially easy: it is clear; it progresses according to clearly established lines. The author's views, while nuanced, are neither confused nor shrouded in mystery. But such an analysis would allow the escape of both the wealth of the developments and what seems to us to be the most new and most praiseworthy. This is the methodology and that concentrated fervour in which we sense a long matured meditation and the profound generosity of the Christian spirit. Let us offer a brief sketch.

Dedicated to humanity, the work is divided into three parts. First, *temporal values*, second, *carnal values* (a chapter each) and finally, at greatest length, *spiritual values*. Despite their appearance, the final part is what seems to us to be the most new, not in its subject – it deals with eternal problems – but in its synthetic methodology which brings the light of speculative reflection and history to bear on eternal questions, along with the most traditional teachings and perspectives most dear to contemporary understanding. A conclusion, which treats its subject too briefly, demonstrates that humanity is a *sacred being*.

Mouroux does not over-use notes and references, but employs them well, and they are discreet testimony to an erudite thought from which the reader too will benefit. He unites a profound knowledge of the documents of Christian tradition (patristic literature, liturgy, conciliar teachings) with great attention to new information. It is in this context that he raises the questions he deals with, showing the way of the

---

[5] The general nature of this article, which deals with the *Sources chrétiennes* and *Théologie* series as a whole, may lead one to believe that here we are questioning the personal thought of Frs de Lubac and Daniélou, who edit the *Sources chrétiennes* and are the most representative contributors to *Théologie*. This is not our aim; or rather, when it is, we shall say so. Frs de Lubac and Daniélou are well able to say what they wish and have no need of interpreters. However, if it seems to them that we have taken aim at them beyond their thought, we will be most happy to receive their corrections and clarifications. This might be an opportunity to warn our dear readers of mistakes, some of which are dangerous.

most common data of modern science, philosophy and literature to most of our contemporaries. In truth, here one does not feel in the company of a specialist (his specialty, of course, being theological reflection), but this openness to culture, which remains honest, is pleasing. It does not throw itself at the first mirage of novelty to agree with it, but is careful not to lose anything which is positively acquired, at the same time as not linking forms of expression of eternal truth to those which arise from an outdated culture and naturally form an obstacle to contemporary understanding rather than opening it up. Here we are thinking in particular of the admirable studies on the person, freedom and love, much more than in the early chapters (which appear to be not only the most new but also, we believe, the least profound, even while offering interesting suggestions).

All this is beautiful, living theology; and if the author unites depth with ease of understanding, this does not appear to us to take away from his mastery and ownership of speculative theology. He handles it with both a very fair sense and constant precision. Whether it is the union of body and soul, the person considered in his subsistence or his openness to God, the historical situation of humanity between the first Adam and the second, original sin and the forces left to fallen nature, the natural love for God and charity, disinterested love: Mouroux's mastery never fails. We are not saying that we accept all his statements as they are, otherwise this would be faint praise indeed. Theological reflection is too personally exercised here, with the author presenting original views which require testing; and we shall not omit to thank him for this even where it seems to us that the solution should be sought elsewhere. But what we appreciate most of all is that, where he innovates or (for at heart he remains rooted in the most classical theology, profoundly assimilated) when he is concerned to shed light on some aspect which is less often emphasized, it is always advisedly: he knows very well what he is doing, for, having seriously weighed up every stance or position he abandons he knows them well. Several theologians, for instance, would find themselves uncomfortable at the point where he deals in various ways with original sin and fallen nature;[6] yet we do not think any could reproach him, not only for ignorance but also for not having examined the end of the question attentively enough. What gives apologetic work its solidity (I mean the obvious aim of finding an audience among minds penetrated by modern culture) might have veered towards more facile arguments. Mouroux gives us proof that Christian thought may enter into contemporary debates without any sense of abandonment, without being ashamed or over-proud of its past, in all frankness and loyalty, with the awareness that has much to learn, for it is still young. He shows us that theological thought may remain very precise and maintain the wealth of its traditional acquisitions by finding its expression in a new formulation. We shall all be grateful to the '*Théologie*' series for offering us books of this worth.

And indeed, not one of the books the series offers is without value, as we shall be able to say in future reviews. Yet we are sorry to see that in several the emphasis on

---

[6] Although not in our case: for us the author seems to rightly maintain the balance which is effectively somewhat 'paradoxical', between the opposing exaggerations of Jansenism and a naturalist humanism.

shedding light on the patristic tradition or the effort of finding a renewed formulation is accompanied by an obvious depreciation of scholastic theology. Far from opposing scholasticism to either the depth of traditional data or attempts at renewed presentation, as though there would be only danger in these routes for it, we feel that scholasticism in precisely in the form which St Thomas gave it represents the truly *scientific* state of Christian thought. This is not to imply any disdain for what went before; one can never emphasize this enough, and the Thomistic synthesis is the first to benefit from earlier work. Neither does it imply that Thomas's teaching must be simply repeated word for word: it is only too true that it would remain inaccessible to many, and it is quite clear that in this way we would lose some beautiful and authentic advances due to work by later Christian (and non-Christian) thinkers.[7] But it remains the case that these advances, at the risk of ruining their own foundations, presuppose and build upon an earlier construction, neither destroying nor replacing it; they are the continuation of a synthesis, not a complete return, making a new 'representation' of the world according to the categories of modern thought, as everything which has gone before has irredeemably aged. Many things, of course, have aged, but we can never agree that such aging has a greater impact than the formulations: an entire world view, characteristic of a particular cultural environment, can also achieve theological truth. We cannot agree that theological wisdom is carried along by the flotsam of impermanence, and that its acquisitions cannot be held to be definitive. This does not mean that they are sealed and cannot be perfected but, on the contrary, implies their capacity for the gradual assimilation of new results of reflection. I am well aware that this idea raises

---

[7] The question of theology's advance and its adaptation to new knowledge in our meaning is thus entirely different from that of Daniélou (*Études*, April 1946, p. 14). Scholastic theology does not encounter modern thought from a closed system of 'categories' irredeemably closed to any assimilation of new information. Its permanence is not that of a finalized construction which has had its day and whose influence now remains strictly limited to only the problems envisaged historically, solutions which it was given then, in formulas in which it will remain forever fixed. On the contrary, we believe that scholastic theology is a way of thinking which is perfectly alive, both ambitious and able to enter into new problems and understand them, to assimilate everything which modern teachings have which is authentic, yet too respectful of truth, too careful to maintain its scientific rigour and to avoid easy conformity, to readily take on with immediate effect ideas and 'categories' which it has not been able to examine and critique previously with maturity. This is surely what Leo XIII sought to restore; and if the restoration has not fulfilled his hopes it is not because scholastic theology is now a worn-out way of thinking, but because it needs more and better servants. Daniélou is welcome to devote himself to a 'dramatic' theology legitimate in its precise aim, not of developing the divine message in terms of speculative truth but of making certain concrete data of the Christian's situation in this world 'open to the heart'; we applaud his success. We desire the development of historical theology no less than him and wish that speculative theology itself had a sense of history as much as he does. Far from thinking this impossible, we think that there are marvellous developments to be found, because speculative theology has potentials which few seem to suspect. It is equally clear that theology must be close to culture, maintain contact with various cultures and be careful to learn everything which cultures teach humanity about its historical situation and existential dimension. But theology must not lose its primordial concern to remain the rigorous scientific expression of Christian thought working on the truths of faith. This is what St Thomas calls us to do, both by his example and by his teaching. The expansion which Fr Daniélou, if we are to believe him, desires will end in a most deplorable loss: the loss of experience in which our most precious intellectual treasure resides and the reduction of scholastic thought to the state of a witness to changing times (no doubt permanent, just as a statue in a museum is). Thomism has no less claim to life than existentialism, Marxism, or Teilhard de Chardin's evolutionism.

problems, and more problems than are within the scope of this article. We shall have the opportunity to return to them, particularly with regard to the wonderful efforts of missionary theology. But have we paid due attention to the fact that the most serious difficulties have no less value against the very formulation of dogma than against the idea of theological *knowledge*, certainly incomplete and always perfectible, but certain of an indefectible truth in its principal teachings and, in many other doctrines, of an ever-greater probability?

Contemporary minds are permanently tempted to judge every intellectual system not essentially according to its conformity with what is (how do we manage that?), but first and foremost according to its relationship with what the author and her time thought and felt. The mysteries of subjectivity are much more interesting than impersonal truth. Thus texts are examined above all for their meaning and *testimony*, their sincerity, the wealth of experience, its resonance; the logical coherence and properly intellectual or 'conceptual' meaning of the analyses and syntheses it presents are apparently secondary. The text must speak to every concept, not only analogy but also symbolism, and judge them according to their expression of a 'lived' human reality. What an impoverished and desiccated expression this is, how reified as soon as we take it to its logical conclusion, alongside the experience from which they gush forth, and about which one could say that they are the leftovers, rather than the fruits. How can life be enclosed in concepts? Above all, how can we enclose the kind of life which is a relationship with God and which culminates in the obscure awareness of a mysterious contact in which we claim the reality of a true experience? Is there not a more precious truth than that which is handed on by clear teaching: that of testimony to a spiritual experience; and should we not look for the significance of the great works of the spirit, or at least those whose object is knowledge of humanity and God?

It seems to me that two habits of the modern mind give a singular power to this temptation. One is born of the formation, in itself of great value, in historical disciplines. There is no need to indicate how their progress seems to us to be an inestimable gain. Thanks to these disciplines we are ever more aware of an authentic 'dimension' of humanity and of human things. Nothing human, and certainly not ideas or scientific knowledge, however impersonal, touched by this engagement in time and place, is not improved when its essential structure is penetrated, its progress is followed, its often slow and hesitant beginnings and later formation by the least expected routes known. Fr Lagrange used to like to remind us of Aristotle's expression: 'The best way of understanding is to consider things from the beginning and to follow their development.' This is why we unreservedly applaud the historical precision demonstrated by the series we are discussing, and we congratulate the authors of the significant debt we already owe them. Once again, we think of the wonderful work of Frs Daniélou and Hans von Balthasar on St Gregory of Nyssa and the questions they raise for us.

But the historical method, and the philosophy with which it is often unconsciously associated, which constitutes a pseudo-philosophy which many think they have acquired through history, is another thing entirely. We need constant vigilance of mind to handle such a specialized methodology with all the intellectual purity that requires. We have been obstructed by pseudo-metaphysical statements (denying metaphysics is a further way of doing it, a way of speaking about metaphysics without getting into the subject), drawn up by physicists or biologists according to methods which have given the same results to biology or physics, but which only end up impoverishing philosophy. Is the law of knowledge not about respecting the legitimate autonomy of these methods? Of course, historical consideration offers much material for philosophical reflection. The philosophy of human activity and culture cannot do without it. But while it is true that this philosophy presupposes a rigorous application of historical methods, there follows on from it a type of reflection which is quite different and which proceeds from quite other principles. The pseudo-philosophy which unconsciously inspires historical methodologies is 'relativism' in its strongest sense: a theory, or rather an intellectual attitude, which replaces the metaphysical idea of speculative truth by the more modest concept of historical truth, like a more or less complete expression of the human experience and mindset of a time or a group of people. The very idea that our mind would be able to grasp and discern a timeless truth in the most assured of its ideas becomes truly unthinkable. The idea that this truth might be a definitive gain for human understanding, a teaching which can transmit to peoples who are most distant from us in time and in cultural differences, seems to be absurd. If humanity is only progressing by surpassing itself, is it not contrary to the very movement of life to attribute an absolute value for the understanding of statements which bear a clear mark of the period and cultural environment in which they were formulated? Is it not precisely what an adult would do when wanting to wear a child's clothing?

But we must renounce any idea of teaching which is universally valid, as a function of the permanent Magisterium; and alongside the idea of acquisition or gain, the very idea of progress fades away. It is quite clear in any case that intellectual progress cannot be conceived of as a linear ascent; thought, like civilization, can undergo tragic periods of regression. But how can we admit that nothing remains of the heights reached by the mind in days gone by, that all that was formulated in ancient times no longer has any value of objective teaching, even if it were still valid as an example of what we must do faced with new problems? Like de Lubac[8] we would like the progress of theology not to be assimilated to the progress of dogma: the differences are only too obvious. But how can we not see that the reasons by which we fight the assurance of theological progress to the benefit of a perpetual rejuvenation of our ideas about God, according to the diversity of time and cultures, would retain all their value to restore the progress of dogma itself to proportions unacceptable to the Church? It is that the most fundamental of these reasons (illustrated by the interpretation of history, although it arises definitively from views entirely different from historical knowledge) is the depreciation of understanding, the shared postulate of every nominalist philosophy, that our reason, in its exercise of clear and formulated knowledge, only directly reaches concepts, and that these concepts are empty abstractions, logical pigeon-holes whose value is entirely pragmatic. We do not see that such a caricature of the life of the mind, which effectively ruins the idea of a theology as a science, is better accommodated to

---

[8] *Surnaturel*, 'Introduction', 5; this book will be reviewed in due course; see the same author's *Corpus Mysticum* reviewed below by Fr M.-J. Nicolas. This work is among the most striking in the series; yet while enriching it with so much work, de Lubac emphasizes his reaction against the speculative theology of St Thomas.

the idea of dogma as proposed by the Church and enables us to take account of the place which the values of *Truth* are accorded in Revelation and Catholic preaching. We need only see what becomes of the idea of *orthodoxy* not only in the church's teaching but also in its practice and life. It is banal to accuse the Roman Church of intransigence in dogmatic questions. Does the constant nature of its practice escape the correcting actions of the divine Spirit which animates it? Is it only the entirely human weight of a certain form of culture? Does it in reality make the essential mystery of the Christian life false? We are the first to agree that the very idea of orthodoxy and the practical attitude which it commands are very often abusively extended by Christian thinkers into statements other than the revealed teaching as it is handed on by the Church; and that the deplorable habit of seeking to answer questions by appeal to authority rather than calm discussion arises from this. We have no sympathy for this sort of argument. It remains no less the case that the divine message is addressed to our understanding, then that consequently it presupposes this and, even in its action of distinct and formulated knowledge, must have something to make the solemn affirmation required in Pius X's anti-modernist oath possible.[9]

We think that knowing the most detailed history of even the most certain of theology's ideas and doctrines is just as infinitely precious in theology as it is in any other realm of knowledge. It is often in this way that we manage to move on from the permanent intelligible content of an idea to a whole collection of contingent designs which have, over the course of history, been more or less associated with it, depending on cultural environments, world views particular to a certain period or thinker, in which this idea can have found a huge system of references which it is often extremely difficult to disentangle. There is no theological synthesis whose understanding does not benefit hugely from a more precise knowledge of the time in which it was born or the cultural environment in which it initially developed and was shaped. But it is true that intellectual activity lives and that, through the concept by which it becomes real, in the midst of a whole subjective conditioning of logical relationships, it reaches the external reality (clearly not as a result of history), every idea expressed offers a very different interest to that of its historical nature, it calls an appreciation of another kind: that of the truth, pure and simple. This is a judgement which history has not been able to bring, even though it has not exactly been brought well by those who know history. It refers to criteria of another order.

The question we are debating here has been raised in the first volume of the '*Théologie*' series by Fr Henri Bouillard SJ. The conclusion of this work is guided by a concern which is similar to our own: to demonstrate that the historical method must not lead to total relativism. Fr Bouillard affirms the permanence, in theological development, not only of 'defined dogma, in other words, propositions canonized by the Church, but also everything which is explicitly or implicitly contained in Scripture and Tradition [including] the invariant or absolute of the human mind, the first principles, and the acquired truths, which are necessary to think about dogma'. But in truth we have poorly grasped the explanation he gives, which consists in distinguishing a collection of absolute statements from the ideas, or systems of idea, in which these statements are

---

[9] Denz. §2147.

made. Ideas are the domain of 'representation' and this is necessarily affected in itself by temporal indications which drag along radical contingency. Now, in our mind these two elements have not been separated and cannot be isolated. We cannot reach absolute statements *alongside* or as though they are above the representation of the whole which we make, we can only reach and think these statements *in* the notions. When the latter change (and they cannot not change), the whole system of representation is established on another type, but according to a group of relationships which in turn translates the same eternal statements.

This laborious explanation is evidence of a worthy attempt to avoid relativism, but we are not sure it succeeds. Some of Fr Bouillard's formulas seem to us to only show off his failure. If these two elements permeate one another to the extent that we can only reach the former through and in the latter (for such is the 'law of the incarnation'), how can we discern them? This discernment can only occur through our 'notions' and will happen in our 'representation' and is as obsolete as they are. Now we find ourselves in the impossible situation of clarifying which truths faith teaches us and which are 'acquired truths necessary to think of dogma'. If we could clarify them, they would form a collection of lasting statements placed *alongside* and *above* transitory representations. Would one entrust the work of declaring which related notions protect 'the eternal statement' and which compromise it to a divinely aided Church, within a system of representation? But is the Church charged with guaranteeing 'the first principles and necessary acquired truths to think about dogma', in addition to 'defined dogma'?

In Fr Bouillard's explanation, the very idea of truth takes on a contradictory meaning. In a Hegelian conception of history this might not be of concern; it is dangerous not only for theology but also for the Christian faith. The same notions must have at one and the same time that actual solidity of being for us both the means of reaching, and of thinking about, eternal statements, from which they are *actually true*, and this instability of letting go to others which are essentially different, by which they become *false for another time* or for a mentality in which their 'representation' is different. Thus it is not, as we originally thought, by distraction, but by the perhaps obscure requirement of a profound logic that, having taken care to define the schemas which belong to St Thomas's theology by contrasting them with the schemas of modern theology, Bouillard ends up saying that 'When the mind develops, an unchanging truth can only be maintained thanks to a simultaneous and correlative development of all ideas, holding them in the same relationship. A theology which is not up to date is a false theology.' At least for those still naive enough to believe in logic, this means that the ideas in which Thomas expressed the theology of grace constitute a theology which was true for his time but is false today.

Next Fr Bouillard raises the question of *notions implied by conciliar definitions*. In using the notion of formal causality against Protestants, did the Council of Trent incorporate it into dogma?

> In no way! It was certainly not the Council's intention to canonize an Aristotelian notion or even a theological idea understood under Aristotle's influence. The

Council simply sought to state, against the Protestants, that justification is an interior renewal and not only the imputing of the merits of Christ, the remission of sins, or God's favour. To this end it used ideas common to the theology of its time. But we can substitute these ideas with others without changing the meaning of the teaching. The proof is in the fact that the Council itself used many more similar ideas drawn from the Scriptures.

But are the 'interior renewal' which is affirmed and the 'imputation of the merits of Christ', pushed aside as a sufficient gift, not *notions*? Are we by any chance finding here one of these 'eternal statements' in its pure state, which Fr Bouillard guarantees to us are inaccessible in any way other than as notions, in a representation which is essentially temporal and changeable? And if these are still notions, can they escape the fate of all the others which, true in one time according to the system they are part of, are later false, when the development of the mind forces the system of representation to change? If at least that statement of renewal is permanent and 'unreformable', why not the statement which expresses that sanctifying grace is the single formal cause of justification (*unica formalis causa*)? We willingly grant Fr Bouillard that the Council of Trent did not seek to canonize either Aristotle or his philosophy, nor such and such a notion precisely because it is Aristotelian, any more than it sought to canonize Thomistic notions because they were Thomistic. But if it is true that human understanding reaches the universal, and if the concept essentially refers to an objective reality which in its essentiality is independent of temporal existence, a notion encloses something other than the reference to the author who formulated it, and something other than the contingent modes of its formulation, that is, an element which is perfectly timeless because it expresses an essential necessity. This is how we can distinguish between what a Council uses (for it is of course in *human* language that divine truth is expressed to us) and that which it does not sanctify; under this precise relationship a notion is no more Aristotelian or Thomistic than it is French, German or Greek: it is purely and simply *human*. Is this distinction not one of these 'acquired truths necessary for thinking about dogma'? I know full well that it is often difficult to discern the difference between the essential content of an idea and its contingent connotations effectively. This is why, in its great and merciful wisdom, the Church avoids using words or notions which have been too involved in controversy when formulating dogma: it has made its own the words and notions of person, nature, transubstantiation and others which are equally precise. This does not mean it has pledged allegiance to Aristotle, Athanasius or Augustine but comes from the need to express divine things in human terms. Here clearly is the real benefit of the historical method, of which we are no less appreciative than Fr Bouillard himself, but which is absolutely not ordered to resolve the problem of universals. It is true that this brings us back to the old debates about nature and the individual, essence and existence, abstract and concrete. We think that these problems are still as alive and acute as in the past and that the response to them has not changed. It is of course true that they are not to today's taste, but the categories of new and old are not a metaphysical criterion. We are aware of the apologetic intentions of many of those who are working on the '*Théologie*' series,[10] but we think that it is vital to maintain the values of *truth* above all and that conformity, of whatever kind, serves truth poorly.

There is a further habit of the modern mind which reinforces the relativism which the historian professes so readily with regard to systems of ideas. This consists of interpreting the term 'conceptual' less from the point of its objective signified, against which it logically claims to measure itself, but first and foremost from the point of the subjective life which it translates. Everyone knows the depth which this method gave to the Freudian theory of dreams. M. Roland Dalbiez analyses this in admirable fashion in his already classic work on the 'psychoanalytic method and Freudian theory'. Without of course in any way assimilating psychoanalytic techniques into a form of reflection which is dependent on many other influences and is focused on another subject entirely, we believe that this relationship is enlightening. The interest in the dream is not its objective significance, whose usual incoherence is enough to decry vanity as an expression of the truth. Interest in the dream cannot be sought as 'face on' but, as it were, *a tergo* from the perspective of its subjective causes, in the life of the instincts and affections of which it is the symbolic projection. Of course many contemporary thinkers show a great tendency to consider any conceptual or imaginative expressions as above all symbolic of an interior life and experience: the experience is more or less rich, more or less authentic, if we need to ask if the symbolic expression is a worthy witness in the place of remaining in the field of simple verbal amplification.

The idea of speculative truth, expressing in itself a relationship of conformity between what is said and things, thus wings its way towards a very different meaning, that of the sincerity of witness and of the expression of authenticity in the formulating of experience. The interest of a philosophy or a theological synthesis is no more than the meaning of the whole, considered in the coherence of its statements, and is no more than the value of teaching as transmission of permanent truths. From this perspective is not every system of ideas subject to aging and death? Its interest, were it a truly human great philosophy, an authentic theology, is above all in the interior experience from which it emanates in its 'spirituality', from which it issues and which makes its true worth.

We would not dream of denying the influence that the 'spiritual climate' can have on the theoretical development of theology constructed within it. Even less would we deny the influence of various experiences on the direction of different theological syntheses, for this is only too obvious, beloved of the historian of doctrines and precious to theological reflection itself. But what we cannot allow is the complete removal of the idea of *speculative truth*, in a similar way of seeing. To anyone who asks whether we believe that truth is accessible to us, we are naïve enough to answer yes. By truth we understand that conformity of a knowing understanding with a reality which is a given for that understanding, and in no way a 'construct'. It is true that the categories

---

[10] Bouillard describes the medieval schemas as unusable:

> In the rich inheritance which it has left us lie outdated explanations, old fashioned schemes, and dead ideas. In their time, they served to hand on the mystery and, to that extent, are venerable. But, like a tool which is too old, or an unfashionable piece of clothing, they hamper the advance of theological reflection. They stop those who no longer understand them from grasping the exact significance of Christian doctrine.

through which we access this conformity are impoverished because they result from abstraction; but we think that these categories help us to grasp an authentic intuition of understanding.

In other words, we hold that St Thomas's philosophical explanation for the problem of knowledge is legitimate in terms of timeless truth. It is legitimate not precisely because we have received it or because we have been given the mission to defend it as an expression of an orthodoxy, but because we believe that it grasps permanent truth and that for us it is more *living* than contemporary theories in which we certainly also find things to teach us, because we understand their interest at the same time as we at least see their failings. There is probably more respect, not only for truth but for different doctrines, with the honest acknowledgement that disagreement may permit loyal discussion, than the constant temptation, well-intentioned as it is, to take advantage of even the slightest convergences to state a substantial and miraculous agreement.

On this matter, despite the esteem we have for the apostolic intentions of his works, and the great value of much of his research, we wonder whether the slightly cavalier fashion in which Fr Daniélou, thanks to the efforts of Fr Teilhard de Chardin, appends the benefits of Marxist, Existentialist and other thought-systems to contemporary theology does not arise from the most irritating desire for agreement, similar to the most superficial encounters. Frs de Lubac and Daniélou seem to enjoy questioning positions which are too easily held to be acquired: we are of course in agreement with them on this point. Such a critical spirit has much use in the Church which of all institutions has such power of conservation and 'tradition' that we should rejoice to see this spirit exercised in it, along with the constant concern for *verification*. We believe enough in the truth of the Church to think that it has no need of our lies and that much of what is 'prudence' is perfectly faint-hearted. But it is precisely that critical spirit which we look for when we see Fr Daniélou's attempt to involve in a renewed theology many of the givens of contemporary philosophy, which are still highly questionable.

The powerful reach of irrational philosophies is doubtless the principal cause of the offensive against scholastic thought in which we are involved. It is not alone, or rather, the experience which brought it to life is also expressed in other fields. Far from denying the value of this experience, or believing it cannot be assimilated into theological thought, we do see its human meaning, but we believe that the categories in which it formulates itself must not escape critique, and we refuse to see theological thought assimilated into it, along highly contestable formulas. It is easy to say that in our days philosophy has often deviated towards literature; thus we are led to appreciate it according to the norms by which we judge poetry and art. I know that the very idea that philosophy might be conceived of as a precise science, attentive towards technical rigour and precision, seems to many to be naïve. I admit that this understanding is compromised by the Cartesian idea of a unified body of knowledge, laid out as it were in a system of immediate clarity, like mathematics. This idea is retained by classical rationalism, but is as opposed as it can be to Thomas's rationalism. Thus we are far from being in full agreement with the claims of, for example, M. Julien Benda and do not much care for his often brief judgements on the masters of our contemporary literature, or the 'philosophy' literally mapped onto the model of sciences, which are another kind of knowledge. This philosophy is really too simple despite its requirements of precision.

But, despite these comments, we are grateful to him for pleading for clarity and rigour, denouncing the use of a vacillating vocabulary and a dubious culture, reminding us of a basic distinction between genres. This distinction is no arbitrary classification but the expression of spiritual activities which are fundamentally different in the very principles and criteria they refer to.

Theology no more lends itself to being judged by the categories of aesthetics than metaphysics – not, I should say, in its expressions, but in the value of universality and the permanence of the truths it defines. This is the default, for instance, of a brilliant and superficial page written by a most distinguished author who, while not appearing in the works of the two series we review here, finds a place naturally in our story: Hans Urs von Balthasar SJ.[11]

But is it as certain as von Balthasar suggests that a historical period only encounters particular problems and that it is always impossible to raise oneself up from simply human problems, whose givens and solutions will reach a level of universal truth? And if it is true that truth and beauty come together and are really identified in the being, expressing its riches which our initial ideas are not enough to explain, they are precisely a different signifier, and hence demand fundamentally different attitudes from our spiritual activities. We expect something more from a teaching than that it awakens in us a sense of beauty or introduces us to an indescribable experience: if it also does this, we are even more indebted to it, but its primary role is to raise us up to notice in our turn, with our living personal understanding of course, truths which others have seen before us and which hold the same value for us as they did for them. A theology is not an exhibit in a museum, only requiring us to seek to do as well in new fields. We ourselves think that in the field of knowledge there are definitive acquisitions: not all of them which seemed to be or which we thought they were. In the history of thought there are many illusions and many steps backwards, but those tested by time are among the most precious jewels of our culture. And if St Thomas is so dear to us, it is because in our eyes he is the theologian who best introduces us, with both self-effacement and boldness, to that 'most fruitful understanding of the mysteries' which, according to the [First] Vatican Council, is what constitutes theology.

---

[11] Here Labourdette quotes from von Balthasar's *Presence et pensée*, ET: *Presence and Thought. Essay on the Religious Philosophy of Gregory of Nyssa*, trans. Mark Sebanc, San Francisco: Ignatius, pp. iii–iv.

10

'The analogy of truth and the unity of the theological method'

'L'analogie de la vérité et l'unité de la Science Théologique', *Revue Thomiste* 55 (1947), 417–66.

Marie-Michel Labourdette OP and Marie-Joseph Nicolas OP

With the title 'The analogy of truth. A philosopher's reflection on a theological controversy', Fr Jean-Marie Le Blond SJ returns to one of the points at the very heart of the debate we have already dealt with in our *Dialogue théologique*.[1] He neither names any of us nor quotes our work, only referring to a 'shrill controversy'. But he claims to show that the neglect of 'elementary points, which all can accept', mostly clearly taught by St Thomas himself, has led us to 'hasty judgements and summary condemnations'. By these words he seeks not only to justify the expressions raised in our controversy, particularly those of Fr Bouillard, but also to denounce the dispassionate students of dogma who plead for the permanence and timelessness of Thomist philosophy and theology alone: they are unconscious rationalists who forget the supernatural nature of faith, in opposition to the Church's current missionary directives, and of course like Spinoza guilty of univocity. They are calm rationalists who plead on behalf of the permanence and timelessness of Thomist philosophy and a single theology. Of course, we do not feel accused of failing to submit to the Church – for this is exactly what he is talking about, as well as a humiliating spiritual vice – any more than we have accused those who hold to a new theology of heterodoxy.

There is no one who desires more than we do that a discussion which has too often deviated into polemic should remain dispassionate exchanges of opinion: we intend of course to renounce polemic. But Fr Le Blond's intervention has the advantage of raising the question in a way which so helps us to clarify the ideas which we are defending that we cannot not take this opportunity to offer a lengthy expose: as Mons. de Solages has

---

[1] M.-M. Labourdette, R.-L. Bruckburger and M. J. Nicolas, *Dialogue théologique. Pièces du débat entre 'La Revue thomiste' et les RR. PP. de Lubac, Daniélou, Bouillard, Fessard, von Balthasar…* (St Maximin: Les Arcades, 1947).

already done, all the weight of the debate needs to be brought to bear on *the analogical nature of truth*.[2]

We begin with a thorough, if perhaps too detailed, summary of the article aiming to justify each of the expressions called into question in 'Theology and its sources' relating to the relativity and the invariability of the conceptual expression of the truth, the links between 'the contemporary' and 'truth', and inseparability of the invariant and the variable and so on. We shall later examine the problem this raises.

The analogy of truth and the diversity of systems according to Fr Le Blond

Our starting point is an application to the transcendental, '*truth*', of the common doctrine of analogy of being.

Only divine Truth is perfect, 'absolutely absolute'. 'All other truths are complex and deficient, they imitate simple truth, without being able to equal it in their multiplicity, that they are, in a word, truths which are *analogous* to the first Truth.' Thus, just as the multiplicity of creatures imitates the simplicity of the Divine Infinity, without any one of these fragments of the image being able to claim to be the perfect image, independent of the cooperation of the other fragments, in the same way the multiplicity of truths imitates the simple, infinite, eternal Truth which infinitely pours into each truth.

As a result,

> to safeguard the transcendence of divine truth, and to avoid any danger of ontologism or proud rationalism, it forces us to maintain an unbreachable divide here below between our human judgements and systematisations – even if we are talking about the clearest and best constructed system – and subsistent Truth ... The best human system ... will never be the *best possible*, 'than which nothing can be thought to be more true' (*quo verior cogitari nequit*) which, in the order of truth just as in the order of perfection or of being, remains the divine prerogative; it simply is the best *in fact*, always separated by a chasm from the simple intuition which is God's possession and which he alone can communicate in a participation of his being. In addition, to talk about an absolute or unique system appears unreasonable; the Thomist synthesis itself, a certain synthesis, consecrated for the use the Church makes of it, prescribed by the Church for the formation of its clergy and in any case singularly opening, cannot be equalled to the subsistent Truth and does not convert all its wealth. In fact in the Middle Ages, other syntheses were aligned to it, alongside it, underneath it: those of St Bonaventure, of Blessed Duns Scotus, of Francisco Suàrez: perhaps less firm, less well constructed, but complementary rather than opposed; they too are part of the Christian treasury and express aspects of it which Thomism does not ignore, but emphasizes less. Other attempts might be ranged alongside the Thomist synthesis

---

[2] 'Autour d'une controverse', *Bulletin de Littérature Ecclésiastique*, 1947, 1.

in the future, which will continue the asymptomatic human effort to approach the absolute, by which we hope to be possessed in our other life. However powerful it is, Thomism always remains a system, a unified multiplicity, irreducibly other from absolute simplicity.

As we can see, Fr Le Blond, who is rather too much of a philosopher, does not even maintain the distinction between theological *science* and theological *system*, to which Fr Chenu held so firmly, as Mgr de Solages has emphasized in his 'Pour l'honneur de la théologie'.[3] In his eyes, any intellectual construction, if it is a 'unified multiplicity', is a *system*.

Thus every human judgement is relative to the absolute but is not absolute; however, it is true, in the analogical sense of the word, 'true'. What is true, what *tends to the absolute*, is whatever participates in divine Truth, the *statement*: the multiple, changing subject this statement is about is the *limit* just as essence limits the act of existence. 'The absolute nature of our truths comes not as representations to which they are applied, but as a statement itself. These representations cannot entirely hold it in their limits, but the statement goes beyond them and reaches out to the absolute.'

We recognize Fr Bouillard's formula on *statement* which can remain identical to itself while the *notions* which it draws together change. But he seeks to show how the statement of truth can take place in an absolute way through relative and replaceable representations, by applying the theory of analogy. Just as a created being is constituted by the union of a finite essence with an act of existence participating in the pure Act which is God, but limited by that essence which it receives, so a created truth is constituted by the statement–representation complex, in which the word 'to be' stated by the action of judging participating in the subsistent Truth, seeking to join it, plays the role of the action of existence, while the representations linked among themselves by the verb 'to be' play the role of the essence.

Have we understood this correctly? And has our attempt to analyse it gone beyond a thought about which the least we can say is that it gets over the primitive intention of being content with basic ideas which are accepted by everyone? Let us at least hold on to this: the human mind, by its action of stating, holds on to the absolute of truth. But *what it states* is irreparably affected by all the relativism implied in its finite and deficient representations. Let us therefore return, as the author himself does at this point in his work, to that factor of the relativism of human truths which is the 'representative', 'conceptual', 'split' aspect of our way of grasping the truth and which is also the way our thought depends on language, which the author is quick to note: 'in our thought which occurs by building and dividing the systems which various languages impose and which do not remain totally external to thought itself'.

'This is the truth which we can attain in our present state, an effort towards the absolute, an affirmation of that absolute, but the effort and affirmation of a human person, limited by the human condition, with all its inheritance, placed in an environment, coming into the history of the world and its ideas at a particular moment.' Thus he can 'speak of successive aspects of the truth'. Truth cannot be analysed outside

---

[3] *Bulletin de Littérature Ecclésiastique*, 1947/2.

of history: to the point that 'actuality thus contributes to the definition of truth', not, of course, in the sense used by Fr Bouillard, that truth changes with the development of the mind, but in the sense that without considering actuality (the relative factor of human statements), it is impossible to fully know human truths. Yet we do not believe that Fr Le Blond wishes to limit himself here to saying that, since the study of atemporal objective truth cannot be done without the help of thinkers who have gone before us and guide us, we must study them historically in order to understand them. Only after or through this should we try to see the truth as it is in itself. 'Each period of history, each school, each person has their original way of leaning towards the absolute and of making out its image, convergent and *analogous* tendencies and images, but which remain differentiated by their starting points.'

Great as St Thomas is, he too is of his time and dated. One can only understand him historically, and therefore what we grasp from this will not be the truth, but the Thomist manner of understanding and expressing it. In reality we scarcely know the Thomist truth. We were wrong to place it above time, and for centuries we have hardly moved forward in our knowledge of this thought system. 'It is true that during the last 20 years the objective and precise knowledge of Thomas' Thomism has progressed ... this work has really only just begun.' Fortunately, this does not stop the author from offering his work as an expression of St Thomas's doctrine on truth and analogy, even without perusing medieval manuscripts.

Yet in any case it is impossible to separate the *invariant* of human truths in order to then establish an absolute and unique system. The movement towards a single theology which encompasses all systems by taking on what is true of each is a claim steeped in modern rationalism's tendency towards a single science. Let us repeat in passing that this statement excludes any distinction between theological science and particular systems. There is no longer a theological science as St Thomas understood it.

What stands out clearly from all this is the need for the Church to adapt its teaching, not only to a range of languages but also to a range of concepts, and, if it does not want to maintain the chasm between seminary and university, to 'actualize it', by honestly adopting the 'situation' of today's thinkers. Since in any case we need a truth, and since pure truth – the most 'just' and 'true' humanly speaking – will be affected, is this not required in the situation we find ourselves in?

It is true that we have added this latter point to Fr Le Blond's considerations, led by the very movement which he transmits to us; and we shall go further yet. Is it not in fact clear that if our destiny is still to affirm the absolute without ever grasping it, we will finish up with more satisfactory results by being content to study history and the forms of truth in the human mind, than by searching out for and in itself? To reach the synthesis which the incorrigibly 'systematic' human mind always seeks, one is even tempted to understand the 'situations' in which humanity finds itself generation by generation as something more than an 'analogy': a succession, progression, ascent, in which superior forms absorb inferior ones, a dialectic of less in which our mind's 'tendency to the absolute' can develop closer and closer, from form to form and contrast to contrast.

Here again we have added to what Fr Le Blond wrote, purely for the pleasure of fully entering into his theory of the analogy of truth. There are minds which will not give up the one theology only to replace it with a systematic interpretation of history or a 'genealogy' of theologies. Would it not be entirely normal for anyone who adopts the 'situation' of a modern thinker, seeking a philosophy of the human mind rather than a philosophy of the real, to replace a theology of the real by a sort of theology of the Christian mind?

It is now our turn to consider a problem which is of major importance both for the formulation of dogma and for the missionary apostolate, as well as for the idea one can make for oneself of theological science.

The specific unity of the human mind and human truth

Here we are faced with a huge subject which is difficult to encompass. We do not at all believe that 'elementary points, which all can accept' is enough. When, in his famous *quarta via*, St Thomas declares that things are more or less beautiful, noble, *true*, he gives no explanation on this latter point. Is truth thus susceptible to more or less? In other words, is it a concept which is realized analogically by a more or less close participation with the divine Truth which is absolute? Yes, of course, but it is important to see closely in what way before drawing over-hasty consequences.

Logical truth and ontological truth

Let us first distinguish between *ontological truth* and *logical truth*. Fr Le Blond does not do so, although he does say somewhere that, 'without the mind, there would of course be no truth'. In terms of the divine Spirit, the source of all created being, since the Idea directs the creative act, the created being is *true*: this means that it responds to the idea that God has of it, its entire essence being that response. The truth of a being is the being as God thinks of it. The 'more or less' of truth cannot be understood here in any other way than the more or less of being as dependent on the divine Understanding whose perfect and fullest expression is none other than the divine Word.

Logical truth is truth which characterizes the mind in its relationship with being; it is the matching of our thought with the thing. Between human thought and the divine Thought which we say is true there is not univocity, despite the use of the same terms, but only analogy. However, there is knowledge of the *same thing* and of the *same (ontological) truth*. Forgetting this elementary point has important consequences. Between the divine Mind and our own, *there is the mediation of things*. It is in these things that our mind finds the principle of its own truth: 'the truth of our intellect is according to its conformity with its principle, that is to say, *to the things* from which it receives knowledge' (*ST* Ia.16.5.ad2).

The thing is measured by the divine idea, in which it finds its ontological truth, but it in turn measures the representation we make of it in which our mind finds its logical truth. And of course the thing is in the divine mind in a totally different way from how it is in our own. Between the way which God, who causes and measures it, knows it and the way in which we, who are measured by it, know it, there is only analogy, properly called, but infinitely distant. In the same way, there is only analogy, properly called, once more infinitely distant, between the truth of angelic knowledge, which yet does not come from the thing but from a participation in divine knowledge, and the truth of that divine knowledge. Likewise, just as things which have more being also have more ontological truth (and we can say in what sense they are more or less true, according to the ascending dialectic of the *quarta via*), created minds realize a more or less perfect logical truth in their knowledge, from where they more or less approach (while always remaining infinitely distant) the only Perfect Truth, the Sovereign Uncreated Truth. In angelic truth there is more truth than in human truth and infinitely less than in divine Truth.

Human logical truth

However, this view of the whole only teaches us that in the scale of understanding – human, angelic, divine – truth is only realized analogically, in other words, in a way which is both proportionally possible and essentially differentiated. It remains to be seen what it is in each of these. We shall pay particular attention to the case of the human mind. If we have correctly understood him, Fr Le Blond believes he can give an account of human truth with this proportion: the statement, 'participating in divine Truth', is to the representation in ideas to which it relates and which limit it, what existence, participating in Pure Action, is to the essence which it realizes and which limit it. The truth of our mind is valued by statement, because it tends to the absolute; it is by the notions on which this statement bears that it is limited and precarious. The value in our truth is thus entirely in its tendency towards the divine absolute, in its participation in the divine Truth: this analogical resemblance measures it. Hence nothing is totally absolute: there is always something more true.

Is this explanation correct? Unfortunately it only ignores the object. 'The truth of our intellect is according to its conformity with its principle, that is to say, to the things from which it receives knowledge', St Thomas tells us, and from him this is indeed a basic teaching. *The statement of human truth is directly measured against the object on which it is based*. It is true that rather than grasping at a glance the whole of understandable reality, as pure spirit does, giving each known element the fullness of its comprehensibility, the human mind can only grasp it little by little, putting it back together in a way which is always incomplete, and then reaching internal knowledge from the outside, to the more certain and the (ontologically speaking) more true from the less certain and less true. This is why (logical) human truth only reaches perfection at the end of lengthy effort. Nonetheless the essential retains its relationship with the object.

The human mind forms ideas about the objects it knows and hopes these concepts will hold for all persons. Later we shall see all the factors which come to limit this hope and shall emphasize the differences and variations which proceed from it.

Here we are speaking about the normal play of understanding itself. It forms concepts about the *things* which are in its reach, which then enable affirmations or negations which truth itself pits its wits against *these things*. It is of course certain that God knows these things in other ways from us and that the truth of the divine mind is infinitely superior to the truth of our mind. But we do not directly read in this the truth of things, according to which each of us would make various but analogically true ideas; what we know directly is not divine Truth but things, and we know them with our human understanding. We form more or less universal conceptions about them which understand them either in their accidental and shared properties, or in their properties which reveal an essence which remain hidden, or in generic essential properties, or (more rarely) in their specific difference. These concepts enable human persons to have a number of shared truths, not only truths of fact but truths of law, and the constitution of human sciences which applies to all humanity.

But not all beings are at our level, because our intellectual knowledge comes from the senses. There is a whole order of realities, which are purely spiritual, even God, which we only reach *in the analogy of realities which are first and foremost directly known*. In our reflection these latter appear to bear inexhaustible perfections, which are presented rather in an inferior and limited condition, implying that they have their cause in a being in which this perfection is fully realized. Starting from the first object directly known and thus conceived of as an inferior analogue of a perfection which is realized in other modes, we form an analogous concept of this perfection. It is thanks to this that we affirm the realization of that perfection in God, as in its cause, in a noteworthy mode whose creation is entirely denied. One can fight this philosophy, as it clearly depends on realist premises. Our aim here is not to justify it but to recall that it underpins the whole of Thomas's treatise on the existence of God and his attributes and to show how this forces us to understand *human truth*.

Thus we form a number of opinions, positive and negative, about God. We affirm that he exists; we deny that he has any of the imperfections of the creature. He is not made, he is not changing, he is not finite, he is not multiple and so on. We affirm that, in a way which escapes us, the perfections with which he has endowed his creatures are realized in him: he is truth, good, intelligence, loving, all-powerful and so on. How do we measure the *proper logical truth* of all these opinions which we say are *true*? It is not *directly* on the truth of the divine Intelligence, because that cannot in anyway fall into our own grasp. These are all *conclusive* judgements. They therefore take as read the human logical truth of the affirmations which directly bear on created realities, in which analogies we show what a human mind can know about God. It is always the same kind of human truth. Of course it is true that God knows himself in a way other than how we know him; that the truth of the knowledge he has of himself is entirely different from the truth of the knowledge we have of him. But this does not in any way invalidate the fact that everything which we say about him essentially boils down to the laws and demands of *human* logical truth.

Unity of the human mind

Fr Le Blond appeals to the analogy of being to explain the analogy of truth: made up of essence and existence, the variety of creatures can only realize being analogically in relation to the divine Being. Alongside this, the various created truths, consisting in statements which tend to the absolute and divided representations, only reflect analogically the divine Truth. But the analogy of being does not only involve created beings, analogous to the divine Being, or all analogous among themselves: if it did there would not be two which *univocally* possessed the same essence. I do not know whether Fr Le Blond would accept such Nominalism, but I am certain that his historical probity does not impute this doctrine to St Thomas. Are there beings, yes or no, which univocally realize the same essence? They are of course all analogous to the divine Being, but this would be according to the same analogy, and they would remain univocal among themselves. At the same time, the fact that the truth of the human mind is only an analogical reflection in relation to the divine mind – so that every time that a human mind moves itself to affirm a truth or deny an error it is, in this, in its infinitely deficient manner, similar to the divine Mind, the Perfect Truth – does not in any way imply that human truths are purely analogous among themselves, immeasurable against one another. Or rather, it would only imply this if the human mind *were not a specifically single nature*.

The question then is to know whether the human mind is one, univocally one, *specifically one*. Do human persons only participate analogically in human nature, or is it *specifically the same* in each one of them? This would nonetheless leave a huge margin for individual differences. This is definitively where the debate led by Fr Le Blond takes up again. *If the human mind is one, specifically one, then univocally one is its proper way of being, its human way of being which is adequate to the real, to true being, to analogous being to the divine Mind.* Of course there has never been any question of denying or doubting that the *logical truth* as it is realized in human understanding is only present with the truth as it is realized in the divine Understanding, an infinitely distant analogy. We are not talking about this. We are asking whether the *human* mind has a specifically single nature and whether, consequently, its proper way of being true, of affirming the truth, is specifically one. This acceptance of the 'human condition' is what we are accused of forgetting.

It is because we claim this unity through the differences we discuss below that we maintain the unity of a human truth about God, to which theological science tends. Faced with the divine Truth, our ideas are terribly deficient, but they are precisely formed and apply to all of humanity. The analogous concepts in which we conceive of them are human no less than univocal concepts. In an ideal world, there is only one perfect and adequate *human* way of representing the divine Truth, and the effort of thought is to raise oneself to this height.

Revealed truths

Does the fact that supernatural divine Truth is *revealed* change the situation of the human mind in this regard? This question leads us to a further consideration, of primary importance in our subject, and one which we risk forgetting as we simple philosophers intervene in a debate about the nature of theology. The *data* which the theologian analyses and explains is not the divine Essence, about which he can only form concepts which are inevitably powerless. This data is a *revelation made in human concepts* in statements whose truth, supernatural and guaranteed by God, is a truth *which is logical human truth*. The Divine Truth to which theological science matches itself is a truth which is already translated and expressed in human language by God, and *God alone*. God alone reveals, and reveals by speaking. The Church does not reveal, and certainly not the theologian: the Church conserves, transmits, explains and adapts but conserves in it the *same supernatural sense* given to it in human formulas, and conserving the *same truth*: 'the same sense, the same sentence'. Human statements tell us about the mysteries which are in God; the relationship between these statements and the mysteries themselves is guaranteed by God, being his revelation; it is indiscernible to us. And this is why we can only reply in our mind to this revelation with an assent of *faith*: we believe, by reason of the authority of the God who reveals, *what God tells us* about himself and his providential plans for our salvation. An essentially supernatural light is what permits us to make such an assent and makes our elevated mind reach its object not in the formula but in the supernatural reality which that formula expresses: but it reaches it by the proper means of the formula, and it is the formula alone which expresses worthily the truth reached by human understanding. The whole of these statements, gradually revealed until the death of the last Apostle and organized in a Creed which is not a philosophy, but the Word of God made present to humanity in its own language, is conferred on the Church. How does Fr Le Blond conceive of its development and permanence? Is it enough that in revealed statements, human concepts in which God has translated the divine Truth should be replaced by other concepts, which are merely analogous to the former, which in scholastic terminology means precisely concepts which are proportionally similar but *essentially different*? Is the permanence due to the *statement* alone, understood as a tendency towards the absolute, independent of what it expresses, the 'notions' it is concerned with? If this is enough, one would slip alongside *meanings* which, down the ages and in differing cultural situations are simply analogous to one another; that is, proportionally similar but essentially different.

To continue to speak as theologians, we would say that such a view, to which Fr Le Blond's theories would lead if pushed to their limits, is clearly incompatible with the clearest and most solemn statements of the Ecclesial Magisterium, from the [First] Vatican Council to the anti-Modernist documents.[4]

We can never emphasize enough the congenital deficiency of human statements in which the object of faith is offered in relation to the transcendent divine reality; and onto this is grafted the call to a knowledge of quite a different kind – essentially obscure, mystical knowledge through love of the very same supernatural God. We must go even further: to express his mysteries in human language, God had to choose one or more particular human languages. We shall no more dwell on 'human language' than on humanity in general. God used the possibilities of the language, be it Hebrew or Greek, raising it to greater purity and truth, but he also accepted its very limitations. It is possible that for the expression of such and such a mystery a different cultural spirit, and thus another language (e.g. that of India or China), would have offered him different resources. But what he did cannot be re-done, and in any case, he alone could re-do it. In the same way, having chosen to be incarnate, the Word of God took a necessarily individual human nature. In the same way, Christ is and will always remain a Jewish worker who lived in a precise time in history, in a clearly determined cultural

---

[4] Of course we do not intend to suggest that Fr Le Blond would not accept all the documents of the Magisterium. It is precisely because he accepts them all that this argument seems to us to be strong.

milieu, speaking in the language of his time and not in the more universal languages of his time of Greece and Rome (and yet we know that the Incarnation involves the whole of the human nature, precisely because it is *one*). In the same way, the Word of God, speaking in human language, was spoken about after the fact in Hebrew and Greek. In the same way, since the death of the last Apostle, this Revelation, which must be taken to the ends of the earth and until the end of time, as a *revelation* properly speaking, is complete. The result is that, whatever language it is translated into, whatever the cultural milieu in which it takes root, whatever the development of humanity in millions of years, if indeed it lasts millions of years, its expression must remain entirely identical to those Hebrew and Greek expressions, expressing the *same* meaning, the same *human truth formulated* by God alone. One can regret that in order to achieve his revelation God did not wait for the total 'planetization of humanity', but once again, we cannot re-make history on the pretext of a historical spirit.

Theological truth

By keeping the debate in this field we are not in any way identifying or confusing theology with dogma, but the idea which each of us holds about theology *is entirely dependent on the idea we hold about dogma*. Theology is not a 'philosophy of dogma', neither is it the application from outside of the philosophy or a philosophical system of the deposit of revelation. It has its original light; it responds to this call to understanding which, for the mind of the believer, is the divine affirmation from the moment that she goes beyond simple adherence and places herself in front of the divine Word *to seek its understanding*. *Fides quaerens intellectum*. It is this understanding that the theologian strives to bring to the humanly perfect state of knowledge which we call science (in a different sense, we should repeat, from the modern term which opposes science and philosophy).

Of course the theologian essentially seeks to know God. He strives to conceive of him as best as is possible for us, but can only do so in applying himself to the *teaching revealed by God*, the statements which express revelation in human language, to best grasp the content which is comprehensible to us, with its implications. The theologian studies divine truths which are already humanized in their formulation, analysing and explaining their meaning. *The truth of our theology is measured against these, not against the truth of the divine Mind*. The theologian does not see God, does not benefit from any new revelation. What he strives for is the best knowledge of God to be had, by means of those truths which have already been formulated in human language, *the human mind* which we are constantly talking about, in the midst of all these historical varieties, *the unity of nature*. This is why we claim the unity of a single theological science: we do not in any way deny the existence and the (inevitably unequal) value of various theological syntheses and systems. We simply state that to the extent that they are diverse, each of them represents a more or less successful effort to reach the status of science, to raise theology to the human unity which is its inbuilt ambition. And this in turn means, not of course that each of these systems, or theological science itself, seeks to be equal to the truth of the divine Mind, but that it strives to reach the best state of *human* truth about God, according to which we learn about his very Revelation.

It does not in any way aspire to become dogma. It will always remain a human thing whose value, like faith, will derive from the quality of the human reflection it bears. It will always be no more than an analogy, infinitely far from the divine Truth, and I know of not one scholastic who would ever have dreamed the contrary! Scholars know it remains human, that is, poor and deficient, a shadow, not even a reflection of the divine Truth, but precisely because they believe that it aspires to value *the human mind for itself*, that is, for every human person and for all times.

Diversity in the human mind and human truths

To demonstrate the innate unity of human speculative truth, we have appealed to the specific unity of the human mind, which implies the specific community of the laws which make it appropriate to the real. The truth of our ideas is not measured directly against divine Truth, more or less approached in the very distant analogy which we maintain with it, but rather against the demands of the *human mind* in its taking possession of the object.

But one would have to have a terribly superficial and partial knowledge of Thomist thought to believe that his understanding of the nature of human truth is initiated by this 'serene dogmatism'. Perhaps that thought emphasized that unity because it finds in it the full prize: Is this not one of the values whose mission it is to conserve? It remains no less the case that it is still perfectly aware of the multiplication of variations of the human mind; and for our part, we think that in its principles it holds what is necessary to explain them in a deeper way than a more empirical, less ontologically based philosophy.

Individual, racial, cultural and historical individuality

Most opportunely, Fr Le Blond reminds us about the composition of essence and existence, and the limiting nature of essence, in relation to the analogy of being. The act is limited only by power, while being is limited by a 'potential to be', and this is what enables its multiplication: the unreceived being is unique and develops in fullness everything which the being alone can be when it is not limited to such and such a partial realization.

But potentiality can be near or far in the composition of a created being. It is always present at least in the essence but that essence can be a pure form; it is therefore simple, and on the precise level of the degree of being and divine resemblance which this essence represents, any multiplicity is impossible, for essence is but a form, so all differentiations reach the kind. This is why St Thomas taught that each pure spirit, each angel, is a kind, a kind which cannot have several individuals. The form cannot be multiplied here because it is not 'received' and no capacity limits a particular realization and exhausts its proper potentialities, enabling them to realize themselves in other ways. In other words, an angel does not participate in its nature according to a certain receptive capacity, but only because of existence, but in a necessarily unique way, it realizes the level of being and participation in God which defines it.

It is entirely different for creatures made of matter:[5] matter enters into the very essence of the being. This is no longer about pure form: form itself is but a limited act with a receptive capacity and it is the form–matter composite which limits the power of a being in relation to its existence: it determines the degree of being according to which it participates in existence. The result is that every material species can be indefinitely multiplied and increased into distinct individuals. Each of these individuals participates not only in the existence which it does not have of itself, like every created being, but even in its nature and proper form. This is inexhaustible: it presents' only a particular realization of this existence, maintaining of course the same formal principles, univocally and specifically keeping the same form, but in a realization which cannot use all the potentialities. It is a part of a specific community: it is a more or less successful realization from the perspective of the individual whose nature it describes. This is not realized in any way – except the divine Idea – in its ideal purity and exhaustive plenitude. Here the realist but anti-Platonic solution of the problem of universals is acknowledged.

Humanity is one of these instances. The human soul is of course spiritual: yet it is no less in the form of the matter with which it composes a single being and substance.[6]

We agree with the Thomist explanation of individuation through matter. We shall not develop this further: it suffices to examine its consequences, which are too often too little considered. Given that the soul, even though spiritual, is only individuated thanks to its relationship with the body, we should not in any way conclude that a human person only differs from another in the body and its dispositions. The soul is individualized to make a single being with the body, and it is according to itself and all its powers, even the *spiritual* ones, substantially distinct from every other individual human soul. The unity which remains, on which we focused so much above, is purely formal, the community of characteristics which constitutes the species. Each realizes the human species, none exhausts it, none is the Ideal Person, fully actualizing all the potentiality of humanity. The individuation of the human mind and its realization in a multitude of beings which are truly distinct and different from one another are by nature able to retain human truth and unity.

In this sense it is true to say that the species goes beyond each of its individual members: it is the form which each of them seeks (metaphysically speaking) to realize as best it can, and which, because it cannot, it has the inclination to transmit it by generation to other individuals which will extend the existential realization beyond its own life, and which will each begin the temporal adventure of being human. In this way we can speak about a great life of the species which began with the first individuals and continues down the generations.[7] In the successive realization of the species, there are successes and failures, and many mediocre and average realizations.

[5] Here of course we are talking about 'matter' in the precise meaning of the word for natural philosophy, in the resolutely ontological meaning which is not in any way that used by modern scientists who seek to decode the physical and observable make-up of the material being, often with the help of mathematical symbols.
[6] Theologians should note the formulation of the Council of Vienne (Denz. §481).
[7] Here we do not envisage the problem posed by the theory of biological evolution of species. See also the valuable comments of J. Maritain, 'Coopération philosophique et justice intellectuelle', *Revue Thomiste* (1946), 442–3.

This increase of the species is not a breaking up into individuals which would have nothing in common apart from their essential nature. It is a constant fact that in this proliferation sub-specific groups are formed, brought together by a certain number of shared characteristics. Obscure as it may be, biologically speaking, in its true breadth and its proper causes, the notion of *race* clearly designates an important fact detected through observation and confirmed in an astonishing way by discoveries from prehistory. Ideas of heredity and of relation introduce us to thinking about the same reality. By taking individuation in a clearly analogical sense, we can speak about 'collective individuation', that is, the interior constitution of more and less numerous racial groups. It is true that categories from the biological perspective alone (and that is still insufficiently precise) are completely inadequate from a human point of view. But already in this field, regardless of the intermixing of races within humanity, and leaving the word open to all possible vagueness, we must say that for racial groups as for individuals, not one is ideal humanity: each represents a particular realization, which is not exhaustive. Just as we speak about failure and success for individuals, so we must discuss this for racial groups – not of course in the sense that not all have the same human nature and thus the same essential dignity, but in the precise sense that all the races do not represent the same successes. History tells us of races which are less gifted and among those which have shown themselves to be less gifted, in terms of the whole, there is still a huge diversity of talent, abilities bent towards widely differing human realizations.[8]

But how far we still are from the true facts about humanity, with such inevitably inferior concepts! These biological differentiations are simply a – no doubt very remote – bedrock of the diversification among historical humanity. To understand these, we need to resort to other notions. Because humanity is not pure spirit, but an incarnate spirit, it does not possess the intuitive intelligence of pure spirits: human intelligence is *reason*. And because the human person is reasonable, he reaches his development only little by little, with the help of other persons. He needs them for even what is most human and most personal. This is why there is a sort of community which is characteristic of the human person, in order that he might develop: this is the social community. This is something completely different from the specific or racial community: it is a society organized from the perspective of human life. As a result the individual person finds himself trapped within the scope of human realizations which are out of his reach. If we consider malleability, in the relatively lengthy time it takes a person to become fully grown, we see what the hold of a human environment has over the members of its collective. This hold goes more or less beyond particularly powerful personalities, though they continue to be active. Family, city, social and political organizations: all these in their most human senses must be essentially ordered to raise the human person to her best human realization, where she will reach the highest and most universal values: yet how hard it is in so many other ways, with the weight of

---

[8] Here is perhaps the element of truth which was able to support the great racist error: an error because it misunderstood, on the one hand, the weight of the primordial and fundamental *unity* of the specific nature and, on the other hand, the transcendence of the human *person* and its destiny in relation to all the *individual* and community conditions.

psychosocial and moral pressures and social determinism. Thus human groups form, which a constellation of circumstances ensures are more or less homogenous and which differentiate themselves profoundly from other groups. The various civilizations and cultures each leaning towards the greatest human truth, but inevitably individualized, characterized in time and space, have grown in this way.

We should also note here that no civilization can exhaust the virtuality of human nature, nor lead it totally to its perfection, although some are more successful than others. And while it is true that each can learn much from others where it is deficient, there are those which have better reached the expression of the permanent elements of humanity and its thought.

Let us add a final comment to this all too brief account of truths, which demands much further development: unlike pure spirits, and because the human person is matter, he lives and acts *in time*. He develops only slowly and gradually. Time is a dimension which affects every aspect of humanity. It is not only an individual reality whose passage we know intimately – infancy, childhood, maturity, old age, death. It is also a social reality, one of the major conditions of humanity's development. This is what makes the reality of history and its profound human meanings, without implying either its necessity (a whole stack of contingencies come together with natural necessities, liberty is at work, at the same time as many more or less determining blind forces, which may or may not be discerned) or its orientation as a fact towards progress or decline.

If the line of individual development is simple, at least from a biological point of view, that of a differentiated humanity such as the one we have described can only be highly sinuous: that of a slow conquest of humanity by itself, with successes here and failures there, sometimes, in favourable circumstances, undergoing marvellous flourishing, sometimes, dominated by the forces of decay, terrible declines. For if the fate of a group is to aim with its own means towards the optimal human realization, many forces at work in history, starting with sin, tend rather towards the disintegration of human society and to its collapse into sub-human species rather than the perfect human realization. No doubt during this evolution a human knowledge or experience has developed, an increasingly penetrating awareness of humanity itself and its 'situation' in the world. Ethnology as a field of study is now sufficiently developed to enable philosophical reflection to understand at what point, in a fundamentally unchanging nature, humanity changes: how does a primitive differ in his ways of seeing the world, representing things, and life itself, from a person who is heir to a lengthy past civilization and culture. This is of course not a value judgement, for this evolution is only inevitably progressive in terms of technology, arts or science, and not in any way in terms of pure intelligence, moral conscience and other higher human values.

But after all these factors of differentiation, it remains the case that things can be considered from the opposite side, to demonstrate the extent to which, under this astounding multiplicity, humanity remains the same always and everywhere, with every person bearing the 'totality of the human condition' in themselves. What is difficult is not holding one or other of these two complementary truths, but rather not forgetting one in favour of the other, and knowing how to unite them if we wish to discuss the philosophy of history.

Diversity in the way of expecting and expressing the truth

What we have just said about the differentiations of the human mind within the very same specific nature allows us to already anticipate in what sense and for what reasons there can be non-identical and yet non-exclusive representations in various human minds of the same objective truth. The human mind as such does not exist. There are only human minds, particular realizations of the same spiritual nature. This multiplicity is simply due to the material, and the proper way of knowledge of such a spiritual nature shows the effects of its condition: the human mind composes and devises, having 'abstracted'. This suggests a 'division' of the real to reach a mental 'reconstruction', an 'order' which reproduces the unity of the real thanks to a collection of relationships of reason. These successive, complicated operations of the mind, slow to reach their result, do not happen without the possibility of error or some other deficiency appearing at every step.

The mental expression of a truth whose nature is not achieved in a single go will be essentially susceptible to mixtures, and progress, of a greater or lesser perfection. From one mind to the next, from one generation or one category of mind to the next, it can vary without contradicting itself absolutely. But this does not in any way prevent there being a universal human truth – the ultimate object of all philosophical research – whose essential elements can or at least could one day be considered to have been definitively achieved, without naive dogmatism.

And this fleshly condition of the mind in the human person does not only bring with it this abstractive and successive way of knowing but even more, as we have said, 'individuation', the multiplication and succession in time of human understanding (which as it is, tends towards unity and plenitude), and also appears as essential to the truth, as much as this is possible for the human person, to feel the effects of the individualizing conditions which come to qualify and limit our intellectual nature. The effects of truth, the relationship of one mind with another, whose type varies with the nature of that mind, are felt by the human person, alongside that which is essentially one, and that which necessarily is multiple and changing. This may be deduced a priori from its nature. But we would like to demonstrate this more surely by examining the various actions by which, in the concrete, the human mind senses the truth and the conditioning which these actions are unable to escape.

Various degrees of truth in human judgement

To speak of human truth, that is, of the truth of human knowledge, is too vague. For the human person, it is one thing to conceptualize and another to judge. Now the truth of the mind is formally *in judging*. It is in the affirmation of an object of thought as existing, as *real*, that the truth of the mind finds itself affirmed at the same time. To say 'this is' (or even 'this is this way') is the equivalent of saying 'it is true that this is' (or 'this is this way'), which may be developed as: the thought which I am forming about this object conforms to the real. Logical truth, by definition, is aware of itself, affirmative of itself: here dwells its proper divergence from ontological truth. It results that a judgement is more or less immediately true according to how its truth appears more or less immediately simply by bringing together its proper terms. There are judgements whose truth appears to me by the intermediary of other judgements which little by little bring me back to the truth, the immediate view of the object. Those non-immediate judgements which are conclusions, the fruit of reason, are themselves more or less perfect, their truth more or less immediately grasped and affirmed to the extent that my mind, by its powers of deduction or by long habit, perceives more quickly and pulls together more easily the group of 'reasons', intermediary statements, which lead it to its conclusion. All our judgements are far from being equally radiant with truth, for they are not all scientific. There are some which are 'opinions' or 'hypotheses'. Of course they materially conform or not to the truth, but this conformity is not always visible in the drawing together of their terms alone, or in necessary reasons. And there are many incorrect 'conclusive' statements, yet which start from entirely correct principles. One may hold internally truths whose consequences one has not been able to perceive clearly, which nonetheless continue to pressure and confuse us with their implications, all the while explicitly denying them or professing some which are even contradictory. A false judgement may thus coexist in the same subject with true judgements which logically destroy it. The 'perfect' coherence within the same mind is but rarely achieved, but it is the condition of perfect human truth. One can therefore certainly say that there is a perfectly and essentially true judgement about every object, which the mind seeks to form and which may be said to be 'the most true possible' (of the type of truth which is that of the *human mind*, and which does not in any way equal the infinitely more true divine Truth).[9]

It is clear too that the judgements which cannot be said to be purely and simply true are often far from being entirely false: they are worth something due to what they affirm rather than what they deny. They are false in their universality but remain valuable in such or such a category of case whose particularity or proper reason would not otherwise have been seen. Is 'sympathetic discussion' not essentially 'distinguishing' between the terms in play, in other words, to clarify the various possible meanings to retain the one which alone will give truth to the judgement? Many opinions could be true 'in a certain sense' which is not always explicitly excluded by those who profess them. But this leads us to consider, not judgement itself, but the elements which form it, which are our representations and concepts.

Various degrees of the truth of our 'conceptualizations'

Whether concepts are strictly speaking true or not, it is bringing them together which gives rise to truth or its appearance, and the truth of our judgements depends on the value of their relationship with the real.

---

[9] One might well wonder whether this 'more or less' to which the concept of truth is susceptible when applied to our judgements is the sign of an analogy. But even if it were – and we think that the same kind of analogy exists between the truth of an opinion and that of a scientific statement as between a virtue itself and the simple disposition to a virtue – this would not prevent the initial analogue of such an analogy being the human scientific judgement and, even better, human judgement of immediate evident, which in turn is more infinitely analogous to that great analogy of which divine Truth is made. Of course, it is because of its participation in divine Truth that human truth realizes its own concept more or less perfectly. But there is a pure and perfect kind of human truth.

There is also a truth of the concept which represents the intelligible object. As long as this representation is not affirmative in itself and does not collapse into subject and attribute, we cannot yet speak about logical truth, but only about that kind of ontological truth of the mind which is its fidelity to its nature, the nature of a concept being to contain its object, just as the truth of that object is to be itself. But it is clear that this ontological truth of the concept prepares the logical truth of judgement. And what is more, more or less implicit judgements often get mixed together in this work of 'conceptualization' and 'definition' which is the first scientific step of the philosopher.

But are we right to call this 'conceptualizing'? 'To conceptualize' is to form a concept, to represent and express in a concept whatever our intelligence grasps about an object. Bergson's philosophy has spread abroad, a way of understanding this which we do not at all accept. According to him, the mind is initially grasped by the object, at a certain level of depth preceding the distinction of the understanding and the will, by means of a faculty which is entirely other than discursive and conceptualizing reason. It is this 'intuition' of the object, this living experience, which should seek to express itself, to formulate itself in 'concepts', in 'images' which are solid and fixed, whose value of representing the moving real is less assured than its practical value, and whose correspondence to the living intuition from which it proceeds is only provisionally assured.

But in our view, the first sight of our understanding in no way precedes our concepts. The human mind does not think without forming for itself a concept of what it is thinking about, even where we are talking about the very first intuitions of the being, of substance, of its proper existence. The concept – a fabrication of the mind to the extent it is a psychological entity – is but this and is representative of such and such a thing only by virtue of a determination imprinted on the mind by the 'thing' in question itself, by the object. The concept is purely intermediary: it 'makes present' the object as understandable by intelligence. But the first concepts, the immediate concepts, not yet reflected upon, not developed or compared to each other, are 'confused'. The initial generalizations, by which we seek to group our particular experiences and notions which are insufficiently intelligible because they are insufficiently universal, are also 'confused'.

To understand in reality, at least virtually, several intertwined concepts, seeing several realities without distinguishing one from the other, leads to equivocal judgements which contain both truth and error. The use of confused concepts in our reasoning is extremely dangerous, because we risk slipping almost unconsciously from one meaning to another. 'To conceptualize' the real by a mental effort of reflection is to obtain a concept which is clear, precise and distinct, from a confused concept, what the ancients called to define, that is, to make a notion which unifies and explains others appear in the field of the mind.

It does us good to consult our own mind in a certain way about what it really thinks, questioning it and forcing it, in Socrates' words, to 'give birth' to the concept proper to the thing as it is distinct from all others.

There is nothing pejorative about the word 'conceptualization', nothing which of itself indicates a translation of knowledge from a superior type into an inferior plane, nothing which might make us think of a 'degraded' or 'deficient' representation, adapted to our needs and our feelings, of a transcendent real. On the contrary, this is a perfecting of knowledge itself.

It is true that in a certain way there is more in our confused knowledge than in our clear knowledge. At this level of immediacy and non-explaining, concepts and felt experience are mixed up. A sort of wider view often brings in its wake a very powerful corresponding feeling, for, as St Thomas saw well, whatever knowledge precedes love, 'one can love perfectly what one knows imperfectly' (IaIIae 27.2.2). The feeling of life often intensely accompanies our confused concepts, and alongside it all those connatural things which give knowledge at least more flavour and another kind of evidence. Clarification and impoverishment are the price of conceptualization which must be pushed to its greatest perfection to restore to the mind that impression of 'fullness' in the view of the real at the same time as immediate contact with it.

A clear concept is always in fact *partial*. It represents such and such an aspect of reality, but not always the most essential. There are generic concepts, others which are specific: both are univocal. Others only reach a reality through analogy with another which is more directly perceptible, after which we form an analogous concept which is completely abstract from those inferior to it. Every *complex* being leads to quite diverse representations of itself. It is particularly striking when we think of conceiving realities which are simple but superior. Goodness, truth, intelligence, love are various 'views' of the one divine Reality. This is all the more the case in concepts in which supernatural truth is revealed. There are always two faces, at first glance opposed in a revealed mystery, Bossuet's famous 'two ends of the chain', whose reconciliation seems external to reason. It is clear that the order in which these concepts present themselves in the human mind can vary, leading to different although not mutually exclusive perspectives, as they do not relate to one another, and that perfect theology will integrate them. In the same way, there can also be two differing analogies which both serve to help us conceive of the same reality – God – such as that of 'Word' or 'Son' to help us conceive of the second person of the Trinity, but far from us considering them as 'equivalent', and substituting one for the other, they *complement* one another and mutually enlighten one another.

St Thomas tells us that the more a being rises in the order of intelligence, the fewer ideas it has, because it has the power to unify the objects of its thought, or rather, to perceive their unity. That is to say, in becoming more perfect, ideas lose their partiality. The intellectual natures which are superior to us see the same things as we do, but in a much wider whole, with *all* of their references to the whole of which they are parts.[10] From one person to the next there are also these differences of perfection in

---

[10] A classic example will shed light on our thought. Faith teaches us that God is absolutely One, and yet also a Trinity of Persons. One might initially conceive of God's unity in seeking to deduce the non-impossibility of a certain aspect of the Trinity of Persons, or, on the contrary, conceive of the Father, the Son and the Spirit as being God, and seek to rediscover the unity of Nature of these three persons. Neither of these two conceptualizations of the revealed data loses any aspect of the mystery, they are equally legitimate as expressions of faith, although not as a principle of scientific explanation. They would be foundations of Trinitarian theology which are unequal as explanations, or in coherence, but the notions and conclusions of each, while appearing to be from another perspective and not equally precise, cannot be mutually exclusive (although of course they cannot be true together). The advantage of the co-existence of these two conceptualizations and systematizations is mutual checks and balances. Both may be thought by the same mind and can be

concepts. We understand that they are not oppositions or incompatible views; that several imperfect conceptualizations of a complex reality may exist; and finally that it is often very difficult to oppose on any given problem the judgement formed by a human mind to that which another human mind forms, without it being necessary to find an analogy between their representations.

Up until now we have been discussing the inherent limitation of all conceptualization, which is *partiality*. But most often we should be discussing a sort of error, at least virtually and implicitly. When I implicitly attribute to a whole collection of realities which I have perceived in confusion a definition which seems to me to have represented their shared essence, their deepest essence, which in reality does not touch them all, my conceptualization is incorrect and leads me to an error of judgement.[11] But it is not necessarily the case that every concept which is inadequate to the object it seeks to define is incapable of being the foundation for true judgements, nor that two concepts which aim towards the same reality, which have been grasped with confusion by two minds, are in contradictory opposition to one another just as two judgements, one positive and one negative, on the same object would be. If such a conceptualization is imperfect because it has not grasped what it is that makes the shared essence of a group confusedly brought together by ideas, or because it has explained only one non-essential aspect, however shared it may be, it is not, properly speaking, false. It is perhaps applicable to some of the ideas which I seek to define, or a particular aspect. One can make use of imperfect concepts in true judgements, when the whole part of the truth is used. This is what explains the possibility of using imperfect philosophical concepts to return, through reasoning, to truths. The use of philosophical concepts in theology is a particular illustration of this. Here the philosophical concept is really only at the service of a truth of faith which seeks to explain itself, and which will often restore the human concept, using what truth there is.

Jacques Maritain has demonstrated this in detail with regard to St Augustine, but emphasizing that his use as a theologian of imperfect philosophical concepts, which are full of errors in themselves, supposes that his faith was enlightened by the gift of the Holy Spirit. What is so manifestly true for Saint Augustine may also be more generally said of all that age of Christian thought, that of the Fathers of the Church, whose proper mission of 'builders' and defenders of dogma implies the aid of the Holy Spirit, but whose less scientific methodology also implies a greater mixing between loving contemplation and rational discourse.

There is therefore more or less precision and success in our 'conceptualizations'. However, let us suppose that our mind has not succeeded in forming a precise and exact concept about what it was thinking of in confusion. Let us suppose a truly false conceptualization, which disagrees with what I hold in confusion in my mind. It often happens that in seeking to clarify, I deform. In this case it is not necessary that my clearly defined idea abolish the confused concept which was prior to it and which led to its development.

---

definitively integrated into a single synthesis. Note that in this example, the diversity of concepts is rooted in the complexity of divine revelation itself.

[11] Cf Ia.60.ad3.

How often have we reached a particular formula or concept only to see later that it did not only not take account of what was but even of what we truly thought. In this way we often continue to think with confusion in truth, using conceptualizations which are inadequate to the truth. In the same way, at least when we use them and manipulate them in our judgements, discussions and research, we often implicitly restore and understand them slightly differently than we think when we consider them alone. Here we must invoke Socrates and his methodology.

Once again our observation, which can be infinitely nuanced, is very important in the field of theology. Theology is an effort to analyse and explain revealed concepts. This explanation is subject to the vicissitudes of the rational work of our mind. But whatever more or less happy conceptualizations we reach, the concept revealed and defined by the Church which was the departure point remains present in our mind. And just as its intelligible content is infinitely greater than what we could conceive, just as the light proper to it is the light of faith, an infused light absolutely transcendent to the rational light of reason and the next principle of infused contemplation, the psychological phenomenon which we have indicated is even more easily observed: a bad conceptualization may ever lead to false judgements, which however do not destroy the truth which I perceive in a confused, obscure state, by the concepts of faith. A theology which is false in many of its conclusions and views may very well coexist with an objectively identical faith to that which leads a theology which is entirely true.[12] This sits alongside what we said above about the very imperfect coherence which habitually exists in the human mind.

Until now these differences in the conceptualizations of the same object have been made at the same level of intelligibility. Thus we obtain complementary representations of the real, or those which are more or less clear and full. But the abstractive nature of our knowledge causes yet deeper differentiations to arise. The conceptualization of the same immediate data is effectively possible at several levels of abstraction. The same objective reality can give rise to several orders of representations, to several systems of conceptualization, to several sciences or types of knowledge. The physicist who considers the being as realized or realizable in what may be observed sees the universe in quite another way from the pure mathematician who considers it to be subject to the pure laws of number and quantity, while the metaphysician, observing the world of perceptions, considers in them what is transcendent above matter, quantity and so on.

The mistake would be to draw all these questions into a familiar system of conceptualization. A physicist would be tempted to keep to his experimental language to talk about realities which are only revealed to metaphysical understanding. The metaphysician would risk drawing everything into too broad a concept, which would be an inadequate response to the questions raised by the mind on an inferior level of abstraction. Such a proposition would therefore be 'true' *if* it were read within a particular 'register' or conceptual 'lexicon'. According to the meaning and, we may say,

---

[12] Yet another example: it is difficult to fully adhere to Cajetan's concept of personality while not simultaneously noticing that Scotus's concept makes a true hypostatic union unthinkable. But at the same time one can very well admit that the confused view (which both seek to analyse) of Christ's personal unity is the same in the Scotist mind as in Cajetan's system.

the degree of the word 'to be', two statements, and two systems of the world which are apparently divergent, are equally true, in different fields. The very range of the word 'reality' is not the same in a science which researches the law of observable fact, and that which researches essence itself, the 'quiddity' of things. This difference is already encountered at the interior of the same order of abstraction. Between experimental or 'empirical' physics and ontological physics, the difference in the type of knowledge is obvious enough for some minds to tend to reduce the second to metaphysics, while reserving the term 'physics' to the former alone. These two types of knowledge have systems of conceptualizing the same object which are not contradictory, yet are fundamentally different: thus the same words cover very different ideas which can give rise to disparate definitions and statements which appear to be mutually exclusive. However diverse they are, these ideas have analogous roles. The philosopher's 'quiddity' is replaced by the physicist's 'possibility of observation'; 'conditionality' is substituted for 'causality'. To reduce observed, measured phenomena, whose laws and conditions are being researched, to a causal philosophical concept seems to be a pseudo-response, absolutely non-existent. The 'conceptualization' of a problem which appears to be identical – that of the 'intimate constitution' of matter – is completely different in the empirical and ontological fields. The very idea of the 'constitution of matter' is different in the two fields. On the other hand, the empirical physicist is easily subject to the attraction of mathematics, precisely because the transposition of observable phenomena into quantitative terms is possible. The type of truth which he reaches in this way is mathematical truth, defined rather as a symbol of reality, and so he reaches the physical universe in statements which it is necessary to be able to read in the appropriate register and which, in that register, remain true.

Let us not emphasize these things, despite their importance, for J. Maritain developed them at length and in great detail in his *Les Degrés du Savoir*.[13] They are of key import in the field of natural philosophy and enable us to note the permanence of not only metaphysics but also of the natural philosophy of the Middle Ages, via the prodigious development of physics in the empirical and pseudo-mathematical fields. The same principles can help us to perceive the possibility with regard to the same revealed data of a profound difference in conceptualization between the ontological and the moral or mystical fields.[14] St Thomas is not opposed to St John of the Cross, nor St Augustine to Duns Scotus.

The multiplicity of conceptualizations of the real also draws to unity. Every extrapolation of concepts, from the field where they are developed and extended, to a field foreign to them, brings in its wake equivocation and error. Every positive misunderstanding of a plan of knowledge implies an error about its deepest structure and the possibilities of human understanding. Finally, metaphysics in the purely natural field, speculative theology in the field of knowledge of revealed data, have the power to reflect on all the ways and degrees of knowledge, and to constitute a synthesis of the whole of our knowledge.

---

[13] *Les Dégrés du Savoir; ou Distinguer pour Unir* (Paris: Desclée de Brouwer, 1932).
[14] Again, Maritain gives too sketchy principles for the solution of both Augustine and St John of the Cross.

Conceptualization and formulation

In everything which we have said about the factors of relativity of human truth there is something lacking. We have not dealt with the question of language; and yet no equivocation requires dispelling more than the terms 'expression' and 'philosophical language', when we do not know whether they refer to concepts or words. It is all too clear that a concept is separated only with difficulty from the word it serves to keep in the mind and transmit outwards. But if reality goes beyond the concept, the latter at least is its natural representation, while the word is only ever but a conventional sign of the concept. The truth of a word is to be adequate to the idea which it seeks to express. But the fixity of its signifying value comes from usage and is only assured at all in practical life, thanks to the perpetual confrontation with concrete things and actions. From the moment we seek to raise the word to the significance of general ideas, a certain fluctuation of the signifying value, a certain arbitrariness in usage becomes possible. But what can we say when it comes to naming those philosophical concepts which are formed slowly and with difficulty at the cost of in-depth reflection? What to say when we need to describe to another person what we are perhaps the first to have clearly seen? It is evident that there is something *relative* in the value of philosophical discourse. Behind the words one must always reach an idea. A vocabulary cannot necessarily be imposed on absolute truth. Revelatory as the analysis of words which express a particular spontaneous philosophical notion in a given language is, it can only be a starting point for the explanation of the concept. But if the meaning of the words depends to a certain extent on what the philosopher wishes to make them mean, it is fatal if on the contrary he produces a certain reawakening of terms which the philosopher of a particular time and place on his own thought. It is difficult to use words which are characteristic of a particular philosophy to express concepts which are different from those which it generally means. Far be it from us to say that human thought should be *essentially* dependent on a language which is essentially variable from century to century, as Fr Le Blond seems to say, 'which occurs by building and dividing the systems which various languages impose and which do not remain totally external to thought itself'. On the contrary, thought only reaches truth to the extent that it is able to use language as an instrument. The powerlessness of a language is its great obstacle, which the historian unceasingly detects, but which the philosopher himself seeks to abolish.[15] The more we have an idea of the natural relativity of thought towards

---

[15] The great obstacle which the 'word' presents for the idea is that power which it has to substitute itself. Who can say how often words and images substitute themselves for concepts in imperfect thought. This is why one can very well have confused truths, immediate intuitions coexisting in one's mind with concepts which seem to contradict them but which one does not really 'think' because they are not thinkable. But it is unfortunately too common that one does not really 'think'!

This substitution of words by concepts can also take place when the concepts are full of reality. Thus we reason about mental signs which have been emptied of their content. It is this sort of algebra, this unhooking from reality which is too often confused with abstraction. There is abstraction, but it is no longer about the particular or perceptible: it is an abstraction of the real. In this way we can end up with statements which are materially true, but not that *flavour of truth* which gives contact with the real. How astonishing therefore that minds accustomed to only working with words lose that 'sense of the true' which would lead them away from so many errors, from incomprehension, from

what the human mind should tend towards, to establish a system of signification which is absolutely objective and fixed, to proceed towards a sort of conventional fixing of language. This at least is what the Church has done for its dogmas and what academic theology tends to accomplish.

What a huge advantage is given by the very precise conventions of language to ensure we are understood! Words drawn from shared language are given an exact and determined meaning: they can evoke the same concept in all minds. The pitfall is that one can play on them too much, reason on them, excuse oneself from thinking and from doing the vital work of *personal* conceptualization and understanding of the real. If the philosopher is to enter into direct personal contact with the profound truths which we live, to not have to create a language is dangerous. But to have to express what one has seen, in a language which is objectively fixed, whose signifying value is given in advance, is a far superior demand! What a victory over approximation! But philosophy has lost its objectivity, its universalism and its claim to be definitive and timeless. It tends to become the expression of a personal way of seeing eternal realities, and it seeks to hold onto the cachet of personality.

The problem with verbal expression is much broader than the problem of vocabulary. As soon as a thought seeks to express itself it immediately obeys certain laws of expression, it constructs itself in a certain order, the one which best favours expression 'ad extra' and communication with others. The 'order of doctrine', and its verbal formation and linking of ideas are the constraints which oblige thought to clarify itself, but communicate to it a certain fixed air which does not come from its own law. Here, varieties of order, method of exposition and style intervene. The same thought can be expressed in many different ways, each of which has an effect on its internal order. The difference in formulation can affect the very conceptualization. Here we may study the variety of literary genres and styles. But it appears obvious that enough profound differences in the form given to the thought will not change the understandable content, except fatally in the nuances, and that one may re-write St Thomas, for instance, in a less didactic, less serrated, more modern style, without in any way changing the concepts.

Conceptualization and systematization

Everything we have just said about the truth of judgements and concepts becomes much more complicated if we are talking about an organized body of ideas, judgements and reasoning, or that rational construction which we call a system. We use the term in a generic sense which includes every mental collection of knowledge linked to another which depends upon the same fundamental concepts. However, we have been unable to talk about conceptualization, without already anticipating the interior constructions of those mental collections which can even seek to reproduce the totality of the real in the human mind and according to the human way. But the truth of a system of science or of wisdom is clearly not as easy to measure as the truth of a concept or a judgement.

misunderstanding of the real in fields which are new to them, and so many arbitrary limitations on their own ground.

It is enough that a rational construction has the strength to support itself in a mind, and in a school, for us to be assured of the truth of the great number of propositions which it holds. It is true, and this is elementary, that this truth must be appraised in the light of the system itself. Concepts which are part of it can only be understood in their true sense when they are considered within the system. Each philosophical system has its invented language, or at least one modelled by its own concepts, often influenced by these concepts even when it is being used to express shared ideas. Again, of course, each system begins from a different place, but while there is not a difference in the path of discovery (*in via inventionis*), it is unusual that it does not affect the whole.

But if the author of the system constructs it on a principle which in reality is only a secondary aspect, he has made a mistake; many truths will remain available, and some, by accident (*per accidens*), will appear to him to have more weight. The fact that these conceptions are incorrect (and, if one examines their content, for conceptions are complex, not everything in them will be incorrect) does not make everything which appears in their realm invalid. If, for instance, I deny the value of intelligence, and consequently I trust my instinct, most of the time in the act which has been carried out (*in actu exercito*) I am not using my mind any the less as though it were dealing with the real, and I will discover many entirely correct things. If I limit human thought to objects which are empirically observable, my view of the world will be incorrect due to what it denies, but I could be led from there to a significant improvement in my faculties of observation.

When we add differences of emphasis to these multiple causes of differentiation, in other words the formal object, we find ourselves faced with 'positions' about the real, whose principal error is their mutual exclusion and of bringing the denial of poorly understood truths because they are seen under a strange light. A 'scientific' (in the modern sense) view of the world is often simply a view of the world where the philosophical emphasis is missing and where only part of the error is derived from negation. In other words, there is truth in all the great systems, and we offer no apology for writing such a banal statement, the more so since it is something to have understood how this is possible. But having said this, we must be able to formally speak not about the truths contained in a system but about the *truth of the system as it stands*, of whether this mental construction is adequate, 'one' particular, very distinct from all others, with the real which it claims made intelligible. In this very precise sense, a system will be true if its fundamental principles are true, if they are truly primary, if the conceptualization implied in these principles is perfect, clear, formal, that is to say, going to the very essence of the thing, and finally if the methodology is correct, responding to the true nature of the mind and all its steps. We should add that to remain entirely true a system must remain 'open', available to all that is real, always ready to criticize itself and to rebuild itself. A system always has a tendency to claim to be the whole, which is in any case its essential aim. It is no error not to embrace *everything*, but it is an error to judge that 'everything' is there, that the whole of reality has been captured. The mind always tends to deny what it cannot find room for in the closed synthesis it has made of itself. Every human mind which closes itself to anything other than what it has conceived, and the more so to what it has learned, in this way makes false the truth which it holds. In its self-affirmation, a system must always be aware of that part of the real which it has not yet assimilated and which could in turn become a principle and a leaven. This is why the most true must save itself from the danger which threatens it by the very fact that it is a system, which is to judge all propositions according to how they correspond with the system as a whole rather than by their proper principles, and soon perhaps no longer having a spirit of research but being an expression of acquired truths. Even supposing that this method protects from many errors, it risks giving the system itself and its coherence as an object for the mind rather than reality. Once one knows no other problems than those from which the system has been born, we risk resting our laurels on what is contingent and accidental, historically conditioned, and what has conditioned its becoming. It is no paradox to say that the 'truth' and the 'life' of a system like this can only go together. But having defined the condition of the truth of a system in this way, it is clear that faced with the same object and in the same kind of knowledge, a single true system is possible, and it is in search of this that the human mind works through its many attempts at synthesis which time devours only because they have not yet reached their aim, while leading the way there, and often by the same path as error. The word 'system' is no longer appropriate for this ideal mental construction whose objective possibility is enough to justify all the non-satisfactions and research which are the true system. This quite generic word which expresses above all the internal coherence of a mental group also applies to the true, to the hypothetical, and for the false. A system worthy of its name is an attempt at science. If it claims and affirms itself to be true, it declares at the same time that it is a 'scientific' expression of the real.

As we have seen, there is no reason why this should not also be the case in theology and even in metaphysics. The disproportion in theology between the human mind and its subject creates an infinite distance between the subject and the representation which the mind can make of it, thus appealing to a super-conceptual knowledge by the pure and direct means of faith, but could only justify the multiplicity of theologies if the human mind were specifically one or if the divine Truths had not been revealed in human concepts.

But the human mind is made in such a way that the essential itself is partial. No system which comes from it can be without error or lacunae. No system which concretely exists in the mind of a human person can fail to bear the individual mark or to lose in it the pure nature of perfect science. Even if all the truths could find a place in the true system, it is often necessary that some appear in the light of other conceptualizations and other methods. This is why, alongside Science, and as long as Science has not reached its state of supreme achievement, systems which perpetually oblige it to verify itself, revise and complete itself, must also subsist.

Mindsets

Moreover, beyond the possibilities of the diversity of attitudes of mind which we have discussed, within the same science the infinite variation remains, which arises from the individual differences of minds. A mind can only entirely copy another mind if it is not in contact in itself with the real. Of course, all aspects of the real will never be embraced by the same mind in their proper order without any kind of personal choice, order of preference, any kind of after-effect of what makes its own intelligence individual. The problems which are raised, the interest taken in them, the basic knowledge we all share, the influences we have, all determine the direction of understanding which can only seek to go beyond these factors which themselves are contingent after having submitted to them. The eternal essences are only reached by humanity through what passes and changes and by an activity which is deeply rooted in time. Everything which comes from the individual in human thought is simply an accidental cloak; but this cloak, and seeing it develop, is essential to this thought. This is what we must now consider more closely in studying briefly what we can call the thinker's 'mindset'.

We would not fulfil our aims if, being attached to locating the different concepts from which our judgements are formed in the context of the great system of ideas in which they find their meaning, we did not replace these systems themselves in the even broader, vaguer and more undefinable context of 'mindset'. The mindset of a thinker, as distinct from their thought system, is everything which they hold in a non-academic frame of mind, which makes up the atmosphere and the presuppositions of their intellectual effort. It includes non-critical, non-academic judgements, even erroneous judgements, value judgements, a sense of life, an *attitude* towards God, the world, humanity and a spirituality. Every new metaphysics is born in a mindset which it sometimes seeks to transform while developing itself, although slowly.

And yet many of the ideas in which one might try (with some difficulty!) to formulate a mindset are accepted ready-made, uncritically accepted because everyone accepts them, into a system which is strongly applied to give its own principles reason. The 'mindset' will never define itself by a collection of ideas but rather by ways of feeling, evaluating, seeing and *imagining* the world, which have for instance determined morals, institutions, the debris of ideological systems which long reigned but have now crumbled.

To understand what we mean here by 'mindset', we must recall what we said about the relationships of the individual with their race, their social category, their milieu. We shall always return to this human condition, *individual* according to the link with the body, and thus *multiplied and begotten*, aspiring to the completeness of its nature by union with fellow creatures, creating a family, life in society. The human mind never thinks *alone*: it *depends* on others for its life of thought. It does not face the object alone: there are already positions taken which determine it, which are imposed or inherited, about which it is not always possible to say whether they are true or false.

However right and true an idea is, however coherent and substantially adequate to reality a system is, it is impossible that references to the 'mindset' in which it is thought do not come to add themselves to the pure conceptual data and affect it with a certain relativity.

'Mindsets' vary even though many conceptions remain worthy. It is impossible that every thinker or time period would not have their own, particularly as the properly scientific approach seeks to liberate itself from these once it becomes aware of them. But if this 'mindset' has something passing which affects the essence or specificity of academic thought, this thought process would not be true, as it has not reached the eternal and necessary. A true thought is only affected accidentally by this relativity, by the relationships between the mental context. The invariant in it can be separated from the variable in the same way as in the mind one can separate the essential and necessary from individuality.

In any case, a mind whose 'mindset' differs from that of a thinker, must, when thinking about the *same* system and the *same* ideas, strip them bare of those references, or, if this is not possible, stymied by the re-clothing, albeit accidental, will make it unable to even sense the objective reality which the ancients grasped, and, the more so, to stick to it.

Truth and history

It is the job of history to help us to discern what is variable and relative from what is essential and permanent, and perhaps to save us from succumbing to the influence of our time. We are far from misunderstanding the need for history in the search for truth. However, we must also avoid that strange confusion in which many are often mired when speaking about the relationship between truth and history. It is said that we must allow the factors of 'history' and 'time' into our conception of human truth. For Hegel, we know that this means that truth is in the process of becoming, just like reality itself which is an Idea. But for us, only one meaning can be acceptable. There is a history of human thought, and a history of truth as seen by humanity. But there is an identical timeless truth which is the specific object of human wisdom. The truth as seen by a thinker, whether St Augustine or St Thomas, is dependent on history, time, and everything which has conditioned their act of thinking and proper limitations. But the final object of our wisdom is not St Augustine's Augustinianism, or St Thomas's Thomism, or the spirit of any other thinker: it is truth itself which my own mind must think about, with the help of those who have contemplated it before me, while avoiding their errors and going beyond their limitations, while trying myself to see what they saw.

Can we allow more to the 'time' factor? Can we think that the duration of humanity, no less than that of the individual, is not only a succession of moments but rather moments begotten by others: 'time' would be 'directional'? The human species, certainly not in a continuous manner, and not without eclipses and steps backwards, without dead ends, fruitless attempts, would undergo a process of development. The human mind, thanks to its incarnation in individual and multiple types of matter, would gradually reach its maturity and its state of adaption to its object, its ability to see the truth. Humankind would rise towards more spiritual, truthful things, according to a particular law, a dialectic whose knowledge would serve to better understand the thought of such and such a point of evolution. But since its nature would not change, and thus neither its way of knowing what is real and adjusting to it, this would not mean there would be a sort of analogy between the successive visions humanity makes for itself from the world. There would be only a gradual elimination of errors, a development of principles, and the reaching of new, perhaps essential, truths, which might fail the very bases of the structure. But we use the conditional because the facts do not seem to make this way of interpreting the history of the human mind correct,[16]

---

[16] Rather, we should say more precisely with M. Brêler (*La philosophie et son passé*) that, through so many great changes, the fundamental attitudes of the human mind remain constant and few.

and no a priori can force us to value *novelty* over truth. It is already a significant that the novelty of discovery gives a greater feeling of life to thought.

In any case, why do we not see that certain times are privileged, that certain people are predestined to see the 'decisive moments' of human history realized in them? Others, bringing only novelty, are simply of their time. The greats go beyond their time, discovering what is necessary and eternal, and are the true masters. And once the essential has been reached, in whatever field, the eternal has also been reached by the fact itself.

St Thomas and the one theology

As we have seen, we agree with Fr Le Blond, and probably with the whole world, that one can find truth in very different thought systems and language and that, in fact, there are factors of 'relativity' and 'variations' in every concrete human thought. But we do not explain this in any way by the necessarily analogical nature of our different representations of the real: first because we find these same factors of variation in every field where there are single representations; second because, just as the real goes infinitely further than the proper object of the human mind, the unity of the mind reduces to a unity the sort of analogy by which it will know the Infinite. Where concepts differ not only by their references to an obsolete system of thought, that is, one which is acknowledged to be false, we have an outdated mindset, but by their content alone we no longer say that it is the same truth, even when we use the same words. We do not think that several systems whose metaphysical bases contradict themselves can be equivalent as expressions of the real. We think that the task of the human mind is to aim towards the unification of knowledge. The effort of a general synthesis of all knowledge, of a total and unique view of the world beginning from faith is not a rationalist tendency but a statement of the unity of the human mind in the face of even divine Truth, and of the objective value of its grip, however partial, on reality, an aspiration towards *wisdom*.

Will we now say that this single theology exists and that our only role is to understand St Thomas and repeat his theology? If this were the case, it would be unforgivable not to dedicate all our strength to an exegesis of his thought, armed with all the resources history can offer. Now, important as this work is, capable of employing whole teams of specialists, and however much desired, we think it is also necessary to continue to contemplate the real as well. St Thomas, clearly, did not say or see everything. He did not drill down into or apply all his principles. He integrated historical knowledge and scientific errors into his synthesis, which strongly influenced several of his philosophical conceptions. In his mind, he held, uncritically, many views of his time, which did not depend on his own metaphysics. He lent little attention to the values which now appear most important to us. He was ignorant of a great many things which would have inspired him to great metaphysical views and admirable theological explanations. He had one determined aim, to teach and then to be a scholar. His language was admirable, since he said exactly what he wished to say, yet it could be enriched; a spiritual temperament marvellously open to the work of a scholar, which was that of his own holiness. Finally, if a mortal were allowed to live for centuries in the fullness of maturity and with the lively innovative curiosity of youth, it is clear that he would never have stopped developing, drawing to himself everything which other minds would have discovered about the truth. But St Thomas is but one man: some years of thought after twelve centuries of Christianity, and how many of human civilization? However, he understood better than anyone before him the essential, primary, most fundamental truths, and he was able to build upon them, in a system which was more open to any truth rather than dependent on a metaphysics, that is, on principles of all things. Something very new and very important in Christianity began with him. In him and with him, Christian thought succeeded in its synthesis with philosophy of pure reason as it had appeared in Aristotle. How could those who do not believe in the truth of this philosophy, or those who do not believe that up until then theology was missing its perfect rational tool, attach the same importance to St Thomas as we do? The fact that this philosophy is true, and thus able to progress, to stretch, assimilate everything which is true to itself, while nevertheless remaining the same thanks to the permanence of its defining principles: we know how hard this is for modern thought. If it is true, so much is false! Even theses permitted and taught in the Church – but the Church only imposes an opinion about what is either of faith or very closely connected with faith. Fortunately! – for who otherwise would be orthodox? 'Justice and truth are two such subtle points that our human instruments are too blunt to touch them with precision; we are apt to miss the point, and groping about, to reach the false rather than the true.'[17]

With regard to a philosophy which is essentially contrary to what St Thomas took over from Aristotle, we can only do what Thomas did for Aristotle by denying Thomas. Thus those who speak about imitating Thomas while baptizing Hegel or Bergson, Kierkegaard or Marx, are questionable, for St Thomas did not intend to give Christianity a provisional expression which was only valuable for a time when it was thought Aristotle was true. Rather he intended to give a rational expression which was objectively and always true of a dogmatic whole offered to the essentially unchanging understanding of humanity.[18]

How is this position *anti-historical*? Are there not decisive moments in the history of the mind, and is what happens in time always necessarily perishable? Are there not discoveries upon which the whole of human history depends? Do they not come about through an evolution which is as often slow as it is sudden, through a shock,

---

[17] Pascal, *Pensées* 207, trans. H. L. S. Lear (London: Rivingtons, 1878).
[18] In his article in the *Nouvelle Revue Théologique* cited above, Fr Daniélou once more distinguishes Christian thought and its essential requirements from the various philosophies in which it can take flesh. To think as we do that a single philosophy is true does not in any way prevent us from also admitting that Christianity contains within it imperious philosophies which risk upsetting the categories of all the purely rational systems. These demands, according to Fr Daniélou, would certainly break open the historical Aristotelianism in terms of what is fixed and closed, but also of course the genius of St Thomas was to fully and explicitly grant it without losing the benefit of the positive truths of Greek wisdom. It is true that his God is both totally independent and at the same time accessible to the creature without any possible confusion with the created being; that he gives a central place to the human person in a universe which today we recognize as disproportionate. This is why, with St Thomas, we speak about an encounter between Christian philosophy and Aristotle.

which gives birth to a newer, more perfect form? To go to its heart, has the Church not needed a theology for the protection and fruitfulness of its faith? And thus, was it not necessary that it should find its own philosophy? Should one therefore be surprised that the Holy Spirit led the development of Christian thought to the point that the faith of the Fathers encountered philosophical principles which are always true? And why name such and such a Father, and St Thomas and Aristotle; it is in fact they who found or decisively expressed such and such a truth, giving it their seal of approval. But whoever thinks about the inventor of the plough? Yet the plough exists and is a perfected machine whose principles have not changed. Some ideas and methods are more precious inventions than the plough or any other tool. And yet we also know that Aristotle and the whole of Greek thought appears to represent a partial view of the human mind, when we think of the world of Hindu thought or even, so different from either, of modern thought. Yet it was not for nothing that the divine Truth revealed itself initially and was taught in Hebrew and Greek concepts. Probably they were appropriate for this and prepared by the Word which illuminates every person who comes into this world. Above all, they were adapted and rectified, given more truth by that divine Truth which expressed itself in them. Plato and Aristotle are our masters, but how transformed by the Faith which found in them concepts which it needed to express itself humanly!

And how would this position also be *insufficiently Catholic*? We have talked enough about how systems which have some error or basic lacuna at their root, some confusion between the accessory and the essential, can still contain many truths. How much more so is this true of Christian systems? The fact that their great doctrinal themes sometimes appear to make the Thomist categories collapse simply proves that often one must go deeper to integrate, and no longer confuse what St Thomas explicitly thought with what he permits us to think, the limitations which his individuality brings to the fruitfulness of his thought with the limitations inscribed within internal possibilities and the essence of that thought.

Often, too, in many cases, Fr Le Blond is correct to say – and we have been careful to analyse his reasons – that the oppositions are less real than verbal, not because the concepts are equivalent or analogous to one another, but because under the different words is hidden the same idea, if one can understand them within the general light of the system. It is all too clear that the human mind, faced despite itself with eternal problems, spontaneously forms concepts which only begin to differ between systems at the very highest level of explanation, or through the relationships which allow them to sustain being part of the whole, often at the cost of the initial intuition. It is not always impossible to translate a philosophy in one language into the language of another philosophy, particularly as it is better to do this in the contemporary language of the culture than to borrow technical vocabulary from a philosophy which is essentially opposed to it. In any case it is necessary to translate many values and realities which have been perceived by thinkers who are foreign to us, into our own philosophical language. It is not at all paradoxical to say that the result of this 'transposition' risks being more fruitful between systems which are entirely foreign to one another, and which have not been born out of a shared opposition on a common data.

However, for the reasons we have discussed above, to purely and simply abandon the scholastic language, and even its most essential procedures of exposition would entail the loss of one of the great strengths of Christian philosophy. We must simply unceasingly enrich it with everything which has become common and classical in modern philosophy, many of whose terms are susceptible to finding a fixed meaning in the whole of the broader Thomist synthesis which imposes itself.

Neither does this position err by *rationalism* or an excess of intellectualism. By making the Christian thinker aim for the as yet incomplete yet solid edifice established by St Thomas of a single Catholic philosophy and theology, we profess through this the academic nature of theology. Having said this, academic theology is not the only theology. It is the most perfect in the order of pure knowledge; but it is not the only means of knowledge offered to the Christian soul, and pure knowledge is not the whole of the human person. The delightful knowledge of a text revealed through the action of the gifts of the Holy Spirit is a more direct contact with God, a more direct nourishing of the faith; even more so the mystical contemplation of God present in the soul. We also think that 'the Word of God in its definitive, unique fullness, is the Word made flesh', but that to reach and quench this as it is, is no longer part of academic theology, but far beyond it. What is more, in addition to all knowledge is charity, not only for its moral value but even more so for the union with God it achieves. God does not only want theologians in the Church, not that any of us limits himself to being a theologian! Conceptual theology can also be less academic by making itself apologetic, 'kerygmatic' and adapting itself to the needs, possibilities and, as much as possible without being untrue to itself, to the ways of thinking of those it seeks to save and to nourish with the bread of truth. On the purely rational field, the same applies. Objective, realist philosophy of an academic structure does not suppress but rather to a certain extent frees philosophy which is more engaged in life and experience, the witness of metaphysical experience, analyses which keep themselves from stripping down their object from its existence and from everything that this brings in terms of what is quaking, personal, impossible to universalize. There is no great metaphysics which has not been born or maintained from a spiritual experience. It is true that some minds refuse, for their part, to release themselves from this. We also need poets to rediscover a truth which is not truth by their own paths. 'Do not stop the music', as the wise say. But it is key that all these forms of the life of the mind do not seek to replace a metaphysics and a theology whose negation would imply a position with regard to understanding and being which is totally incompatible with the possibility of fixed, permanent dogmas.

We affirm what every Catholic must believe about the permanence and unity of the dogmatic formulas across the diverse cultures, as a necessary consequence of theological science, with the difference that that theology is still incomplete and not necessary for salvation. If we may be permitted to quote here what we wrote in our article on the missionary apostolate:

> The fact that the absolute truth of faith can be expressed in substantial and personal concepts demonstrates that these concepts, in the sense they are understood in the Church's definition, are certainly very true for every human person and can be

assimilated into every culture. But if the Church, for instance, put down roots in India and wished and could express its faith in concepts familiar to Hindus, these concepts would in turn be true and able to assimilated by Latin thought, with more or less effort. Western philosophy has been much more deeply transformed by Christian faith than that faith has been conditioned by western philosophy; and in the same way, Christian faith would profoundly transform eastern philosophy. *It would be a factor of unity for the human mind* which, left to itself does not find in the unity of its structure a sufficient force to dominate the thousand elements in which human intelligence expresses itself.[19]

Finally, does this mean that we must say that *in broadening itself in this way our position ceases to be Thomist*? It is enough to recall the fundamental concepts which we said were essential and permanent for us to realize that Thomist thought, enriched as it is by all the foreign elements, or by new observations and reflections, will always reconstruct itself organically from them, maintaining in a (perhaps remodelled) mental context what makes it characteristic among the philosophies and theologies which history has seen: realism of knowledge, conception of science, structure of being, notions of object and nature, doctrine of action and potentiality, of causality, anthropology, relationships between knowledge and love: in a word, everything which is the basis of logic, metaphysics, psychology, morals and finally the principles and methods which enable us to use all of this in theology. It is in fact for this reason that the best introduction to theological science is in the direct, literal, deep study of the very work of St Thomas, in which these fundamental principles appear in full light and emphasize these fundamental principles which remain such a leaven for anyone able to enter them. Here is the whole meaning of the place which the Church has given him: he is the Master of theological science.

Conclusion

The claim to unity and universality which St Thomas's scientific form of theology implies is also a natural need of the mind.

An attitude of extreme tolerance of theological liberalism can only be provisional. Already we can see an otherwise positive claim breaking through. Already, more or less consciously, people seek to follow St Thomas with other things, another view of the world inspired by modern science, by the feelings of human people today, with another philosophy and then, with another theology. Why can we not do for the philosophy of evolution what St Thomas did for the philosophy of being: to rethink Christianity in the light of new science, a science which thinks it contains a whole wisdom? Some even think of course that, thanks to a supple game of analogy, this renewed view of Christianity will agree with the Catholic tradition and even with St Thomas. Perhaps they expect no more permanence from this 'updating' of Christianity than from that championed by St Thomas. Above all they dream of making Christianity 'reach out to'

---

[19] *Revue Thomiste* (1946) 46/3-4 582-583.

those who, drenched in the positivist and evolutionary mindset, are more at ease in that kind of conceptualization, so that the Kingdom of God should be no more closed to them than a Middle Ages imbued with the dangerous Aristotle. But then there are some with a further ambition! They think that finally humanity has discovered 'science' and that after twenty centuries Christianity is encountering a moment of evolution and culture which will enable it to realize its full agreement with reason. A great enthusiasm runs through these minds. They feel in continuity with many of the Christian themes which have been little examined in a world of thought which is too keen to be determined. They truly believe they are the ones who have found the truth. If they think it impossible to integrate the results of science and history into St Thomas's metaphysics and consequently into what is particular about his theology, at the same time they share with the Thomas they are abandoning a search for a total vision of the world by the union of their faith and their reason, which they can believe definitively, at least in its essential structure. They should also share with him the academic search for the state of the soul, as independent as possible from everything which can cause thought to shudder, the subjectivity and the particular. How can they not see that Thomism (and with it all the traditional theological schools, for none would survive its ruin except as itself: by way of the sparse themes repeated and transformed in entirely new intellectual constructions) is at a critical juncture? Is it a straitjacket which Christian doctrine must break out of? Or on the contrary, does it remain the most perfect and perfectible academic design? In any case, it is not an 'analogical' relic which can suit it: it conforms most to its most essential claim by giving up its place.

Part Three

Further thoughts on *ressourcement*

Introduction

11 Jules Lebreton, 'The "sources chrétiennes"'

Lebreton (1873–1956) was the editor of the *Recherches de science religieuse* from 1927 until he was replaced by de Lubac in 1946. A member of the Paris province of the Jesuits from 1894, he taught the History of Christian Origins at the Institut catholique de Paris from 1905, holding the newly created chair in the History of Religions from 1907. His original training in classical philology led him to focus as a Church historian on the 'primitive Church' – the development of Christianity in the Mediterranean world during the first four centuries – and on the origins of Trinitarian doctrine. In 1910 he, along with Léonce de Grandmaison SJ, the first editor, founded the *Recherches de Science Religieuse*, to publish research into the origins of Christianity, the development of Christian beliefs and other religious traditions.

The series '*Sources chrétiennes*' had been founded by the Fourvière Jesuits de Lubac, Daniélou and Claude Mondésert, under the guidance of the Rector of Studies Victor Fontonyont. Although they had been planning it since 1938, it only took shape in 1942; yet some dozen volumes were prepared for publication between then and the end of the Second World War. Lebreton, himself an expert on historical theology, immediately recognized the immense potential of the series, with its range of subjects from the second century until the fourteenth, across the Eastern and Western Churches. His positive review is in stark contrast to the lambasting the series received at the hands of the Dominicans Garrigou-Lagrange, Labourdette and Nicolas, who regarded the series above all as a threat to the thought of Aquinas and the neo-scholastic model.

12 Henri de Lubac, 'Memories'

In this brief article, de Lubac offers some memories of the often trying circumstances in which the '*Sources chrétiennes*' series was founded. It is extraordinary to recall that the series was founded, and the first four volumes published, in the midst of the Second World War. It was further complicated by the division of France, with Daniélou and Mondésert in Nazi-occupied Paris, and de Lubac and Bouillard in officially 'free', Vichy-run Lyon. The fullest account to date remains Étienne Fouilloux' volume marking

50 years of the Sources chrétiennes, *La collection «Sources chrétiennes». Éditer les pères de l'église au XXe siècle* (Cerf, 1995, 2011). The series, as de Lubac notes, sought to offer up-to-date critical editions and translations (into French) of key texts in the history of Christianity; as of July 2020, 607 volumes have been published.

13 Yves Congar, 'Collective responsibility'

This chapter originated as the first appendix of Congar's *Vraie et fausse réforme dans l'Église* (Paris: Cerf, 1950), volume 20 of the '*Unam Sanctam*' series. For years it remained one of the very few of Congar's works not to be translated into English, and Paul Philibert's 2011 translation omits this appendix. Famously it was said that the then Nuncio in France, one Angelo Roncalli, read the book and mused whether such reform of the Church was really possible: as Pope John XXIII, he called the Second Vatican Council. Congar's primary theological interest, which most scholars attribute to his upbringing in the Protestant city of Strasbourg, was ecumenism.[1] His travels in Germany during the inter-war period and his incarceration as a prisoner-of-war for most of the Second World War enabled him to study the Reformed churches more closely, and he was an early preacher at services of prayer for Christian Unity. His series, '*Unam Sanctam*', was founded in 1937 to promote Christian unity, and his own *Chrétiens désunis* was its first volume.

---

[1] See, e.g. Gabriel Flynn, *Yves Congar's Vision of the Church in a World of Unbelief* (Aldershot: Ashgate, 2004).

11

'The "sources chrétiennes"'

'Les «sources chrétiennes»', *Recherches de Sciences religieuses* 31 (1943) 251–56.

Jules Lebreton SJ

The '*Sources chrétiennes*' series, founded and edited by Frs de Lubac and Daniélou, has, in the last two years, given us four volumes,[1] which have made this new work better known and appreciated than it could be through any curriculum. Of the four authors whose works have been published, two are from the second century, one from the fourth and one from the fourteenth. The first two are apologists, the third introduces the mystical life and the last interprets Byzantine liturgy. We can see from the range of subjects and historical periods the huge breadth of Christian thought which, it is suggested, might be better known. The choice of works tells the same story: the four books translated here are only familiar to experts in Christian writing, they escape the attention of most students, and even more so the interested public; and yet they are wholly characteristic of their time periods and countries of origin. The series editors, whom we congratulate, have not sought to draw readers by offering books closer to us in time, but have sought to teach them by placing in front of them the most representative works of different schools.

This characteristic is particularly evident in Gregory of Nyssa's *Life of Moses*. The introduction allows the reader to grasp the interest of this masterly work. In his commentary on the 'Exodus', Fr Daniélou first of all unravels the secular culture which the former Athens student assimilated so deeply and which continued to mark his thought. It is evident not only in the style but also in the movement of the thought, the Platonic élan which lifts the soul, not towards the world of ideas but towards the living God. Scripture guides and inspires Gregory's contemplation further and deeper than the works of the philosophers: the life of Moses suggests to him the ideal of the mystical journey. Philo preceded him with this exegesis, but St Paul even more so, making him discover figures of the life of Christ and the destiny of Christians not only in the realities of the images of the intelligible world but also in the history of the patriarchs and the prophets. The classical problem of the essence of perfection

---

[1] Gregory of Nyssa's *Life of Moses*, ed. J. Daniélou SJ; Clement of Alexandria's *Protrepticus*, ed. C. Mondésert SJ; Athenagoras's *Plea for the Christians*, ed. G. Bardy; Nicholas Cabasilas's *Commentary on the Divine Liturgy*, ed. S. Salaville.

is seen in this light. The solution seems paradoxical: Gregory says that in terms of virtue, perfection does not exist, and that, in effect, as long as the person is on earth, perfection is his progress; but, and this is a further paradox, this progress is only real when it is simultaneously stable. The ground on which we are to advance is not sand which collapses under our feet but a rock, which is Christ. The spiritual life may only be understood in relation to Christ. It is Christ who, through his redemptive work, has restored it; it is he who, uniting himself to it, fertilizes it; the whole mystical journey is towards him. It begins with the crossing of the Red Sea, the passage from senses to spirit; then it is the desert, the life of faith, stripped of all human charms and tasting the sweetness of God; it is the ascent of the mountain, the dark night of the soul, the shadows of the spiritual night; and finally, the manifestation of the tabernacle to Moses, in other words, the revelation of the world above, which the Word of God reveals to us; contemplation is consumed in love. This progress, sketched out in the present life, will continue in heaven, when the soul is full of all the blessedness it is capable of, and its capacity develops with contemplation. 'Thus, the one who ascends never stops.' This mystical theology, firmly and clearly expressed, introduces the reader to the very heart of St Gregory's thought: the *Life of Moses* has no further mystery and any small detail or difficulty here or there is resolved with a note.

The same method is followed in the other works: a 'broadly cultural' introduction introduces the author and the text, the translation makes it accessible to all, the notes shed further light.

Clement of Alexandria's *Protrepticus* opens up a completely different world, two centuries earlier than that which we encountered with St Gregory of Nyssa. The Alexandrian elite, whom Clement addresses, has not yet been won over to Christianity; pagan and frivolous, it has started to feel the attraction of Christ, and the speaker is determined, in his *Exhortation* or *Protrepticus*, to make this draw stronger yet.

The twentieth-century reader who joins this audience feels the charm of these discreet and enthusiastic words deeply. In the *Protrepticus* we do not find the high speculations and exegetical work of Origen, nor Irenaeus's strong theology; yet we are touched by the sincere and fervent emphases in which we recognize a broad human sympathy alongside a profound Christian faith. This little book is simply a call, not a curriculum or a theological *summa*; but the call is vibrant and allows a glimpse into a still obscure past, a glimpse of a truly human life, lifted up by the Word of God towards a new ideal, enlightened by a knowledge (*gnōsis*) which transforms human wisdom without despising it. All the elect are united in a new society, a mystical and celestial Church which is beginning here on earth, sanctified by the pure and holy mysteries which are the sacraments. Fénelon and Newman greatly appreciated Clement; Fr Mondésert will draw new disciples to him, through his introduction which is loaded with a warm sympathy, and by his faithful translation.[2]

Athenagoras, a contemporary of Clement and almost certainly like him an Athenian, has left us an Apology which is different in a number of ways from the *Protrepticus*. This is not an exhortation addressed to a chosen audience, but a little book in which

---

[2] There appears to be some uncertainty; for example, the introduction appears to question whether Clement was familiar with the Bible, while the note states that he did.

the life and the teachings of Christians are laid out and defended. Entitled *Plea for the Christians* it is dedicated to the Emperors Marcus Aurelius and Commodius, but this dedication is fictitious.[3]

This text is distinguished among the Christian *Apologies* by its firmness of writing, clear features and sober, sincere expression. The author does not parade his learning: he does not know the Bible well; he is unaware of Latin authors; he unashamedly warns us that he is using a *florilegium* to report the opinions of philosophers. This sincerity does him credit and the confidence it inspires is confirmed by the whole book: the reader appreciates the Apologist's respect for the emperors (p. 17) and also for the great thinkers of the Hellenic world, such as Plato (p. 21), who is acknowledged and appreciated as 'a type of average man, a friend of wisdom and of justice, for whom the defence of Christianity appears to be a work of reason as much as morality' (p. 27). The theologian is one whom the Apologist anticipated: a sincere Christian, firmly presenting and defending his faith, and reserving the contemplation of the highest mysteries, which our reason, here on earth, is incapable of understanding and explaining, for a future life (p. 61). His morality is harsh, but we should not associate him with Tatien's encratism (p. 29). M. Brady reminds us (p. 44) of Bossuet's admiration for Athenagoras's *Apology*; the readers of this excellent introduction will also understand it. The translation of the book is attentive and faithful, and the plentiful notes shed much light on points and allusions which second-century readers would understand but which today only scholars would grasp.

By presenting the *Commentary on the divine liturgy* Fr Salaville transports us to the fourteenth-century Byzantine Church. The author, Nicolas Cabasilas, was not, as he has often been described, a bishop. This theologian, highly visible and dedicated to the cause of Cantacuzen, remained a lay person. We have his *Life in Christ* and *Commentary on the divine liturgy*, here translated with commentary, as well as a number of other less important writings. The *Commentary on the divine liturgy* was quoted with high praise by the authors of *The perpetuity of the faith of the Catholic Church regarding the Eucharist*[4] and by Bossuet.[5] Fr de la Taille, too, held Cabasilas in high regard and cited him with praise in his magisterial work on the Eucharist.[6]

The treatise translated here is entirely worthy of this praise. Cabasilas is separated from us only by the role which he assigns to the epiclesis.[7] In all other questions he faithfully transmits the ancient tradition of the Greek Church. I was delighted to learn this, in order to better understand the venerable liturgy he explains to us, which remains the liturgy today of many uniate [sic] Oriental Churches.

In his introduction, Fr Salaville explains not only Cabasilas's Eucharistic and liturgical doctrine but the whole of his spiritual teaching as expressed in his treatise, *Life in Christ*. It is entirely dominated by the theology of the mystical body of Christ.

---

[3] Does it predate or follow the persecution in Lyon? Bardy leaves the question open, concluding that 'Only the year 177 answers the information of the problem; we shall leave it there' (p. 16).
[4] Migne, vol. I columns 466–80.
[5] *Explication de quelques difficultés sur les prières de la messe à un nouveau catholique* (1689), n. 28; here Bossuet calls Cabasilas, 'one of the most solid theologians of the Greek Church'.
[6] *Mysterium Fidei* 3rd edn (1931), 108, 496, 576, 676.
[7] See ch. 29, p. 150. Fr Salaville discusses the question carefully, pp. 150–78.

I would like to compare this doctrine by an Oriental theologian to the Sovereign Pontiff's recent teaching.[8] It will be noted that the Byzantine theologian does not depart from the traditional teaching expressed by the pope with his full authority;[9] and this work, full of doctrine and piety, will be read with great sympathy. The editor was more qualified than anyone to help us understand and taste Byzantine theology; we thank him for having done this so well through his introduction and notes.[10]

To the four volumes reviewed here, the series has just added the works of Diadocos of Photius, edited and translated by Fr des Places.[11] Photius describes this author, bishop of Photius in Egypt, as having defended the dogma of the two natures of Christ against the Monophysites. This defence may in fact be read in the *Sermon on the Ascension of the Lord* published by Cardinal Mai in 1840. Diadocos's main work is a 100-chapter treaty on 'spiritual perfection', completed by a brief work on 'vision'. These three books are published for the first time in French translation, and we hope that the edition of the Greek text will be available shortly.

In 1912, Tübner of Leipzig published the 100 chapters in a critical edition by Weis-Liebersdorf. In 1937 Fr Dörr wrote a careful study on them in which he shed light in particular on Diodocos's polemic against the Messalanian heresy,[12] but he was interested above all in making Diadocos's spiritual teaching and his personality known. I read with great interest the critical analysis of this book so long forgotten and yet in many ways so close to us, for example, the doctrine of the 'sense of the soul' which allows us to see 'the taste of God and the divine' and gives us an impression of assurance and plenitude (pp. 33–5); and above all the study of 'spiritual discernment' (pp. 40–6). One feels the Bishop of Photius values and experiences the things of God, at the same time as deep thought and sure judgement; and it is a pleasure to discover, through his transparent style, the fervour of an ascetic who is not unaware of the beauty of nature, the 'beautiful shadows, beautiful wells', but turns away from this to see only God, 'keeping his wings clipped of love for visible things' (p. 114).

---

[8] Translator's note: Here Lebreton refers to Pius XII's Encyclical Letter *Mystici corporis Christi* (On the Mystical Body of Christ), published in 1943.

[9] Differences of expression may be noted here and there but they have no doctrinal importance. For Cabasilas, too, Christ is not only the head but also the heart of the mystical Body. Fr Salaville rightly draws attention to this (pp. 59–60) and has judiciously explained this using one of Cabasilas's own comments: God's unions with humanity goes beyond all human analogy, and this is why we have so many comparisons, as a single one would be insufficient to make a mystery this intimate be understood.

[10] We would only wish for more attentive writing: the reader follows the guide, but the path is not always certain. I was surprised to read (p. 63) about the manuscript which was the basis for this edition that 'this excellent *papyrus* was written by monk Joasaph at the end of the fourteenth century'.

[11] Diadocos of Photius, *One Hundred Chapters on Spiritual Perfection; Vision; Sermon on the Ascension*, ed. E. des Places SJ.

[12] *Diadochus von Photike und die Messalianer* (Fribourg: Herder, 1937).

12

'Memories of 1940–1945'

'Souvenirs (1940–1945)',
ΑΛΕΞΑΝΔΡΙΝΑ: *mélanges offers à Claude Mondésert SJ* (Paris: Cerf, 1987), 9–13.

Henri de Lubac SJ

(From the third volume [1943] until the twenty-eighth [1951], the following heading appeared on all the volumes of the 'Sources Chrétiennes' series: 'SOURCES CHRÉTIENNES, a series edited by H. de Lubac, s.j., and J. Daniélou, s.j.'. The name of Fr Mondésert, initially editorial secretary and from 1960 (volume 73) editorial director, was also associated with this work. From its laborious beginnings, Cardinal de Lubac was one of the inspirations and remains a valued witness. We are grateful to him for having shared these extracts from his unpublished memoirs, to appear at the start of this homage to the man to whom he handed over the baton. To help the reader, we have, with his permission, added notes in brackets signed 'S.C.')

[...] During that awful period, life carried on somehow or other, with its daily obligations. But one thing was abnormal: we lived *intensely*. Everything seemed to be going to the dogs: hope was never stronger. In the *atmosphere* of spiritual warfare, plans which until then had been confused took shape. These plans were not just developed, but we started to fulfil them. The horror of the evil which we were fighting acted as a foil: thanks to the divine gift of Revelation, the conscience was enlightened. From this came a spiritedness, a greater speed in tasks which should help to pass it on. (Here of course, once again I can only offer some comments on my own narrow field of experience.)

Hardly had Fr Chaillet[1] returned to France at the start of 1941, taking up his classes again at Fourvière and hastily preparing his clandestine action, than he nursed a

---

[1] [Pierre Chaillet (1900–1972). Professor of theology in the Fourvière Scholasticate from 1932 until 1942, is best known for his publications on Möhler ('Introduction' to *L'Unité de l'Église* [1938]; *L'Église est une* [1939]). During the Occupation he founded the *Cahiers du Témoignage Chrétien* (no. 1, November 1941), Gaston Fessard, 'France, prends garde de perdre ton âme' ('France, watch that you don't lose your soul') and with others, the *Comité des Œuvres Sociales des Organisations de Résistance* (COSOR: *The Committee for the Social Works of Resistance Organisations*), to which he dedicated himself until the end of the war. S.C.]

grandiose scheme which he had firmly decided, one day or other, in some form or other, should be started. He met with Fr Fontoynont, who had long planned a collection of the Greek Fathers.[2] This would be a single publishing house, with the Eastern Fathers, Latin Fathers and classics of Christian thought in every modern language to be added to the Greek Fathers. Dominating these various branches was to be a scholarly yet accessible edition of the *Biblia* of both Testaments. He would not achieve any of this himself, but his impetus was related to the beginnings of the '*Sources chrétiennes*'. The embryonic institution was founded in 1941, and the first volume was published in 1942. His influence was also felt – although even less well known – on the publication of the *Bible de Jérusalem*.[3] In his memoirs (*Histoire de Dieu dans ma vie*, p. 464), Stanislas Fumet talks about meeting Chaillet in Lyon, noting that 'Fr Chaillet dreamed of a great development for the spread of the Bible in his country'. While the sentence is rather confused, it nonetheless alludes to very real facts.

An initial project in which I was involved, but which soon seemed impossible to achieve, was to appoint Fumet himself as the editor for the series of the Greek Fathers, with which we wanted to begin.[4] Shortly afterwards, at the university seminar of our Catholic departments, hosted by the Sulpiciens, M. Georges Villepelet, one of the directors, arranged a meeting with me and Fr Chifflot, O.P., who was improvising the Éditions de l'Abeille in Lyon, as a provisional substitute for the Éditions du Cerf.[5] Fr de Vaux, then in transit through Lyon, was able to join us. (Villepelet, de Vaux and Fr Voillaume, the founder of the Petits frères de Jésus, had studied together at Issy-les-Moulineaux and were known as the 'three Vs'.) During this private meeting, it was agreed in principle that Cerf would publish our '*Sources chrétiennes*'. Following my explanation of the wider project as conceived by Chaillet, Fr de Vaux retained the idea of using individual booklets for the translation of the Bible which he was then undertaking. The '*Sources chrétiennes*' series was started by Frs Jean Daniélou and Claude Mondésert, swiftly followed by M. Bardy (Dijon Seminary) and Fr Salaville, A.A., my own colleague in Lyon.

In this way, thanks above all to Fr Henri Bouillard, newly arrived from Rome where he had drawn up the programme, the Fourvière theological series began, with the beautiful and simple name of '*Théologie*'. Fr Daniélou, who had returned to Paris

---

[2] Victor Fontoynont (1880–1958), the former director of studies at Fourvière, had stayed there, admired by all. Of an ecumenical mindset, he saw this project as a means of *rapprochement* with the Orthodox Churches. An excellent Greek scholar, he understood that the missions of our Jesuit Lyon Province in the Middle East, which put us in touch with a number of Orthodox, were in some way predestined to demonstrate to them that the Catholic Church continued to acknowledge the Greek Fathers as their own. [All students of Greek knew of Fr Fontoynont thanks to his *Vocabulaire grec commenté et sur textes*, never out of publication from 1935 until 1957, when its author said he would be 'happy, in this his 78th year, to hand over the future of the "Vocabulaire" to Fr Mondésert' (5th revised edition, p. xvi) and from 1957 until 1985. S.C.]

[3] Translator's note: this was the French forerunner of *The Jerusalem Bible*.

[4] Fr Chaillet was initially appointed editorial director, but mobilization in the summer of 1939 saw him sent to Budapest. Fr Henri Rondet, crushed by circumstances, had to decline. Our superiors thus called me. … H.-I. Marrou encouraged us. Fr Daniélou ensured its flourishing in the occupied zone, and Fr Mondésert, in Lyon, was first of all the editorial secretary and then, from 1960, the director.

[5] Translator's note: the Dominican publishing house, Éditions du Cerf, was based in Paris and thus subject to the full restrictions of Nazi occupation.

shortly before, ensured it was accepted by the publisher Fernand Aubier, who was very interested in it. The first two volumes came off the presses in 1944; they were the doctoral theses of Frs Bouillard and Daniélou. The first, *Conversion et grâce chez S. Thomas d'Aquin*, was a thesis for the Gregorian University, but as travel to Rome had become impossible, it was defended at Fourvière in front of a panel presided over by Fr Charles Boyer, dean of the theology faculty at the Gregorian. (No one could be in any doubt that two years later, this would give rise to an unbelievable theological war.) The second text, on St Gregory of Nyssa, was a thesis for the Sorbonne. The third volume, on Clement of Alexandria, was once again a Sorbonne thesis: that of Fr Claude Mondésert.[6]

[...] We were caught up in the daily tragedy of the Occupation, soon faced with the huge round-ups of Jews and the invasion of the southern zone. There was no respite from some in an entirely different action against what they seemed to reckon to be the most pressing danger of the hour. Here I simply note these two examples, from which I still have traces of writing [...] On the other hand, it was a *Note* 'on the patristic collection, "*Sources*"', which I must have written in response to certain accusations [...] which were floating about from the first announcements of the project. Here it is, with all its ridiculous clarifications, which at the time seemed necessary.

Note on the Patristic Collection '*Sources*'

§1. The translations of the Greek Fathers planned in this series are all complete translations, and no patristic author is excluded. This means that there is no tendentious preference governing this undertaking.

§2. The works of the Fathers deal variously with dogmatics, exegesis, apologetics, liturgy, history or controversy; there are also works of asceticism in its original meaning, or of mysticism. This is why in the first six volumes to be published, we have two apologetic treatises (Athenagoras's *Apology* and Clement of Alexandria's *Protrepticus*), two works of exegesis (Origen's *Homilies on Genesis* and Gregory of Nyssa's *Life of Moses* – the latter also a key work of mysticism), a liturgical and dogmatic work (Nicholas Cabasilas's *Commentary on the Divine Liturgy*) and a work of asceticism (Maximus the Confessor's *Centuries on Love*). This last work is edited and has an introduction by Fr Viller,[7] which offers a triple-lock guarantee of competence, orthodoxy and the Jesuit mindset.

---

[6] [From 1944 until 1984, the *Théologie* series published eighty-four volumes. Among these, for readers of the 'Sources chrétiennes' series, we draw particular attention to de Lubac's *Histoire et Esprit. L'intelligence de l'Écriture d'après Origène* (vol. 16, 1950); *Augustinisme et Théologie modern* (vol. 63, 1965) and the four volumes of *Exégèse médiévale. Les quatre sens de l'Écriture* (vols 41, 42, and 59, 1959–64); as well as to the works of G. Bardy, *La conversion au Christianisme durant les premiers siècles* (vol. 15); J. Moignt on Tertullian (vols 68–70 and 75); F. Bertrand and H. Crouzel on Origen (vols 23, 34, 52); R. Bernard on Athanasius (vol. 25); M. Pontet, J. M. Le Blond, H. Rondet, M. Le Landais, A. Lauras, C. Couturier on Augustine (vols 7, 17, 28); R. Roques on Pseudo-Dionysius (vol. 29); and H.-U. von Balthasar on Maximus the Confessor (vol. 11). How and why this series was brutally interrupted is not relevant here. S.C.]

[7] [Marcel Viller (1880–1952) was professor of patristics at the Oriental Institute in Rome and later taught history of dogma at the Enghien Scholasticate in Belgium. He was the author of a small book which has not been bettered, *La spiritualité des premiers chrétiens* (1930), and founder of the *Dictionnaire de Spiritualité*, the first volume of which appeared in 1937. S.C.]

§3. At least in French, the terms 'spiritual' and 'spirituality' often have a wider meaning than the field covered by the two words asceticism and mysticism. Whatever the tendency or school to which one is attached practically in ascetical or mystical terms, a Christian must nourish her understanding with living doctrine or, if another metaphor is preferred, enable a world view which is inspired by the Christian truth. One cannot be content to stick to this truth only later to allow oneself to be inundated with strange doctrines (as happens often in our own time, when such doctrines solicit the very minds of believers from every direction). This itself is what is claimed when one talks of providing minds with a Christian spirituality; the holy fathers are one of the main sources from which the Church invites us to draw.

§4. I cannot see, therefore, how in any way the holy fathers might encourage a 'false spirituality' nor, as a consequence, how this idea could be developed from them. Only a heretical thought could reach such comment.

§5. Assuming that the *Spiritual Exercises* are perfectly orthodox and traditional, they can only find themselves to be fully in agreement with the teachings of the Gospel and of the holy fathers. But we cannot see how this doctrine of the Gospel and the fathers should have to be *made* to agree with the *Exercises*. Such an idea would imply the supposition of a possible disagreement, rejected by orthodoxy, and a certain demand of the method which rejects the honesty of academic work.

13

'Appendix 1: Collective responsibility'[1]

'Appendice 1: Responsabilité collective', *Vraie et fausse réforme dans l'Église* (Paris: Cerf, 1950), 579–596.

Yves Congar, OP

There is certainly novelty in the contemporary awareness regarding the question of collective responsibility. Doubtless the great revolutionary crises and ideological battles which, initially in Spain (1936–1939) and then through the whole of Europe, turned into unending war shocked already active consciences into powerful action. If, as St Paul says, heresy is needed to test the purity of the true faithful, is a certain level of the horrendous and the tragic in shared modern drama the condition of progress in moral ideas and the refining of the conscience?

For while there is no progress in that morality which is properly called personal, and whose achievements pass with those who have reached them, there may be – and I believe there is – progress in moral ideas. It is a slow and limited progress but real enough. Because humanity is evil, we no longer allow the questioning by torture of the accused or witnesses (although it is still practised), while in days gone by it was not only practised but also permitted. We are hardly better than our forebears in terms of justice or human fraternity, but we have more developed, perhaps more refined ideas. It is therefore not impossible that the contemporary conscience is aware of a whole order of things which constitute the field of collective responsibility. In fact, I believe this is precisely what is happening.

This is linked to a second and interdependent achievement of the modern mind: that of the sense of history and of the more realistic analytical knowledge of social entities. These are areas where the modern mind has recognized elements of understanding and the explanation of the real. The conjunction of these two things and their systematic exploitation explains to a great extent the attraction which Marxism holds over some minds. It is undeniable that Marxism has done much to develop a new sense of historical and collective responsibility, but one can make use of its true notions without being in thrall to its conclusions or postulations, and the supports for our ideas go far beyond the field of Marxist analysis.

---

[1] A fuller version of this text was published in *La Vie Intellectuelle*, March 1950, pp. 259–84, and April 1950, pp. 387–407.

History, in the sense of knowledge of the past through critical work on documents, is certainly not something recent. In terms of Church history, for instance, who would claim to surpass the erudite giants of the seventeenth century? But curious as it may seem, one may have great historical knowledge without having *a sense* of history. A sense of history means something other than knowledge of the past, that is, a sense of the movement of things, their development, their existence in successive time periods. Things are not only dated, located by their coordinates in time and space, but come from something and lead to something. History is not only the reconstitution of dead things according to their time and date but an attempt to find explanatory sequences in how they happen or develop, a genetic understanding of how events took place and the interplay of powers and battles.

In this sense, popular revolutions which, while not unheard of in the past, are rather more characteristic of the modern period have given humanity an exceptionally lively historical experience, and thus given the sense of history a sort of maturity. There is something profound in Lacordaire's comment that 'the eighteenth century was too young for history: it read history as a child and, thanks to the revolutions which have matured our age, we read it in human beings' (6th Toulouse Conference, 1854). Helped by the great development of historical studies, our contemporaries are perfectly well aware of their place in the development of history. They not only have quite detailed knowledge but are also *historically enlightened* about the sequences and crises of the past to analyse the present historically and to be aware of their own situation, and eventually their own role in that history which is being made. Thus, among many of our contemporaries a sort of historical dimension of the conscience has been awakened, which also represents a prophetic dimension, if by prophet we mean someone who perceives a sense of time, opens and foresees developments, explains the meaning of an event. We are now sensitized to the previous history and to the consequences of our attitudes, not only in terms of personal morality but also in terms of properly historical – and of course also social – realities. Today the awareness of living history, of making history, is not just the prerogative of prophets or apprentice prophets, of dictators or apprentice dictators (what a dangerous role this has played since the Great War!) but also commonly shared among all those who have followed the developments of the century.

The same may be said of the awareness of the social dimension of humanity and of every earthly human reality. Here again, moderns have discovered but not invented. The idea that every human being is only a member of a social group was lived out and admitted through much reflection in antiquity, during the Middle Ages and in the France of the ancien régime. In one sense, the novelty of the modern age is much more in the individuality of the person and the sometimes anarchic individualism of his actions. In part as a reaction to this, and in part under the pressure of a new socio-economic situation and imbalance to the extent of exasperation, the nineteenth century nonetheless discovered the social dimension of humanity in a new way. More precisely, a new analysis was made, using new tools. When in 1839 Auguste Comte coined the term 'sociology',[2] it meant something other than a crazy desire to establish an artificial

---

[2] *Cours de philosophie*, 47th lesson.

image of the sciences. In these conditions, this word would not have stuck, but it soon came to represent one of these nouns which had become necessary to describe a new reality unleashed by the mind. Thus, around 1817, the word 'proletariat' appeared and around 1919, the term 'ecumenism'. Socialism (still a new word which criticizes a new awareness) and Marxism imposed certain categories and perspectives in the analysis of social facts. Under the names of class, class warfare, rising class and so forth, there are certainly authentic realities. Marxism works hard to be the most complete philosophy of history, assuming a 'prophetic' value of an explanation of a movement of things. I believe that it is wrong to diminish all historical explanations into a single element, but this is not the place for that criticism. Certainly, in the wake of Marxism, we can no longer think about these subjects exactly as we thought before. Mercilessly, allowing no escape, it has imposed the idea that every person is engaged in a history which is a battle between opposing forces; that with regard to this fight, to refuse to take sides is to support the conservative or reactionary forces; that even without having personally made a choice, one's contribution to collective historical forces which have weight and meaning is made by one's situation and belonging to a group. The argument by which the judge proves to Koestler's Roubashov that he is a traitor, an agent of reaction, has given us a transcription in a novel which any contemporary Marxism might have spoken, an experience indeed, which any Marxist might have had.

A term which has been greatly used over the last years expresses the new perspective acquired in this way in the order of moral ideas well. We speak about having a good or a bad conscience, by which we mean that beyond what we can blame someone for given the morality they have received (e.g. the examinations of conscience printed for the attention of our parishioners), we may be yet more accountable, having to respond to attitudes, acts or omissions which relate to the solidarity of the group which we accepted or did not denounce. Many of us have thus felt responsible not only for what we have personally done or failed to do but for a state of affairs or events whose cause is social. This is also why, over the last years, we have seen these acts of rupture, in which the desire to reject solidarity with a state of things which we think contrary to the truth and the purity of human life is expressed. How many young people, from the middle classes, even the aristocracy, sometimes young clergy, have broken with their family background in this way, just as, from the earliest days of Christianity, souls seized by the absolute nature of God unceasingly rejected a corrupt world. Many of these gestures are critical, and often it is in this way that generous people take on new interdependencies which are hardly purer than the previous ones, but this does not change the facts and their obvious meaning. These are demonstrations of the discovery of a tomorrow whose responsibility has until now been poorly explored.

Of course, we have always been aware of the obligation not to participate in injustice or to profit from injustice even when we have not committed it ourselves. St Elizabeth, princess of Thuringia, was instructed by her confessor, Fr Conrad, not to eat or wear anything which she could not be certain did not have any kind of injustice attached: the very word 'good conscience' is scattered throughout the text which reports this story.[3] Similar gestures have existed throughout the long history of Christianity until today;

---

[3] I quoted this text in an article on St Elizabeth in *La Vie Spirituelle* of January 1932, p. 71.

but they remained in the sphere of a desire for personal purity and did not reach the idea of a responsibility in a state of affairs, a desire for purity in that part of ourselves which exists collectively in the solidarity of a group, even a group which itself has a certain historical role.

For in a field which is as open to feelings as responsibility, contemporary conscience appreciates things by marrying a sense of history to a social sense, just as we suddenly perceive the depth of objects when we look at them with binoculars. This is the field of what we should call historical as well as collective fault. Responsibility bears not so much on my own impurity as on an impurity in the state of affairs or a historical event in whose causes I acknowledge my own participation. Everyone's life goes this far. And of course, at this level, that life largely escapes us. In truth, aside from a few thousand individuals, no German sought Auschwitz or chose to liquidate entire populations; the young captain of Mun (Armand de Melun), who heard a communard say, one day in March 1871, 'You are the insurgents' neither chose nor sought the oppressive and unjust state of affairs against which he would soon fight. Responsibility here is total, with no subjectivity; it cannot be grasped at the level of personal intentions, aware of this and that, perhaps without some exceptions who represent truly monstrous moralities. It is rather to be grasped in its terrible results, which we can see in the facts. But the true subject faced with this result is a collectivity or even a collection of collective realities, whose existence and action raise questions about a host of extremely complex factors. If we look at these from a linear perspective, we would reach an idea which we find today in the limitations of the new feeling of collective and historical responsibility: a limitation which in reality comes from another thought world. We would locate moral qualifications, goodness and evil would no longer be the subject, but rather impersonal objective realities; we would move from a morality of intentions, the purity of consciences, to a morality of results, from the position and efficacy of acts considered in their materiality of action, to looking at the end which would only be the immanent finality of history, the sense of the movement of things. Clearly, dialectical materialism has to see things in this way. Its materialistic quality consists precisely in the fact that it denies that an idea, and thus a mind, has any antecedents, with regard to the fact represented in the world. There is hence no morality which may be defined in relation to a transcendent law raised by a mind which would also have ordered the cosmos, but only results which are appreciated in relation to the sense of the evolution of the world. One of the difficulties which this position raises, to say nothing of the metaphysical idea implied by the denial of God, is that it does not make a normative and transcendent character secret – in the way evolution does – but keeps the character as purely fact, purely a 'result'. In this way Marxism has often criticized the reintroduction of an ethical perspective, in other words, a criteria of evaluation which is outside of the fact itself. Once again, our purpose here is not to criticize Marxism, but these few words were necessary beacons to mark the limits we do not want to go beyond, or even reach: the limits of a 'morality' of result, without subjectivity, which has passed from the field of intention to the field of efficacy.

To think about the problem of collective responsibility and historical or social guilt, traditional morality offers us resources, the details of which we shall not discuss here but rather only retain the general direction.

Guilt, properly speaking, is strictly personal. It resides in individual 'subject' guilt in particular physical persons, that is, it is individually imputed to those persons. From the point of view of moral imputation, I do not think the position of speaking about common guilt, that is, the fault of the community as such, is felicitous, as the community is the subject of rights and duties in which individuals share as members of that community.[4] This way of treating the individual seems to me to push the realism of social unity too far. It presupposes an organic, almost biological, unity and solidarity among the members of the group. This is doubtless the idea of primitive societies which come together in little natural groups: family before clan, clan before tribe.[5] But society is not gifted with its own freedom and knowledge. Whatever responsibility and, above all, whatever guilt lie in society result from actions or omissions committed by physical persons; it is just that, among these persons, there are those directly responsible and those who, acting as representatives of the group or in the name of the collective, bring a certain responsibility to bear on every member of the group.

Guilt is broken down individually on all those who freely engage in reprehensible actions. In principle, one could say who and to what extent; the fact that we cannot does not change the question of principle. This guilt is clearly diverse and graduated. In the first place, it resides in the individual guilt of those who definitely committed the crime. Among these, it bears primarily and most heavily on those who ordered it, and then, and less weightily, on those who executed it. In moral terms, as in penal and social terms, some of the latter may even be more or less forgiven: every normal human jurisdiction[6] allows attenuating circumstances, such as ignorance, constraint, even passion.

In the second place, guilt resides in the individual crimes of those who encouraged or helped the malefactors of the first degree by their moral consent, their economic or political help or simply by the weakness which made the omit standing up against the crime or those who carried it out or omitted to criticize their solidarity with the former. This responsibility (in moral terms of guilt) is real; it is founded in social solidarity but goes beyond simple material solidarity. Material solidarity is simply a state of fact: solidarity in the consequences of a defeat as in an epidemic, as in the enjoyment of the fruits of victory. This suffices for the foundation that the non-guilty should share in

---

[4] According to reviews, this would appear to be the position of Professor R. Egenter, *Gemeinschuld oder Strafhaftung*, in his *Aus der Theologie der Zeit* (Munich Catholic Theological faculty, Ratisbon, 1948). Egenter argues from the case of Adam; but Adam is entirely particular, linked to a unique situation as head of the race and a positive desire for God ordered by his offer of grace.

[5] This system of collective responsibility is very clear in pre-Christian Celtic society, which was based on unity through blood relationships. Cf. J. Chevalier, *Essai sur la formation de la nationalité et les reveils religieux au pays de Galles des origins à la fin du VIè siècle* (Lyon/Paris, 1923, pp. 115ff, 149–50). Christianity eliminated this idea, p. 366. See too *Journal of Religion*, January 1944, p. 22. The same article demonstrates (p. 21) that in Israel the whole life of the people was dominated by the covenant, the principal of the very existence of Israel as a people of *God*. Any sin which broke the covenant attacked the connection between Israel and God and justified rejection in place of election.

[6] I say 'normal' to exclude jurisdictions of martial law which only know material facts and do not consider either the intention or extenuating circumstances. At heart, the Marxist idea of the morality of efficacity, which is continued and concretized in the revolutionary justice of popular tribunals, is linked to the idea of class warfare and to a warrior view of existence.

punishment.[7] This has no moral qualification. Solidarity must have existed in the field where moral responsibility reigns, and this requires at least a minimum of knowledge and power. From the moment one knows and one could have done something, one is complicit to a certain degree in the evil one has done nothing to prevent. St Augustine already told us this with a clarity which cannot be improved[8] and Péguy's Joan of Arc was, in her charity, overwhelmed by the feeling that 'complicity is the same as actor. The one who allows something to be done is like one who does it. It is all one. It is all together.'[9] Fr Gratry said that a Europe which allowed the events in Poland in 1863 to happen without protest was in a state of mortal sin.

Of course everything depends on the level of knowledge and power which a person may reach. It is clear that in Nazi Germany, a Barth or a Guardini had other possibilities and thus other responsibilities than those of the country's various underlings. Of course we should say that in complex situations one is often poorly informed and only slowly, often too late, acquires the knowledge of exact contexts, the experience which enables us to foresee consequences; finally, we discover in such or such a place that one is forced to take on real inconveniences, other solidarity, which encourages further evil. And even supposing that one were able to form a conscience, what can one do? How can one act against the tide of crushing social pressure, in a system of constraint, a police state, terrifyingly efficient? And how do we avoid falling from solidarity with injustice into solidarity with other injustices, from a limited but defined evil into yet greater evils? We do not always see this. Let us consider, for instance, some national war, and the violence which accompanies it. How do we form a judgement? What do we do when, having loyally tried to know and understand, having questioned a dozen respectable and well-informed persons, one finds oneself for and against, and unable to disentangle one from the other? How do we pronounce judgement against military victories if we do not want, for entirely worthy responses, to give the vote to the party which rejects them? And these are but a few questions: a hundred others are waiting in the wings.

It is beyond doubt that responsibility is thus highly mitigated by the difficulty of knowing and of foreseeing, and then the limits of 'being able to do something'. However, one can always do something; one can participate in opinion making, in emotion, one can do something which truly breaks solidarity. One must not placate the pricking of conscience too much; difficulties are not excused by our flabby or cowardly attitude. There is a whole area here on which examinations of conscience are generally silent, but which is nonetheless a field of real responsibility.

It is in this perspective that we can raise the problem of collective responsibility and socio-historical guilt in the area of the historical life of the Church itself, which is of direct interest to the subject of this book.

---

[7] In the sense that they are deprived of goods which they would have enjoyed if those from or with whom they should have received them had not been justly deprived of them; for instance, the children of a guilty party whose goods have been removed for a fine. These sanctions suffered through real solidarity do not, properly speaking, have a nature of *punishment* for the non-guilty.
[8] *City of God* I.9.
[9] *Le mystère de la charité de Jeanne d'Arc*, Pléiade, p. 57.

One can view the question of Catholic responsibility in some of the great tragedies from a historical perspective. One can ask what their role was in the eleventh-century schism, the rending apart of the sixteenth century, the massacre of St Bartholomew's day and so on. The answer to this question is to have a good critical knowledge of the facts, a full and astute historical method and finally a certain penetration of the mind and a wise judgement on a subject which is extremely complex. Something of this is in Dvornik's work on Photius, or Lortz's on Luther. Participating in a general movement of self-criticism, purification of attitudes and awareness of a historical-social dimension in humanity, contemporary historical science will probably be more and more interested in such research. We can expect from this an effect of abating, a real freedom in sectors which have been literally poisoned by polemic and 'esprit de corps'.[10]

We might view the question from a prudential and pastoral perspective. Here one might ask if, through research and admissions of this kind, we do not risk shaking the confidence of the faithful and working in reality for religious indifferentism which is the vestibule of Neopaganism. Entirely hypothetically, can we throw out self-critical texts, which accuse ourselves, into the wider public without imprudence? Is the current taste for such texts entirely healthy?

One can view this question from a spiritual perspective. Here it appears to be extremely important, whether with regard to the work of the Holy Spirit in us, whose first act is *to convince us of our sin*, or from the perspective of the very truth of our attitudes as moral and Christian: this truth in fact will never be reached without the conviction and avowal of our guilt; or finally, with regard of the need of this avowal to obtain various fruits of peace and communion. Christian reconciliation, which is the proper task of the twentieth century, offers certain analogies with the restoration of peace and communion between peoples. Those who have investigated the problem of the reunion of Christians in one Church, not only with their mind and authentic information but with their soul, their prayer and, in some ways, on their knees, are in agreement in thinking that only a conviction, an avowal and a forgiveness of the sins which we have, all of us, committed in the time of separation will allow the Spirit of unity to do its work.

Still from the perspective of the spiritual attitude, one must emphasize the seriousness of the cause. In many self-critical texts which have been published in the last years, one does not always sense the serious nature of a true sentiment of collective responsibility; one senses rather a certain enjoyment of iconoclasm, the delight of the child who, having reached the age where its voice is heard, feels the need to beat down a few idols and to ridicule the masters. Among others, the desire has taken on a resonance which makes us fear for the seriousness of the venture; true penitence has another sound, its very seriousness making it rather showy. In this case, the conviction and the avowal lack that seriousness if one does not feel it to be truly in solidarity and if one does not suffer by criticizing it. We need only transpose St Exupéry's admirable

---

[10] E.g. my preface to Dvornik's *Photius*, and 'Luther vu par les catholiques', *Revue des Sciences philosophiques et théologiques* 34 (1950), 507–18.

text onto the Church and Christian categories. The text has power in the pages which were lived through and signed by blood.[11]

Do not these lines illustrate the places in the present study where the truly Catholic reformer appeared to us as the one who does not despair of 'saving the Church by the Church' and does not accept to consider it other than his family home?

Finally, we can view the question of collective responsibility in the Church from the perspective of ecclesiology, that is, a theology *de Ecclesia*. The distinctions suggested in Part One, chapter 1 of the main text appear capable of shedding light on a problem which is not that difficult when we come to examine it simply.

We say that there is an aspect according to which the faithful – and churchmen – make the Church: it is the aspect of community and people, a people who must be the people of God who objectively have all the means of being the people of God but which sometimes, in such and such a portion of itself, acts as a people of Mammon, Venus or Jupiter, giving in to the temptations of money, the flesh, power or pride. We know that the history of the Church is full of failures of this kind and we can locate them according to worthwhile categories. Once this is done, we should not return but try to draw out the collective aspect of the responsibilities incurred.

Empirically considered as a people or community, the Church lives according to laws analogous to those of any community. That is, in great tragedies, in impure states of affairs where a complex and ultimately collective responsibility is to be found, there are those responsible in the first degree, and those responsible in the second degree, by solidarity of non-criticism, cowardice or connivance. In the Church more than in other societies, there is a connection between the impure states of affairs and great tragedies; perhaps we might even say that the latter are materially the product of long maturation, of inveterate and accepted malfunctions at the level of a certain state of affairs in the field of custom, above all pastoral customs, devotions, current preaching or non-preaching, theological doctrine and so forth; in short, all those things in which we have acknowledged a very real field of reformism as much as the very order of the most ordinary collective responsibility. Let us make all this concrete by rapidly mentioning three or four examples from history – and what history!

In what has been called the 'Eastern schsim', there was clearly fault on both sides. But whether we consider the significant faults of Patriarch Cerularius or those of Cardinal Humbert, whose intransigence and impatience were such that it seems they made him clearly go beyond the authority he had received from the pope, we do not find the true causes and the most decisive responsibilities at this level. To reach this, we need to go to the heart of the slow and complex process by which the East and West, the two halves of the Christian body, gradually became strangers to one another and ended up accepting this 'estrangement'. The true sin of the schism is the acceptance of it. From this it is clear that not only is responsibility for it collective, that not only did churchmen commit the sin before it even began, but that we continue to commit it as twentieth-century Christians, to the extent that we accept the 'estrangement' which caused it and that we remain in solidarity with the attitudes which themselves fed this estrangement.

---

[11] *Pilote de guerre* (1942).

At this level, collective responsibility straddles time. Did not Paul say that those who fall after having tasted the Word of God crucify the Son of God again, themselves (Heb. 6.6.)? To maintain solidarity with the state of affairs or a system which brings evil is to consent to it. Luther said that he felt guilty of the deaths of John Hus and Wycliffe by being part of the papal and monastic system which was the true author of these deaths: He did not then cry out 'John Hus was unjustly burned'.[12] Luther had poor doctrinal criteria to judge with, but if we abstract from this his judgement was correct. We need to give him better tools. We may discover some traces of blood on our hands, which we think we washed clean long ago. Every time we allow the 'liquidation' of those who do not think like us, we approve of the St Bartholomew massacre; every time we do not unambiguously denounce the use of force in conscience, we cooperate with the dragoons. And, note it well, this is not simply a sin of thought: we strengthen the system and contribute to its existence and exercising of power. It is an indirect, even distant, cooperation, but it cannot be entirely negated.

Möhler saw schisms and heresies linked to the responsibilities of earlier generations.[13] How true this is, and how it is verified particularly in the case of the Protestant Reformation. More than one churchman of the time and more than one contemporary Catholic historian have proclaimed the Catholic responsibilities in the great rending of the sixteenth century.[14] But we must see the extent to which these responsibilities go beyond the few thousand people whose acts may be known, how they called into question a whole state of affairs which had lasted without serious remedy for three centuries, in the triple fields of pastoral government, piety and theology. Reform of the Church 'in its head and its body' had been demanded for more than two centuries, the head describing the Roman court with its benefice and tax systems which brought the appointment of all ranks in its wake. For longer yet, with a continuity whose recent discovery personally made a great impression on me, men living unhappily on the fringes of Orthodoxy and even beyond its limits challenged the temporal character of the Church, the wealth and secular authority of its prelates: a state of things which, in line with the historical ideas of the times, they said went back to Constantine's donation to Pope Sylvester. They were wrong to mix into this various often seriously erroneous ideas, many of which were simply puerile; but was the Church right to refuse to listen – for this is what it did – to this calling into question of the temporal implications which it would only finally abandon when forced by the hand of history?

The invasion of religion by practices is denounced as having occasioned Luther's protest. Here is not the place to sketch out, even in its simplest form, a history of devotion and its relationship with the causes of the Reformation. I will simply mention one fact. Throughout the fourteenth and fifteenth centuries, it was said that St Francis would free from purgatory the souls of those who had worn the habit of his Order or his Tertiaries, on his feast day,[15] and the same was said of the Virgin Mary and

---

[12] Sermon in 1529, in Weimar XXIX 49ff.
[13] *Die Einheit in der Kirche* §6.
[14] To cite the most recent: J. Lortz, *Die Reformation in Deutschland*; *Die Reformation also religiöses Anliegen* (Trier, 1948); K. Adam, *Una Sancta in katholischer Sicht* (Düsseldorf, 1948); U. Valeske, *Die Stunde ist du. Zum Gespräcg zwischen den Konfessionen* (Stuttgart, 1948).
[15] Cf. e.g. L. A. Veit, *Volksfrommes Brauchtum und Kirche im deutschen Mittlealter* (Fribourg im Briesgau, 1936); J Hashagen, *Staat und Kirche vor der Reformation* (Essen, 1931).

other saints. It was preached with the knowledge of the Church authorities. The Franciscans as a group, and to a certain extent the whole Church, and particularly within it the superiors, bishops and theologians, were supportive in their tolerance of the propagation of the legend. They were also happy to profit from it, which they did. I agree that this is a detail, but we should not be too quick to shake it off by saying it is of little importance, for in its place would rise up a host of others whose quantity alone would be indisputable. There were hundreds, thousands, of false relics, from which hundreds of religious centres made their livings. Since this brings us back to the source of the Reformation, let us simply read the 1509 list of the relics venerated in the chapel of Wittenberg Castle, at whose very door, on the eve of All Saints, Luther would pin his theses: 5005 items, most claiming provenance from major biblical characters, of which probably no more than ten had the slightest chance of being authentic.[16] Of course, it would be unintelligent and unfair to restrict religious life at the end of the fifteenth century to these examples, but I think that at that time there was a system of religious praxis which, as a whole, represented a state of affairs in which the responsibility of clergy superiors was deeply involved. Luther was not the first to mention it, but no one wanted to listen because the 'received ideas' are more convenient than the '*ressourcement*' and the acceptance of the questions raised. 'Let us keep our prejudices, they keep us warm.'

I place a similar responsibility on the teachers of theology – not only those of the two centuries which preceded (and prepared for) the Reformation: 'scholasticism bolted', as Clerissac said, the Nominalists' semi-pelagianism; even those whom the Reformation found in the breach of the Fortress-Church. I know their merits and the genius of several of them; years ago I spent enough time studying Cardinal Thomas de Vio, Cajetan, in charge of Luther's hearing at Augsburg in 1518. I have read more than one treaty by a Catholic apologist of the period. I am astonished to note that these men, who were perfectly capable of rejecting and above all condemning Luther in terms of his confrontation with received doctrine, absolutely failed to perceive, in fact did not even try to perceive, the profound need in which this Augustinian monk's protest was rooted. Neither Cajetan, with his real benevolence in 1518, nor Eck, in 1530 with his catalogue of Luther's errors in 400 articles, like a professor who counts up errors in an exam. But even today, who among official theologians has really made this effort? Once again, we may find ourselves retrospectively in solidarity with those responsible for a tragedy when we agree with their attitudes. On the contrary, after more than 400 years, we are called to do what those greater and better than us failed to do. Borne on their shoulders, we may perhaps see further than them. In any case, we can profit from the lessons of history. I believe that one of the meanings of the current movement of theological thought is to redo the work of the generations who have gone before who in a certain way prepared the great readings of the eleventh and sixteenth centuries. By profiting from a lesson which dissidents have brought right to us, to create in the holy Catholic Church a state of affairs which, if it had existed in place of that which has been allowed to form itself, would probably have meant this grief did not arrive.

---

[16] See Miret, *Quellen zur Geschichte des Papsttums*, 411.

I would have liked to say something about the Galileo affair, so full of teaching, even from my own perspective. We could have seen a new example of the collective responsibility of the churchmen and theologians in a state of affairs, a collection of received ideas which, as sometimes happens, were incorrect and which were not criticized in time. It so often happens that those who do not know criticize and condemn those who know because the latter say things which one is not used to hearing. Once again we would have seen how historical guilt has a heavy price, for today again we bear, and have not finished bearing, the consequences of the excesses committed in the 'centuries of faith' and that continuation of a tutelage which was benevolent but was also anachronistic and abusive. There are many things which could be said on all this but the subject is infinite: after this example, others would appear.[17] Those we have sketched so briefly are sufficient to let us see how, in the perspective of the historical life of the Church, there are tragedies and states of affairs full of tragedies, where the faithful and churchmen, each according to their position, collectively bear a real responsibility.

---

[17] For example, the process by which the nineteenth-century Church 'lost the working classes', described by Pius XI as a major scandal. There can be no scandal without responsibility. Who would dare to say that there was no responsibility by Catholics? Another example could be the collective responsibility of Christians for ideas which for so long brought about the savage treatment of 'witches'.

Bibliography and further reading

Papal and magisterial documents

Pius IX. Dogmatic Constitution *Pastor Aeternus* (18 July 1870); http://w2.vatican.va/content/pius-ix/la/documents/constitutio-dogmatica-pastor-aeternus-18-iulii-1870.html (accessed 16 July 2019).

Leo XIII. Encyclical Letter on the Restoration of Christian Philosophy, *Aeterni Patris* (4 August 1879); http://w2.vatican.va/content/leo-xiii/en/encyclicals/documents/hf_l-xiii_enc_04081879_aeterni-patris.html (accessed 16 August 2019).

Leo XIII. Encyclical Letter on the Study of Holy Scripture, *Providentissimus Deus* (18 November 1893); http://w2.vatican.va/content/leo-xiii/en/encyclicals/documents/hf_l-xiii_enc_18111893_providentissimus-deus.html (accessed 16 August 2019).

Pius X. Encyclical Letter on the Doctrines of the Modernists, *Pascendi Dominici Gregis* (8 September 1907); http://w2.vatican.va/content/pius-x/en/encyclicals/documents/hf_p-x_enc_19070908_pascendi-dominici-gregis.html (accessed 16 August 2019).

Pius XII. Encyclical Letter on the Mystical Body of Christ, *Mystici Corporis Christi* (29 June 1942); http://w2.vatican.va/content/pius-xii/en/encyclicals/documents/hf_p-xii_enc_29061943_mystici-corporis-christi.html (accessed 16 August 2019).

Pius XII. Encyclical Letter on Promoting Biblical Studies Commemorating the Fiftieth Anniversary of *Providentissimus Deus*, *Divino Afflante Spiritu* (30 September 1943); http://w2.vatican.va/content/pius-xii/en/encyclicals/documents/hf_p-xii_enc_30091943_divino-afflante-spiritu.html (accessed 16 August 2019).

Pius XII. Encyclical Letter Concerning Some Opinions Threatening to Undermine the Foundations of Catholic Doctrine, *Humani Generis* (12 August 1950); http://w2.vatican.va/content/pius-xii/en/encyclicals/documents/hf_p-xii_enc_12081950_humani-generis.html (accessed 16 August 2019).

Benedict XVI. 'Christmas Greetings to Members of the Roman Curia and Prelature (22 December 2005); http://w2.vatican.va/content/benedict-xvi/en/speeches/2005/december/documents/hf_ben_xvi_spe_20051222_roman-curia.html (accessed 16 August 2019).

Tanner, Norman P. SJ (ed.). *Decrees of the Ecumenical Councils* (London: Sheed & Ward, 1990).

Selected English translations of works by *ressourcement* theologians

Chenu, Marie-Dominique. *Aquinas and His Role in Theology*, trans. Paul Philibert OP (Collegeville, MN: Liturgical Press, 2002).

Chenu, Marie-Dominique. *Nature, Man, and Society in the Twelfth Century*, trans. Jerome Taylor and Lester K. Little. MART reprints 37 (Toronto: Toronto University Press, 1997).
Congar, Yves. *Divided Christendom: A Catholic Study of the Problem of Reunion*, trans. M. A. Bousfield (London: G. Bles, 1939).
Congar, Yves. *I Believe in the Holy Spirit*, trans. David Smith, 3 vols (London: Geoffrey Chapman, 1982).
Congar, Yves. *True and False Reform in the Church*, trans. Paul Philibert OP (Collegeville, MN: Liturgical Press, 2011).
Daniélou, Jean. *A History of Early Christian Doctrine before Nicaea*, trans. J. A. Baker, 3 vols (London: Darton, Longman & Todd, 1964, 1973, 1977).
Daniélou, Jean. *Origen*, trans. Walter Mitchell (New York: Sheed & Ward, 1955).
De Lubac, Henri. *Catholicism: Christ and the Common Destiny of Man*, trans. Lancelot C. Sheppard and Elizabeth Englund (San Francisco: Ignatius, 1988).
De Lubac, Henri. *Corpus Mysticum*, trans. Gemma Simmonds CJ (London: SCM Press, 2006).
De Lubac, Henri. *At the Service of the Church: Henri de Lubac Reflects on the Circumstances That Occasioned His Writings*, trans. Anne Elizabeth Englund (San Francisco: Ignatius, 1993).
De Lubac, Henri. *The Splendor of the Church*, trans. Michael Mason (San Francisco: Ignatius, 1999).
De Lubac, Henri. *Theology in History*, trans. Anne Englund Nash (San Francisco: Ignatius, 1996).

Selected secondary reading

Ayres, Lewis, and Volpe, Medi Ann (eds). *The Oxford Handbook of Catholic Theology* (Oxford: Oxford University Press, 2019).
Baum, Gregory (ed.). *The Twentieth Century: A Theological Overview* (Maryknoll, NY: Orbis Books, 1999).
Blanchette, Olivia. *Maurice Blondel: A Philosophical Life* (Grand Rapids, MI: Eerdmans, 2010).
Boersma, Hans. *Heavenly Participation: The Weaving of a Sacramental Tapestry* (Grand Rapids, MI: Eerdmans, 2011).
Boersma, Hans. *Nouvelle Théologie and Sacramental Ontology* (Oxford: Oxford University Press, 2009).
Bullivant, Stephen. 'Newman and Modernism: The *Pascendi* Crisis and Its Wider Significance', *New Blackfriars* 92/1038 (2011), 189–208.
Flynn, Gabriel. *Yves Congar's Vision of the Church in a World of Unbelief* (Aldershot: Ashgate, 2004).
Flynn, Gabriel (ed.). *Yves Congar: Theologian of the Church*, Louvain Theological and Pastoral Monographs 32 (Louvain: Peeters Press, 2005).
Flynn, Gabriel, and Murray, Paul D. (eds). *Ressourcement: A Movement for Renewal* (Oxford: Oxford University Press, 2012).
Fouilloux, Étienne. *La collection « Sources chrétiennes ». Éditer les pères de l'Église au XXe siècle* (Paris: Cerf. 2011).

Fouilloux, Étienne. *Une Église en quête de liberté. La pensée catholique française entre modernisme et Vatican II 1914–1962* (Paris: Desclée de Brouwer, 1998).
Fouilloux, Étienne. '«Nouvelle théologie»' et la théologie nouvelle', in *L'histoire religieuse en France et en Espagne*, ed. Benoît Pallistrandi (Madrid: Casa Velasquez, 2004).
Grumett, David. *De Lubac: A Guide for the Perplexed* (London: T&T Clark, 2007).
Holsinger, Bruce. *The Premodern Condition: Medievalism and the Making of Theory* (Chicago: University of Chicago Press, 2005).
International Journal for Systematic Theology 7/4 (2005).
Jodock, Darrell (ed.). *Catholicism Contending with Modernity* (Cambridge: Cambridge University Press, 2000).
Ker, Ian, and Merrigan, Terence (eds). *The Cambridge Companion to John Henry Newman* (Cambridge: Cambridge University Press, 2009).
Kerr, Fergus. 'Chenu's Little Book', *New Blackfriars* 66/777 (1985), 108–12.
Kerr, Fergus. *Twentieth-Century Catholic Theologians* (Oxford: Blackwell, 2005).
Knasas, John F. X. *Being and Some Twentieth-Century Thomists* (New York: Fordham University Press, 2003).
Loughlin, Gerard. '*Nouvelle Théologie*: A Return to Modernism', in Flynn, Gabriel, and Murray, Paul D. (eds). *Ressourcement: A Movement for Renewal* (Oxford: Oxford University Press, 2012), 36–50.
McCool, Gerald A. SJ. *Nineteenth-Century Scholasticism: The Search for a Unitary Method* (New York: Fordham University Press, 1989).
Mettepenningen, Jürgen. *Nouvelle Théologie New Theology* (London: T&T Clark, 2010).
Murphy, Francesca Aran. 'Gilson and Chenu: The Structure of the *Summa* and the Shape of Dominican Life', *New Blackfriars* 85/997 (2004), 290–303.
Potworowski, Christophe E. *Contemplation and Incarnation: The Theology of Marie-Dominique Chenu* (Montreal: McGill-Queens University Press, 2001).
Scully, Eileen J. *Grace and Human Freedom in the Theology of Henri Bouillard* (Bethesda, MD: Academic Press, 2007).
Sorrel, Christian. *La république contre les congrégations: Histoire d'une passion française 1899–1904* (Paris: Cerf, 2003).
Wood, Susan K. *Spiritual Exegesis and the Church in the Theology of Henri de Lubac* (Edinburgh: T&T Clark, 1998).

Index of names

Albert the Great 36, 37, 39, 57, 57 n.85, 58 n.93
Aristotle 8, 12, 34–6, 39, 41, 46, 47 n.13, 90, 107, 110–11, 143–4, 143 n.18, 147,
Athanasius 4, 50 n.11, 111, 157 n.6
Augustine 12, 28, 34, 36, 55, 55 n.60, 64, 65, 68, 111, 133, 135, 135 n.14, 141, 157 n.6, 164

Balthasar, Hans Urs von 107, 114, 114 n.11, 115 n.1, 157 n.6
Barth, Karl 67, 68, 164
Bergson, Henri 64, 83, 131, 143
Blondel, Maurice 83, 91, 91 n.4
Bonaventure 28, 39, 43, 56, 58, 58 nn. 92, 97, 80, 116
Bouillard, Henri 1–3, 6, 8, 12–14, 84, 89–91, 93 n.9, 102 n.3, 109–11, 112 n.19, 115, 115 n.1, 117–18, 149, 156–7

Cajetan, Thomas 1, 23, 134 n.12, 168
Cano, Melchior 2, 19
Charlier, Louis 3, 83, 85–6
Chenu, Marie-Dominique 1–3, 5–7, 7 n.24, 11, 14, 45 n.8, 83, 85–6, 117
Clement of Alexandria 28, 50, 52 n.35, 53 n.37, 64, 101 n.1, 151 n.1, 152, 152 n.2, 157
Congar, Yves 1–2, 4, 6–7, 150

Daniélou, Jean 1, 6, 14, 84, 101–2, 101 n.1, 102 nn.2, 3, 104 n.5, 106 n.7, 107, 113, 115 n.1, 143 n.18, 149, 151, 151 n.1, 155–7, 156 n.4
Denzinger, Heinrich 5–6, 17, 90, 94 n.14
Duns Scotus 28, 30, 43, 43 n.5, 116, 134 n.12, 135

Féret, Henri-Marie 70, 70 n.4
Fessard, Gaston 93 n.12, 102 n.3, 115 n.1, 155 n.1
Fontonyont, Victor 149

Gagnebet, Marie-Rosaire 86
Gardeil, Ambroise viii, 11, 15–16, 18 n.1, 19, 21–4, 28–9, 85
Garrigou-Lagrange, Réginald 3, 6, 11, 12, 14, 83–4, 149
Gilson, Étienne 11 n.1, 43 n.5, 45–6, 45 n.8
Grandmaison, Léonce de 63, 149
Gregory of Nyssa 50, 50 nn.7, 9–11, 15–16, 18, 51 nn.20, 26, 53, 53 nn.39–41, 54 n.44, 46, 50, 52, 55 n.66, 64, 69, 101 n.1, 107, 114 n.11, 151–2, 151 n.1, 157

Hegel, Georg W.F. 64, 141, 143

Irenaeus 52, 52 nn.33, 36, 64, 67–8, 152

Kierkegaard, Søren 14, 66–8, 76, 143

Labourdette, Marie-Michel 3, 6, 7, 12–16, 73–7, 81, 82, 84, 149
Lagrange, Marie-Joseph 4, 22, 22 n.4, 63, 94 n.13, 107
Le Blond, Jean-Marie 2–3, 8, 12–13, 115, 116–23, 123 n.4, 125, 136, 142, 144, 157 n.6
Lebreton, Jules 149
Leo XIII, Pope 1, 1 n.7, 4, 4 n.19, 93, 97, 106 n.7
de Lubac, Henri 1–3, 2 n.12, 3 n.16, 5–7, 7 n.25, 8–9, 13–14, 64, 84, 93, 101, 101 n.1, 102, 102 n.3, 104 n.5, 108, 108 n.8, 113, 115 n.1, 149–50, 151
Luther, Martin 16, 27, 165, 167–8

Maritain, Jacques 126 n.7, 133, 135, 135 nn.13, 14
Mandonnet, Pierre 45 n.8, 85
Marx, Karl 64, 68, 143
Möhler, Johann Adam 4, 6, 23–4, 86, 155 n.1, 167, 167 n.13
Mondésert, Claude 101 n.1, 102 n.3, 149, 151 n.1, 152, 155–7, 156 nn.2, 4

Montcheuil, Yves de 7, 61–2, 70

Newman, John Henry 2 n.8, 4, 4 n.20, 5, 23, 152
Nicolas, Marie-Joseph 3, 6, 12–13, 14, 84, 108 n.8, 149

Origen 28, 50, 50 n.19, 51–3, 51 n.23, 52 n.27, 53 n.38, 55, 55 n.57, 64, 101 n.1, 152, 157, 157 n.6

Parente, Pietro 3, 83
Pius IX, Pope 4

Pius X, Pope 2 n.9, 4, 4 n.18, 85, 92–3, 97, 98, 109
Pius XI, Pope 169 n.17
Pius XII, Pope 2, 2 n.11, 3, 62 n.2, 93, 154 n.8
Plato 26, 52, p.52, n.30, 144, 153

Rousselot, Pierre 5, 80, 81, 84

Suárez, Francisco 2, 43, 116

Teilhard de Chardin, Pierre 67–8, 76, 84, 95 n.15, 106 n.7, 113

www.ingramcontent.com/pod-product-compliance
Lightning Source LLC
Chambersburg PA
CBHW070641300426
44111CB00013B/2201